COMMUNICATIONS AND MULTIMEDIA SECURITY

IFIP – The International Federation for Information Processing

IFIP was founded in 1960 under the auspices of UNESCO, following the First World Computer Congress held in Paris the previous year. An umbrella organization for societies working in information processing, IFIP's aim is two-fold: to support information processing within its member countries and to encourage technology transfer to developing nations. As its mission statement clearly states,

> *IFIP's mission is to be the leading, truly international, apolitical organization which encourages and assists in the development, exploitation and application of information technology for the benefit of all people.*

IFIP is a non-profitmaking organization, run almost solely by 2500 volunteers. It operates through a number of technical committees, which organize events and publications. IFIP's events range from an international congress to local seminars, but the most important are:

- The IFIP World Computer Congress, held every second year;
- Open conferences;
- Working conferences.

The flagship event is the IFIP World Computer Congress, at which both invited and contributed papers are presented. Contributed papers are rigorously refereed and the rejection rate is high.

As with the Congress, participation in the open conferences is open to all and papers may be invited or submitted. Again, submitted papers are stringently refereed.

The working conferences are structured differently. They are usually run by a working group and attendance is small and by invitation only. Their purpose is to create an atmosphere conducive to innovation and development. Refereeing is less rigorous and papers are subjected to extensive group discussion.

Publications arising from IFIP events vary. The papers presented at the IFIP World Computer Congress and at open conferences are published as conference proceedings, while the results of the working conferences are often published as collections of selected and edited papers.

Any national society whose primary activity is in information may apply to become a full member of IFIP, although full membership is restricted to one society per country. Full members are entitled to vote at the annual General Assembly, National societies preferring a less committed involvement may apply for associate or corresponding membership. Associate members enjoy the same benefits as full members, but without voting rights. Corresponding members are not represented in IFIP bodies. Affiliated membership is open to non-national societies, and individual and honorary membership schemes are also offered.

COMMUNICATIONS AND MULTIMEDIA SECURITY

8th IFIP TC-6 TC-11 Conference on Communications and Multimedia Security, Sept. 15-18, 2004, Windermere, The Lake District, United Kingdom

Edited by

David Chadwick
University of Salford
UK

Bart Preneel
Katholieke Universiteit Leuven
Belgium

A C.I.P. Catalogue record for this book is available from the Library of Congress.

Communications and Multimedia Security/ Edited by David Chadwick, Bart Preneel

p.cm. (The International Federation for Information Processing)

ISBN: 1-4614-9893-7 / (eB00K) 0-387-24486-7 Printed on acid-free paper.

9 8 7 6 5 4 3 2 1 SPIN 11382324 (HC) / 11383185 (eBook)
springeronline.com

Contents

Part IV Security in Microsoft .Net

Part V Cryptography

Part VI Multimedia Security

Part VII Application Level Security

Preface

This book contains the papers presented at the Eighth Annual IFIP TC-6 TC-11 Conference on Communications and Multimedia Security, held in Windermere, The Lake District, UK, on 15-18 September 2004. This was a working conference that facilitated lively debate and discussions between the participants and presenters. Thirty three papers were submitted with one being withdrawn prior to review. The reviews were conducted by an international program committee with acknowledged expertise in communications and multimedia security, many being well known authors of books, papers and Internet RFCs. They were aided by a small group of external volunteer reviewers. As a result, eighteen papers were shortlisted and fifteen were presented. In addition, there was a keynote speech and a Panel Session.

The keynote speech was given by Karl-Heinz Brandenburg, the inventor of MP3, who talked about issues in Digital Rights Management.

The Panel Session addressed security in the Microsoft .Net architecture, and the threats that builders of web services applications need to be aware of. The Panel Session consisted of six short papers followed by a question and answer session. The papers were a result of research sponsored by Microsoft at five European University research centres, and the authors presented the results of their findings. This session provoked a very lively discussion.

Holding a successful working conference requires the hard work of many. The conference was organised by a group of staff and research students from the University of Salford. The editors would like to thank the authors for their submitted papers, the program committee and external reviewers for their conscientious efforts during the review process, the organising committee for their tireless efforts to ensure the smooth running of the conference, and the Beech Hill Hotel, Windermere, for their helpful service in providing the conference facilities and the wonderful food which was some of the most delicious we have tasted at a conference.

Conference Program Committee

Program Chair

David Chadwick, University of Salford

Program Committee

Jean Bacon, University of Cambridge, UK
Steve Bellovin, AT&T Research, USA
Elisa Bertino, CERIAS, Purdue University, USA
Howard Chivers, University of York, UK
Stephen Farrell, Trinity College Dublin, Ireland
Russ Housley, Vigil Security, USA
Stephen Kent, BBN Technologies, USA
Herbert Leitold, TU Graz, Austria
Javier Lopez, University of Malaga, Spain
Chris Mitchell, Royal Holloway, University of London, UK
Ken Moody, University of Cambridge, UK
Sead Muftic, Stockholm University, Sweden
Sassa Otenko, University of Salford, UK
Günther Pernul, University of Regensburg. Germany
Bart Preneel, Katholieke Universiteit Leuven, Belgium
Sihan Qing, Chinese Academy of Sciences, China
Pierangela Samarati, University of Milan, Italy
Wolfgang Schneider, Fraunhofer SIT, Germany
Frank Siebenlist, Argonne National Laboratory, USA
Leon Strous, Chairman of TC11, De Nederlandsche Bank, Netherlands
Mary Thompson, Lawrence Berkeley Laboratory, USA
Von Welch, National Center for Supercomputing Applications, USA

External Reviewers

Ji Qingguang
Linying Su
Torsten Priebe
Bjoern Muschall
Christian Schlaeger
Alex Biryukov
Christope De Cannière

Conference Organising Committee

Organising Committee Chair

Grahame Cooper, University of Salford, UK

Organising Committee

Donna Bailey
David Chadwick
Carlos Delgado
Helen Hayes
Peter Langley
John Larmouth
Joanne Perrot
Janice Whatley
Gansen Zhao

DUO-ONIONS AND HYDRA-ONIONS – FAILURE AND ADVERSARY RESISTANT ONION PROTOCOLS *

Jan Iwanik, Marek Klonowski, and Mirosław Kutyłowski
iwanik@im.pwr.wroc.pl, klonowsk@im.pwr.wroc.pl, Miroslaw.Kutylowski@pwr.wroc.pl
Institute of Mathematics, Wrocław Univ. of Technology, ul. Wybrzeże Wyspiańskiego 27, 50-370 Wrocław, Poland

Abstract A serious weakness of the onion protocol, one of the major tools for anonymous communication, is its vulnerability to network failures and/or an adversary trying to break the communication. This is facilitated by the fact that each message is sent through a path of a certain length and a failure in a single point of this path prohibits message delivery. Since the path cannot be too short in order to offer anonymity protection (at least logarithmic in the number of nodes), the failure probability might be quite substantial.

The simplest solution to this problem would be to send many onions with the same message. We show that this approach can be optimized with respect to communication overhead and resilience to failures and/or adversary attacks. We propose two protocols: the first one mimics K independent onions with a single onion. The second protocol is designed for the case where an adaptive adversary may destroy communication going out of servers chosen according to the traffic observed by him. In this case a single message flows in a stream of K onions – the main point is that even when the adversary kills some of these onions, the stream quickly recovers to the original bandwidth – again K onions with this message would flow through the network.

Keywords: Anonymity, onion protocol, adaptive adversary

1. Introduction

Protocols for anonymous communication in computer networks attracted a lot of interest. Their importance increases together with growth of the threats in public networks. Many solutions were proposed, such as Chaum's DC-Nets (Chaum, 1988) and many variations of MIXes (Chaum, 1981). DC-nets pro-

*Partially supported by KBN scientific project 2003–2005 – grant number 0 T00A 003 23

vide information-theoretic security, but computational overhead is very high. For this reason, this solution is not regarded as practical for large scale applications. The second major proposal are Onions described in (Rackoff, 1993) for the very first time. In fact, it is based on idea of MIXes introduced in (Chaum, 1981). Anonymous communication based on onions is scalable and in certain scenarios meets very high demands on privacy (in other scenarios it provides essentially no protection). In order to provide anonymity, a message is sent not directly from the source to the destination, but through a path of randomly chosen nodes, where each node recodes the message with cryptographic tools, so that one cannot see any relationship between different versions of the same message. This protocol has many possible variants, see for instance (Freedman, 2002). Onions are the crucial component of Onion Routing (see for instance (Syverson, 1998) as a starting reference point).

1.1 Provable Security of Onion Routing

In certain scenarios one can really *prove* that onion protocol is secure, even if the adversary traces all traffic. The first rigid mathematical analysis was provided in (Rackoff, 1993). However, the authors assume that a large number of onions are sent at the same time and that the choice of intermediate nodes is somewhat restricted. The result, very interesting from theoretical point of view, is not sufficient for practical applications – security is guaranteed only for the onion paths which have a length that is polylogarithmic in the number n of servers (with a two-digit exponent). The last problem can be avoided by using another estimation (Czumaj, 1999) – the path length can be reduced to $O(\log^2 n)$.

A major breakthrough has been achieved by the change of adversary model in (Berman, 2004) – it is no longer assumed that the adversary can see all the traffic, but only a certain fraction of it. Even if some preferences of the users are known to the adversary, it is shown that the onion protocol does not reveal information through traffic analysis. Neither assumptions about the number of onions nor special addressing limitations are necessary. The path length required is a small degree polynomial in $\log n$. Finally, we have proved (Gomułkiewicz, 2004) that a path length of $O(\log n)$ is sufficient (which is optimal).

1.2 Drawbacks of Onion Routing

A systematic overview of adversary scenarios and their capabilities in real live situations was presented in (Syverson, 2000). The security proofs, mentioned above, should not give us any illusions that the onion protocol is secure in all circumstances. There is a number of tricks that can be used here, based on the fact that connections are not static, exist over a certain time, and that the users have a certain behavior.

A timing attack exploits the fact that closing (resp. opening) a connection causes disappearing (resp. emerging) of one link both at the source and the destination. Monitoring these two hosts reveals immediately that the connection has closed (opened) without any complicated traffic analysis. A predecessor attack (Wright, 2003) is a refinement of this technique. An intersection attack (Berthold, 2000) may occur for instance when a user fetches a certain Web page (in an anonymous way) every time he starts a browser. An adversary records the users that are active at the time when this page is requested. The user in question appears quite often in these records... New attacks, also sophisticated ones, may emerge.

1.3 New Results

In this paper we propose how to deal with two problems. The first problem are node failures in the network. If a path of an onion goes through a node that is down, the message encoded inside the onion cannot be delivered. This is a consequence of the fact that private keys of the node that is down must be used to decode the message and to find out the next node on the path. In Section 3.1 we show that this is not a serious problem, since at each level we can encode alternative nodes through which the onion can be processed. Last but not least, this protocol is as secure as the original protocol in a passive adversary scenario considered in (Berman, 2004).

The second problem considered here is an adversary who can eavesdrop a certain fraction of the communication lines at each step; based on this information he may destroy all messages sent by arbitrarily chosen servers at the next step (however, the number of such servers is bounded). Of course, the original onion protocol is in a hopeless situation against such an adversary: he simply kills the onions one by one (not caring about their contents and destinations). In Section 3.2 we show how to cope with this problem. We propose a protocol such that K onions encoding a message m travel in parallel through the network. A major point in the construction is a mechanism that enables the stream of K parallel onions to self-recover, even if the adversary succeeds in killing all but one onion transporting m. The recovery mechanism must be not too aggressive, since the traffic induced may reveal to the adversary the points where the same message m is located. Then the recovery would bring more harm than profit: the adversary could destroy all messages transporting m. For this reason we propose a method that uses sparse communication, which is harder to be detected. In Section 3.2 we discuss shortly graph theoretic motivation of our solution.

2. Onion Protocol and Anonymity

2.1 Classical Onions

We consider a network with n servers, where each pair of servers may communicate directly. Each server has a pair of a public and a private key, all public keys are widely accessible.

Let us recall the onion protocol in one of the simplest versions. Assume that a message m has to be sent from node A to node B. For this purpose node A chooses at random λ intermediate nodes, say, $J_1, \ldots, J_\lambda$ (they need not to be distinct) and random strings $r_1, r_2, \ldots, r_{\lambda+1}$. Then A builds an *onion* $\mathcal{O}$ encoding m using the following recursive formula (Enc_X means encryption with the public key of X):

$$\begin{aligned} \mathcal{O}_\lambda &= \mathrm{Enc}_B(m, r_{\lambda+1}) \\ \mathcal{O}_i &= \mathrm{Enc}_{J_i}(J_{i+1}, \mathcal{O}_{i+1}, r_{i+1}) \quad \text{for } i < \lambda \\ \mathcal{O} &= \mathcal{O}_1 \end{aligned}$$

Then $\mathcal{O}$ is sent by A to J_1. Node J_1 decrypts the message with its private key. The plaintext obtained contains J_2, the name of the next server on the path, and $\mathcal{O}_2$ – the message to be sent to J_2. This is like *peeling off* the onion $\mathcal{O}_1$: we remove the out-most layer and forward the subonion obtained to the next server. This process of peeling off is repeated at each subsequent server until B gets finally the message m.

The idea behind is that each server J_i cannot see what is the contents of the subonion it sends to the next node – decryption of $\mathcal{O}_{i+1}$ requires knowledge of the appropriate private keys. So J_i cannot see the destination of the message for the subonion it possesses. However, note that additional measures are necessary to protect anonymity of communication. For instance, without the random strings r_i the following simple attack could be carried out: an adversary traces outgoing communication from J_{i+1}. When he detects a message Z sent from J_{i+1} to server U he checks whether $\mathcal{O}_{i+1} = \mathrm{Enc}_U(U, Z)$. If it is so, then $U = J_{i+2}$. This test can be carried out for each single step, so finally the adversary could detect the destination of the message encoded in $\mathcal{O}_i$ without breaking encryption scheme used.

In fact additional measures are necessary. For instance, the size of the packets sent could betray the path along which m is sent. So the encoding must be combined with appropriate padding (Chaum, 1981).

2.2 Adversary Models

There are many different models for an adversary who tries to break the onion scheme. This is a major issue, since a protocol resilient to attacks in one model might be vulnerable in another one. Also, too strong and unrealistic assumptions about the adversary may lead to difficulties in showing security relevance of a protocol.

A passive adversary. A passive adversary may only eavesdrop messages transported along the network. We assume that the cryptographic encoding is strong enough, so the only information available is *where and when the messages have been sent.* It is often assumed that additionally an adversary may get information from a constant fraction of the servers.

There are few variants of the passive adversary:

1 Rackoff-Simon model: all communication lines can be traced by an adversary (Rackoff, 1993)

2 Berman–Fiat–Ta-Shma model: only a constant fraction of communication lines can be traced (Berman, 2004); these lines are determined in advance (with possibility that at each step a different set of lines is tapped),

3 the same as above, but the adversary can adaptively change his choice based on the traffic observed till this moment.

The second case is that an adversary is *active* and can get control over some number of servers. In this case the adversary may detour a subonion: instead of sending it directly to the next node J_{i+1}, a malicious server can encapsulate it with additional layers and send to J_{i+1} through a path of additional servers. This kind of attack can be traced by attaching some encoded confirmation that can be checked by the recipient of the message. Another idea is to send again the same subonion and trace where we can see subonions that have already appeared in the network. Repetitions reveal a path of the message traced. Through careful monitoring all the traffic such an attack can be detected, but it is unrealistic that the routers store and check all messages processed. As a defense one can use time stamps inside the packet (Kesdogan, 1998) – the subonions that do not arrive in predicted interval of time are immediately rejected. However, even with this approach not all problems are solved. A malicious server can postpone for a short moment all incoming traffic except one message. In place of the postponed onions it sends his own bogus messages with known routes ($(n-1) - attack$ from (Kesdogan, 1998)). Then analyzing the traffic is much easier: many routes are known by the adversary.

We consider the model of an adversary who removes the packets (either due to faults or with the aim to bring chaos into communication). This is a great problem: in the network with $n/\log n$ malicious servers and $\lambda = \log n$ each packet gets killed with probability $\Omega(1)$.

2.3 Vertex mixing vs. layer mixing

The adversary model has a big impact on the anonymity mechanism. The original idea of Chaum is that when at the same time two or more onions get

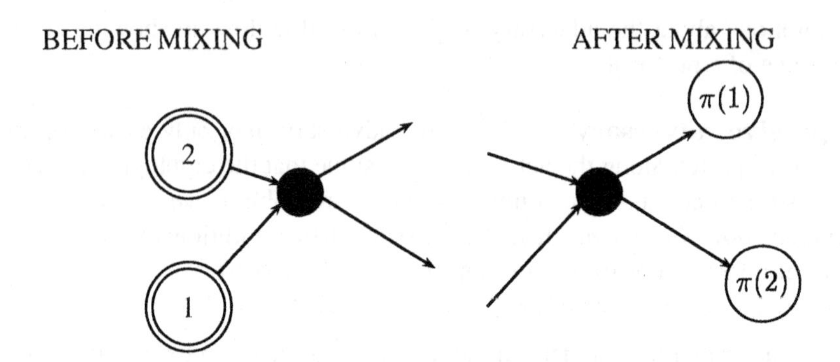

Figure 1. Vertex mixing: what an adversary can see.

into the same server that is not under the adversary's control, then this node acts as a mix: no relationship between incoming and outgoing onions can be found by an external observer. The problem is that if number of onions is moderate the chances that a given onion meets another onion are small. So a large number of onions is necessary to hide their routes.

In (Berman, 2004) Berman et al. pointed to this weakness and introduced "layer mixing" (to distinguish it from the "vertex mixing" discussed above). It is based on the assumption that an adversary may eavesdrop only a constant fraction of all communication lines. Then some number of onions are processed through hidden communication lines. Even if the adversary knows which nodes have received these messages, they are perfectly mixed. So the probability of mixing the messages within a layer of the protocol gets substantially larger.

3. *K*-Onion and Hydra-Onion Protocols

In this section we present modifications of the onion protocol that are aimed to make it robust against communication failures. Two kinds of failures are considered. Either the faults occur at random, or an adversary observes the traffic and tries to hit vulnerable points.

A general idea is that alternative routes for an onion are provided. At each hop, there is not one but at least two servers that may process the onion. So if one destination fails, the message can be sent to another destination.

3.1 DUO-Onions for Random Server Faults

3.1.1 Protocol Description. First we are concerned with random communication failures. All participants use a symmetric encryption scheme SEn. Let SEn_k stand for symmetric encryption with key k and Enc_X for encryption under public key of X.

The simplest version of the DUO-Onion protocol looks as follows: in order to send a message m to node B, node A chooses at random λ intermediate pairs of nodes, say, $(J_{1,1}, J_{1,2}), \ldots, (J_{\lambda,1}, J_{\lambda,2})$, random strings $r_1, \ldots, r_{\lambda+1}$, and keys for symmetric encryption $k_1, \ldots, k_\lambda$.

For each i, we demand that $J_{i,1} \neq J_{i,2}$, but the same server may be chosen to more than one pair. The onion $\mathcal{DO}$ is built via the following recursive formula.

$$\begin{aligned} \mathcal{DO}_\lambda = &\ \big(\mathrm{Enc}_B(k_{\lambda+1}), \mathrm{SEn}_{k_{\lambda+1}}(m, r_{\lambda+1})\big) \ , \\ \mathcal{DO}_i = &\ \big(\mathrm{Enc}_{J_{i,1}}(k_{i+1}, 1), \mathrm{Enc}_{J_{i,2}}(k_{i+1}, 2), \\ &\quad \mathrm{SEn}_{k_{i+1}}(J_{i+1,1}, J_{i+1,2}, \mathcal{DO}_{i+1}, r_{i+1})\big) \quad \text{for } i < \lambda \ , \\ \mathcal{DO} = &\ \mathcal{DO}_1 \ . \end{aligned}$$

The onions are processed in the following way: at a stage i, either $J_{i,1}$ or $J_{i,2}$ has $\mathcal{DO}_i$. First, using its private key, it retrieves k_{i+1} either from $\mathrm{Enc}_{J_{i,1}}(k_{i+1})$ or from $\mathrm{Enc}_{J_{i,2}}(k_{i+1})$. Then, with k_{i+1} it deciphers the third part of $\mathcal{DO}_i$, getting $J_{i+1,1}$, $J_{i+1,2}$, $\mathcal{DO}_{i+1}$. Then it tries to contact $J_{i+1,1}$. If it is down, it contacts $J_{i+1,2}$. Then it sends $\mathcal{DO}_{i+1}$ to the server which has responded. If no server responds, the transmission of the onion dies.

K-Onions Protocol works analogously – we have K possible destinations during a single hop instead of two.

A certain drawback is that each K-subonion contains K ciphertexts of the same symmetric key. However, this is not a problem since we expect to use only small values of K.

3.1.2 Delivery Probability. In this section we check that K-Onions are more efficient than just sending the same messages for many times.

Let us assume that r out of n servers executing the onion protocol are down. Since the onion paths are chosen at random, the location of these servers does not matter. Let $P(\lambda, k)$ denote the probability that a random k-onion reaches its destination server.

For the case of the classical onion protocol we get

$$P(\lambda, 1) = \left(\tfrac{n-r}{n}\right)^\lambda = \left(1 - \tfrac{r}{n}\right)^\lambda ,$$

where λ denotes the length of the onion path. Choosing $\lambda = c \log n$ (which is a secure length for an adversary eavesdropping a constant fraction of communication (Berman, 2004)), we get $P(\lambda, 1) = \Omega(1)$ for $r = O(n/\log n)$.

For k-onions we get:

$$P(\lambda, k) = \left(\frac{\binom{n}{k} - \binom{r}{k}}{\binom{n}{k}}\right)^\lambda = \left(1 - \frac{r}{n}\frac{r-1}{n-1} \cdots \frac{r-k+1}{n-k+1}\right)^\lambda \approx \left(1 - \left(\frac{r}{n}\right)^k\right)^\lambda ,$$

For $\lambda = c \log n$, we get $P(\lambda, k) = \Omega(1)$ for $r = O(n/\sqrt[k]{\log n})$. For practical values of n, we may assume something like $\log n < 30$, so for $k = 5$ we get $\sqrt[k]{\log n} < 2$.

On the other hand, it is worth to say that it does not make sense to take large k, since the ratio between $P(\lambda, k)$ and $P(\lambda, 1)$ grows, but the rate of growth goes down. The biggest change occur for $k = 2$ and $k = 1$. Namely,

$$\begin{aligned}
\frac{P(\lambda, k)}{P(\lambda, 1)} &\approx \left(\frac{1 - (r/n)^k}{1 - r/n} \right)^\lambda \\
&= \left(\frac{(1 - r/n)(1 + r/n + (r/n)^2 + \ldots + (r/n)^{k-1})}{1 - r/n} \right)^\lambda \\
&= (1 + r/n + (r/n)^2 + \ldots + (r/n)^{k-1})^\lambda \approx (1 + r/n)^\lambda .
\end{aligned}$$

Practical example. Let us consider a network consisting of n servers where the number of faulty servers equals $r = 0.3n$ and the path's length $\lambda = 3$. In this case the usual onion reaches its destination with probability $P(3, 1) \approx 0.34$ while $P(3, 2) \approx 0.75$ and $P(3, 3) \approx 0.92$.

3.1.3 Anonymity Issues.

Unlinkability. For an external adversary analyzing the traffic the k-onion protocol behaves just as the original onion protocol. So the results from (Berman, 2004) *do apply*.

On the other hand, the naive solution of sending the same message using multiple onions going through different routes may lead to weakening anonymity – traffic analysis might be facilitated by the fact that for each pair (sender, destination) there is a prescribed number of paths.

Adaptive attacks. A malicious server $J_{i,a}$ may send the subonion $\mathcal{DO}_{i+1}$ to $J_{i+1,2}$ instead of $J_{i+1,1}$, if $J_{i+1,2}$ collaborates with $J_{i,a}$. This enables them to reduce a little bit the unknown parts of the onion paths. By using similar arguments as in (Gomułkiewicz, 2004), one can show that it has the same effect as increasing the number of malicious servers by a constant factor.

On the other hand, a malicious server may start a small repetitive attack: it sends $\mathcal{DO}_{i+1}$ both to $J_{i+1,1}$ and $J_{i+1,2}$. Then both of them send a message to the same server – in this way the adversary may identify the server used on step $i + 2$. On the other hand, the attack and the malicious server would be detected easily, so the attack is not attractive for the adversary.

Note that this trick does not reveal any useful information to the adversary – the only case in which the adversary obtains additional knowledge is when $J_{i+1,1}$ is malicious and pretends that it is down. The only knowledge he may gain by tracing communication sent by $J_{i,a}$ is the name of $J_{i+1,2}$. This knowledge is of no advantage for him, since he may get the names of $J_{i+2,1}$ and $J_{i+2,2}$ by executing the protocol without any tricks.

3.2 Hydra-Onions – Fighting against Active Adversaries

Now we assume that the adversary traces a constant fraction of all communication lines and once it identifies the servers holding the same message, it blocks the outgoing communication from these servers. Of course, it is necessary that a message is transmitted via many routes – otherwise the adversary would win by simply killing the messages one by one.

The general idea is that we send a stream of messages encoding the same m. At each moment we have k subonions corresponding to m (provided that the adversary has not succeeded to kill some of them). Since the adversary may kill some of the subonions, we propose a mechanism that enables the stream to regenerate quickly, so that again we a have k subonions corresponding to m.

The construction must be careful, since a stream of messages encoding the same message may facilitate traffic analysis.

3.2.1 High Level Protocol Description. Assume that A has to send a message m to B. Then K intermediate nodes $J_{i,1}, J_{i,2}, \ldots, J_{i,K}$ are chosen by A for each $i \leq \lambda$. The main change to the previous protocol is that each of the servers $J_{i,1}, J_{i,2}, \ldots, J_{i,K}$ sends the onion to two servers from the list $J_{i+1,1}, \ldots, J_{i+1,K}$. Namely, $J_{i,j}$ sends a subonion to $J_{i+1,j}$ and to a randomly chosen server $J_{i+1,a(j)}$ where $a(j) \neq j$. The choice of $a(j)$ is made by A during onion construction.

In this way we achieve the following goals:

- since random bipartite graphs have expansion properties, if only a fraction of servers $J_{i,1}, J_{i,2}, \ldots, J_{i,K}$ received the subonion encoding m, after step $i+1$ the fraction of servers $J_{i+1,1}, J_{i+1,2}, \ldots, J_{i+1,K}$ holding a subonion encoding m increases with high probability;

- sending a copy of the subonion from each $J_{i,j}$ to all servers $J_{i+1,1}$,$J_{i+1,2}$, $\ldots$, $J_{i+1,K}$ would guarantee immediate recovery of the whole stream of K copies of subonions containing m. However, the communication pattern could betray that certain servers are holding a subonion corresponding to the same message. This could make killing m much easier. A sparse communication pattern proposed does not reveal such information to the adversary.

3.2.2 Protocol Description. For the sake of simplicity we describe and discuss the protocol for $K = 3$. Server A builds an onion $\mathcal{RO}$ via the following recursive formula:

$$\begin{aligned}
\mathcal{RO}_\lambda &= \left(\mathrm{Enc}_B(k_{\lambda+1}), \mathrm{SEn}_{k_{\lambda+1}}(m, r_{\lambda+1})\right)\\
\mathcal{RO}_i &= \Big(\mathrm{Enc}_{J_{i,1}}(k_{i+1,1}, r_{i+1,1}), \mathrm{Enc}_{J_{i,2}}(k_{i+1,2}, r_{i+1,2}), \mathrm{Enc}_{J_{i,3}}(k_{i+1,3}, r_{i+1,3}),\\
&\qquad \mathrm{SEn}_{k_{i+1,1}}(J_{i+1,1}, J_{i+1,a(1)}, k'_{i+1}),\\
&\qquad \mathrm{SEn}_{k_{i+1,2}}(J_{i+1,2}, J_{i+1,a(2)}, k'_{i+1}),\\
&\qquad \mathrm{SEn}_{k_{i+1,3}}(J_{i+1,3}, J_{i+1,a(3)}, k'_{i+1}),\\
&\qquad \mathrm{SEn}_{k'_{i+1}}(\mathcal{RO}_{i+1})\Big) \quad \text{for } i < \lambda\\
\mathcal{RO} &= \mathcal{RO}_1
\end{aligned}$$

In this protocol it is not the case that subonions are sent. Namely, when a server J has to send $\mathcal{RO}_i$ to server J', then $\mathcal{RO}_i$ is encrypted together with a random nonce with a public key of J' before it is sent to J'. Alternatively, we may use a probabilistic asymmetric encryption scheme (such as ElGamal) for encapsulating $\mathcal{RO}_i$.

Let us describe how a subonion is processed. Assume that J receives an (encapsulated) subonion $\mathcal{RO}_i$. Then J decodes $\mathcal{RO}_i$ and deciphers the first three components of $\mathcal{RO}_i$ with the private key of J. In this way, J obtains three symmetric keys k, k', k''. Then J deciphers the 4th, the 5th and the 6th components of $\mathcal{RO}_i$ with the keys, respectively, k, k', and k''. In one case, J obtains the valid key k'_{i+1} and the names of two servers J', J'' for the next hop. (If necessary, we may include some characteristic string in the plaintext in order to detect easily which of the keys k, k', and k'' is valid.) Having k'_{i+1}, server J deciphers the last component of $\mathcal{RO}_i$ and retrieves $\mathcal{RO}_{i+1}$. Then J encapsulates $\mathcal{RO}_{i+1}$ as described above and sends the results to the servers J' and J'', respectively.

3.2.3 Recovery Properties. Assume that the adversary is not blocking the communication at the moment and there is only one server with a subonion holding m. Then after one step we get 2 servers with a subonion holding m with probability 1. If there are already two servers keeping subonions with m, then after one step we have still 2 such servers with probability $\frac{1}{4}$ and 3 such servers with probability $\frac{3}{4}$. Since the numbers $a(j)$ are chosen independently at random, our experiment corresponds to Bernoulli trials with success probability $\frac{3}{4}$. So there is no success within t trials (meaning that we have still only 2 servers holding m) with probability $\frac{1}{2^{2t}}$.

For the case when $K > 3$ the arguments are more tedious. However, let us point that the following Markov chain $\mathcal{S}$ converges quickly. The states of $\mathcal{S}$ are nonempty subsets of $\{1, \ldots, K\}$. The transition function of $\mathcal{S}$ can be described as follows: let U be the current state of $\mathcal{S}$; then for each $a \in U$

choose independently at random an element $r(a) \in \{1, \ldots, K\} \setminus \{a\}$. Then the new state of $\mathcal{S}$ is the set $U \cup \{r(a) | a \in U\}$. Due to expansion properties of random graphs, the chain $\mathcal{S}$ converges quickly to the state $\{1, \ldots, K\}$. We skip further discussion on this problem, since we think that small values of K are most important and for these values the convergence rate can be easily estimated.

3.2.4 Resilience to Attacks. As mentioned, an adversary who analyzes the traffic at step i may locate the servers holding the same message m and kill all packets sent from servers holding m at step $i+1$. In this way m would disappear, even if the adversary does not know the contents and the destination of m.

We assume, as in (Berman, 2004), that the adversary may eavesdrop only a constant fraction of communication lines. Recall (Berman, 2004) that servers $J_1, \ldots, J_m$ and $J'_1, \ldots, J'_m$ form a *crossover structure*, if no communication line (J_a, J'_b) for $a, b < m$ is eavesdropped by the adversary. The number m will be called *crossover size*.

The ideal situation is when the servers $J_{i,1}, \ldots, J_{i,K}$ and $J_{i+1,1}, \ldots, J_{i+1,K}$ from the definition of an onion $\mathcal{RO}$ form a crossover structure at step i. Then the adversary has no trace that they belong together to a certain message m. What is the probability that such a case occurs? It is hard to answer this question: the adversary may adopt some clever strategy to choose the links eavesdropped so that as few as possible crossover structures occur. It turns out that there are graph theoretical limitations on the adversary. Noga Alon (Alon, 2001) (Corollary 2.1) shows the following result:

LEMMA 1 *For every fixed $\epsilon > 0$, and every fixed integer $t > 0$, and for any graph G with n vertices and at least ϵn^2 edges, the number of subgraphs of G isomorphic to $K_{t,t}$ (bipartite complete graph with t vertices on each side) is at least:*

$$\frac{1}{2}\binom{n}{t}\binom{n}{t}(2\epsilon)^{t^2}.$$

In our case we say that an edge (J, J') belongs to G, if the communication link between j and J' is not eavesdropped by the adversary. The main point in Lemma 1 is that a lower bound on the number of crossover structures does not depend on the structure of G, that is, on the strategy of the adversary.

In order to examine the case $K = 3$, let us note the following: the probability that $J_{i,1}, J_{i,2}, J_{i,3}$ and $J_{i+1,1}, J_{i+1,2}, J_{i+1,3}$ form a crossover is at least $f^9/2^{10}$ for a fraction f of links that are not under the adversary's control. In this case the probability that the adversary kills all packets holding the message processed by these servers is about $(r/n)^3$, where r is the number of servers that can be blocked at step $i+1$.

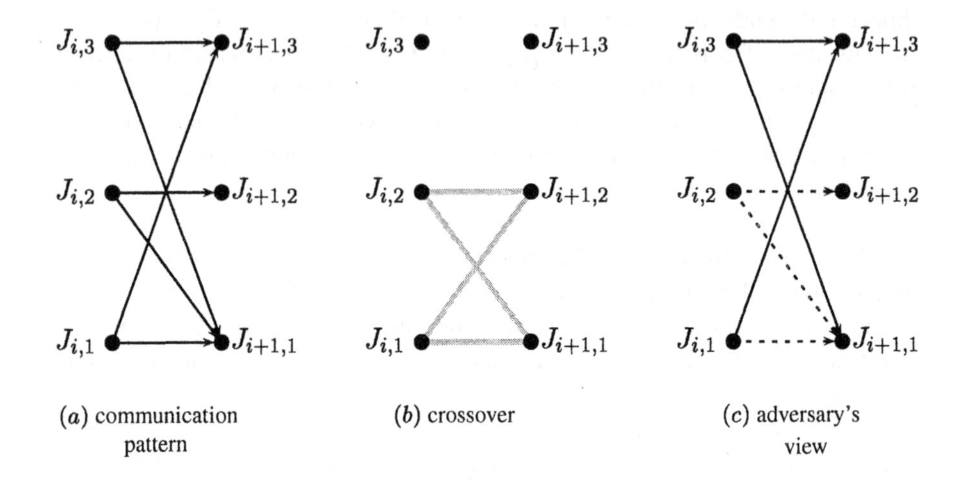

Figure 2. Crossovers of size 2 and the viewpoint of the adversary.

The adversary may be in trouble even if no crossover of size 3 occurs. With probability at least $f^4/2^8$ a crossover of size 2 is formed by two of the servers from $J_{i,1}, J_{i,2}, J_{i,3}$, say J_{i,x_1}, J_{i,x_2} and by two of the servers from J_{i+1,x_1}, J_{i+1,x_2}. By a simple case inspection (see also Fig. 2) we can check the following fact:

LEMMA 2 *Assume that a crossover of size 2 is formed by two servers J_{i,x_1}, J_{i,x_2} from the list $J_{i,1}, J_{i,2}, J_{i,3}$ and by two of J_{i+1,x_1}, J_{i+1,x_2}. Then for every choice of $a(1), a(2), a(3)$, the communication lines between $J_{i,1}, J_{i,2}, J_{i,3}$ and $J_{i+1,1}, J_{i+1,2}, J_{i+1,3}$ where the adversary observes a traffic corresponding to message m does not form a connected graph.*

The meaning of Lemma 2 is that when a crossover of size 2 occurs, then the adversary cannot link together the nodes $J_{i+1,1}, J_{i+1,2}, J_{i+1,3}$ – at least one of then is an *orphan*. Since we expect that there are many such orphans the adversary is in trouble: killing m will succeed only if all three servers $J_{i+1,1}, J_{i+1,2}, J_{i+1,3}$ are blocked.

For larger parameters K, the adversary should be even more confused (we postpone the analysis to the full version of the paper). Let us explain some intuitions behind. For the moment even assume that the adversary knows the relationships of the kind $J_{i,j} - J_{i+1,j}$ and that these relationships are the same for each onion. We draw a directed *additional link multi-graph* $\mathcal{A}$ describing step i. It has n vertices, with vertex j representing the jth server. We draw an arc $\vec{JF}$ in $\mathcal{A}$ when at step i server J sends a message to F, where F is the "second location" indicated by function a. Let us consider the arcs related to processing the same onion. Since each node has out-degree at most 1, we get a subgraph of $\mathcal{A}$ with some specific properties (see Fig. 3): there are exactly K arcs, each connected component contains a single circle and some number of directed paths leading to the circle. The unlucky case for the adversary is when there is more than one connected component in this graph – the adversary cannot link the servers appointed to the same message provided that there many other components due to other messages. It is known that for large K the size of largest connected component divided by K is a random variable with probability distribution that converges with K to a Poisson-Dirichlet distribution.

However, even if there is exactly one component, the adversary might be in trouble, since we assume that the adversary does not eavesdrop all communication links, but only a certain fraction of them. In this case the graphs such as depicted in Fig. 3 get disconnected, since the adversary does not know the status of a constant fraction of communication lines (see Fig. 4).

4. Conclusions and Open Problems

We disregard the problem of different degrees of vulnerability of the servers and communications lines. However we should be able to assign different elements of the network different probabilities of failure or corruption by an adversary. It is yet unclear how to adopt the onion protocols to this situation.

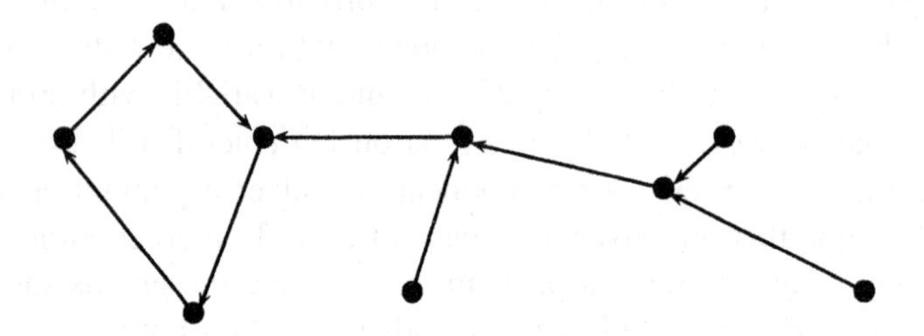

Figure 3. Example arcs in $\mathcal{A}$ corresponding to the same message.

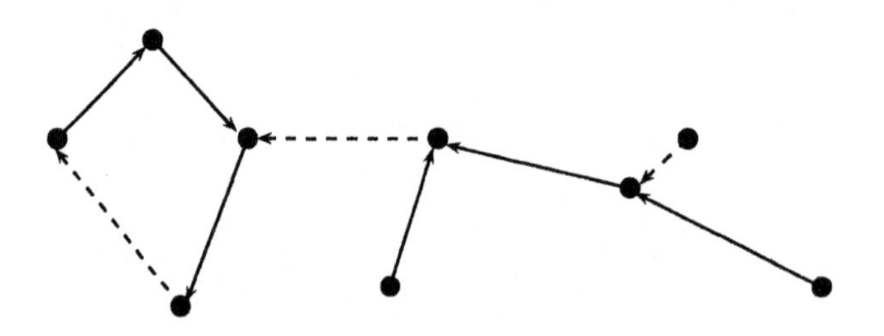

Figure 4. Adversary point of view for the situation depicted by Fig. 3.

References

Alon, N. : Testing Subgraphs in Large Graphs. ACM-SIAM FOCS 2001, 434-439.

Berman R., Fiat A., Ta-Shma A.: Provable Unlinkability Against Traffic Analysis. Accepted for Financial Cryptography 2004.

Berthold, O., Federrath, H., Köhntopp, M.: Project "Anonymity and Unobservability in the Internet." Workshop on Freedom and Privacy by Design / CFP2000, ACM, 2000, 57-65.

Chaum, D.: Untraceable Electronic Mail, Return Addresses, and Digital Pseudonyms. CACM 24(2) (1981) 84-88.

Chaum, D.: The Dining Cryptographers Problem: Unconditional Sender and Recipient Untraceability. Journal of Cryptology 1(1) (1988), 65-75.

Czumaj, A., Kanarek, P., Kutyłowski, M., Loryś K.: Distributed Stochastic Processes for Generating Random Permutations. 10 ACM-SIAM SODA, 1999 271-280.

Freedman, J., Sit, E., Cates, J., Morris, R.: Introducing Tarzan, a Peer-to-Peer Anonymizing Network Layer 1st International Workshop on Peer-to-Peer Systems (IPTPS02), Lecture Notes in Computer Science 2429. Springer-Verlag, 2002, 121-129.

Gogolewski, M., Kutyłowski, M., Łuczak, T.: Distributed Time stamping with Boomerang Onions. Manuscript.

Gomułkiewicz, M., Klonowski, M., Kutyłowski, M.: Provable Unlinkability Against Traffic Analysis already after $\mathcal{O}(\log(n))$ steps!. Manuscript, 2004.

Kesdogan D., Egner J., Büschkes R.: Stop-and-Go-MIXes Providing Probabilistic Anonymity in an Open System. Information Hiding '98 Lecture Notes in Computer Science 1525. Springer-Verlag, 83-98.

Syverson P. F., Reed M. G., Goldschlag D. M.: Private Web Browsing. Journal of Computer Security Special Issue on Web Security 5 (1997) 237-248.

Syverson P. F., Reed M. G., Goldschlag D. M.: Anonymous Connections and Onion Routing. IEEE Journal on Selected Areas in Communication. 16(4) (1998) 482-494.

Syverson, P., Tsudik, G., Reed, M., Landwehr., C.: Towards an Analysis of Onion Routing Security. Workshop on Design Issues in Anonymity and Unobservability, July 2000.

Rackoff C., Simon D.R.: Cryptographic Defense Against Traffic Analysis. 25 ACM Symposium on Theory of Computing (1993) 672-681.

Wright, M., Adler, M., Levine, B., Schields, C.: Defending Anonymous Communication Against Passive Logging Attacks. IEEE Symposium on Security and Privacy 2003, IEEE Computer Society, 28-38.

PERSONAL ATTRIBUTES AND PRIVACY

How to ensure that private attribute management is not subverted by datamining.

Howard Chivers

Department of Computer Science, Univeristy of York, Heslington, York, YO10 5DD
chive@cs.york.ac.uk

Abstract: The aggregation of personal attributes into user profiles is a significant privacy concern. Existing attribute management systems support the controlled release of attributes and unlinkability between session protocols, but do not address the problem that attributes distributed in this way may be data-mined for features that allow user profiles to be reconstructed.

This paper identifies the aggregation problem as the missing element in the protection of personal attributes, and introduces attribute management principles that are sufficient to provide an overall framework to protect users from profile aggregation. The principles are clarified by formalizing them as constraints on primitive operations in a service-based architecture, and this analysis is the basis for a proof that they support system wide privacy. These results are of particular value in the decomposition of business processes into services, and a location-privacy problem is used to show how they can be applied in practice.

Key words: privacy protection, distributed-system security, web-services security, privacy-enhancing technology, electronic commerce, pseudonymity

1. ATTRIBUTE MANAGEMENT PRINCIPLES

1.1 Introduction

Privacy is a fundamental right in the UN Declaration of Human Rights, and in the European Union a Data Protection Directive [1] is enforced by legislation in member nations [2]. These data protection requirements embody the concepts of *necessity, purpose* and *consent*: personal data can be processed only if it is necessary for the application, and only for the purpose for which it was provided. Although the US has not adopted the same legislative approach, similar principles are described in the influential Code of Fair Information Practices [3].

The subject of privacy is of growing importance because of the ease with which information can be assembled and processed, and because of public sensitivity about commercial trading in personal profiles [4]. Technical trends toward highly distributed systems also exacerbate privacy management issues, including the balance between privacy and accountability [5].

These social, statutory and technical pressures have motivated researchers to develop protocols that limit access to personal data. The general approach is to regard any fact about an individual as a *private attribute* whose release should be subject to a policy that takes into account the subject's consent and the needs of the application. For example, Shibboleth [6] manages user authentication in this way, and researchers have proposed pseudonomous PKI attribute certificates [7]; other approaches do not provide enforcement, but specify contracts [8] or policies [9].

These systems use temporary pseudonyms to ensure that different user sessions cannot be linked by a primary identity. The type and degree of unlinkability depends on the protocol, but the pseudonymous user must still present private attributes in order to access the service. Unfortunately, little attention has been given to the threat that these attributes may be directly consolidated by data mining, bypassing the unlinkability of the access protocol and enabling the profile aggregation that is precisely the issue of public concern.

This paper addresses the problem of attribute aggregation; it shows how private attributes can be partitioned and their distribution constrained in order to ensure that attribute release policies set by a pseudonymous user cannot be subverted by aggregation in the distributed system.

The remainder of this paper is in three parts; the first is a discussion of the problem, and proposes *attribute management principles* as criteria for system design. The second part clarifies these principles by formalizing them as constraints on the services and security tokens of a service-based distributed system. Proof that these constraints are effective is given in Appendix A. Finally, a location-privacy problem is used to show how these results can be applied during the system design process.

1.2 Privacy and Aggregation Management

User concern about profile aggregation suggests that privacy is fundamentally related to the linkage or correlation of private data [4], and although data protection legislation is not framed directly in this way, it supports this view: the UK legislation [2] defines a relevant filing system as *structured*, and the linkage of census data to individual population records led to the landmark constitutional challenge of the 1983 German census [10].

The defining nature of linked data is also argued by Wallace [11] who defines anonymity as *noncoordinatability of traits in a given respect.* She provides a powerful example: a criminal (the Unabomber) was completely specified by the single trait of his crimes, but remained anonymous until another trait (writing style) became known. This suggests that linkability of personal traits is a more fundamental issue than the number of individuals determined by any given attribute.

Managing the aggregation of private data is therefore a defining feature of privacy-supporting technologies, implying that *the extent that personal attributes remain independent constitutes the degree to which privacy is maintained.* This definition has the benefit that it naturally includes threats such as aggregation or data mining. Previous work has addressed unlinkable privacy mechanisms, but has not made the case for the fundamental importance of unlinkability as a criterion for technical privacy.

Authentication by attribute, rather than identity, requires an authority such as the user's organization to vouch for the attribute, and a temporary binding between the user and the target service that avoids providing further information. The user expects that this arrangement will preserve privacy by preventing the aggregation of attributes released in different sessions.

Systems that pseudonymously manage attribute release have already been mentioned [6, 7]. There is also an important body of research on unlinkable protocols; much of which is based on blind signatures [12] and variations [13] that provide accountability, or on MIX networks [14]. However, these still require a user to provide authentication information to obtain a service.

Existing work therefore provides only part of the solution. It is also necessary to ensure that private attributes released to services cannot be aggregated directly, for example, by using statistical techniques to identify and exploit overlapping values. This paper proposes attribute management principles to address this problem; unlinkable protocols are important supporting mechanisms, but are not discussed further.

1.3 Indirect Transactions and Attribute Partitioning

Consider the flow of private data in an electronic purchase (for the sake of discussion, of some CDs). The identity of the CDs is not a privacy concern unless they can be associated with the user making the purchase, which requires an identifier such as a bank account number. Privacy concerns multiply as more attributes are collected, for example, adding the user's address provides both a marketing target and information about social and economic group.

The user reveals information about buying preferences by selecting the product and may also provide credit card information to pay for the purchase. The association of these two attributes of private data allows the long term tracking of the user's buying profile. This violates the data protection *purpose* principle, because it is not necessary.

The supplier might argue that credit information is necessary to perform their contract with the subject, but many forms of payment, including cash, do not identify individual accounts. Even complex financial transactions can be carried out indirectly, for example via escrow accounts or international letters of credit. It is arguable, therefore, that this pattern of electronic business has not been established because of a financial or business precedent, but because it is technically convenient.

An alternative pattern for the transaction is that the user obtains an opaque 'electronic check' from their bank that is presented to the supplier. This provides separation of purpose between the private attributes held by the bank and those available to the supplier. There are a number of possible implementations of electronic cheques[1]; this paper uses the generic term 'authorization token', implying that such a token does not carry private data.

This example motivates general principles for the design of systems that manage attribute aggregation: private data provided to any service provider should be partitioned by *trait* (or type); and where a service provider needs to invoke the services of another, then the data subject's authority should be conveyed by an opaque authorization token, rather than by the provision of additional personal information.

1.4 Attribute Management Principles

These ideas can be expressed as attribute management principles that are sufficient to ensure that *no part of a system can aggregate an individual's private attributes:*

[1] Such as electronic cash [12] [15], but recall that this paper is concerned with the management of personal attributes themselves, not the underlying protocols.

1. An individual's private attributes should be grouped into a number of sets (named by 'trait' or 'type').
2. Private attributes provided to any single service provider should be limited to a single trait.
3. Where a service provider needs to invoke the services of another, and the second requires attributes of a different trait, delegation of the user's authority should be via opaque tickets, rather than by the provision of additional private data.

These principles do not specify how private attributes should be grouped into *Traits*, a privacy policy for a specific system needs to balance privacy and feasibility when making this choice. A trait should represent a class of information about a user, for example: buying preferences for particular products; address and location; employment; bank and credit information.

The next section formalizes these principles, to clarify the constraints that they represent, and this provides the basis to prove that they are sufficient to maintain privacy.

2. ANALYSIS

2.1 Introduction

The attribute management principles are intuitively appealing, but their usefulness must be demonstrated in the context of the rich range of services that are supported by practical distributed systems. From the privacy perspective these services can all be viewed as moving data of various types and origins between *principals*[2]. This section models the movement of data in a service-based system in order to clarify the constraints implied by the attribute management principles, and shows that they result in the desired privacy properties for the system as whole.

Both the operation of services, and the distribution of security management information are important. The primitive operations modeled are therefore:

- The creation of authorization tokens.
- The distribution of authorization tokens.
- The use of an authorization token to invoke a service.
- The transfer of an authentication token, or other privacy sensitive data, between principals.
- The transfer of non-privacy sensitive data between principals.

[2] The term *principal* is used to denote an application that can both invoke and provide a service, and is administered by a single authority

2.2 Formal Model

The following model captures the flow of information between principals as a directed graph. The main data types are modeled as vertices and the possible movement of information as directed edges. The information flow implied by each service is expressed as a relation between vertices, and the edge set is the union of these relations. This form of modeling is conservative, because of the implicit assumption that all information flows are transitive; however, it provides a compact and direct representation of the service primitives and allows straightforward reasoning about the overall system. The graph is specified using set theory, in Z syntax [16].

2.2.1 Static types and relations

The base types in this model are the disjoint sets introduced in table 1.

Table 1. Base types

Type	Name	Description
P	Principal	Service providers and users
A	Private Attribute	Private Data, including authentication data
D	Public Data	Data that is not private
K	Authorization Token	An opaque token
T	Transaction	An atomic business transaction
Y	Attribute Trait	The trait, or type, of a private attribute

Principals are active system entities that can provide or invoke services; *Private Attributes, Public Data* and *Authorization Tokens* are types of data that can be accessed by Principles, or transferred between them.

Transactions are data types that model system state. Distributed business transactions are often a sequence of operations with intermediate state held by the service provider. For example, an on-line purchase may involve the selection of goods, followed by setting delivery and payment options. Atomic transactions are an instance of this more general case.

Traits (Y) are used to constrain the model, rather than represent information sources or sinks. This has the effect of neglecting information flow through the type system, which is justifiable because Traits are expected to be static and knowledge of the Traits in the system is not a privacy concern.

The set of vertices in the model is therefore the union of the base types, except **Y**:

$$V = P \cup A \cup D \cup K \cup T \tag{1}$$

Both Private Attributes and Principals have identifiable Traits. It is also convenient to define a trait matching relation between Private Attributes and Principals:

$$YP = P \rightarrow Y^{3} \tag{2}$$

$$YA = A \rightarrow Y \tag{3}$$

$$MATCH = \{(a,p) \mid \exists k((a,k) \in YA \wedge (p,k) \in YP)\} \tag{4}$$

Both Public Data and Private Attributes are owned by specific Principals:

$$PUB = D \rightarrow P \tag{5}$$

$$PRIV = A \rightarrow P \tag{6}$$

The information flows present in the initial system are therefore:

$$IS = PUB \cup PRIV \tag{7}$$

2.2.2 Transactions

As noted above, Transactions record state. Since we are not concerned with functional behaviour it is sufficient to record data items that have contributed to state as a vertex from that data item to a Transaction. The primitive operations are directly modeled in this way, together with any constraints required to uphold the attribute management principles.

A Transaction is owned by particular Principal, so any data accumulated by that Transaction is also available to the Principal:

$$TA = T \rightarrow P \tag{8}$$

A Transaction may make use of local Public Data:

$$TB = \{(d,t) \mid \exists p((t,p) \in TA \wedge (d,p) \in PUB)\} \tag{9}$$

[3] When relations are introduced, $Z = A \times B$ represents $\{(a,b) \mid a \in A \wedge b \in B\}$ as usual, but additionally where A and B are sets of vertices, the pair (a,b) is a directed edge from a to b. Functions such as $Z = A \rightarrow B$ similarly have their usual meaning with the additional connotation of a directed edge.

Creating an Authorization Token. The purpose of the token is to identify one or more Transactions. The Token must not carry information about the state of any Transaction.

$$CA = K \leftarrow T \tag{10}$$

Distributing an Authorization Token. The Token can be distributed to any Principal.[4]

$$DA = K \times P \tag{11}$$

Distributing an Authentication Token. This binds Private Attributes from one Principal to a Transaction owned by a second Principal. It models the provision of user attributes for the purpose of authentication, or more generally any operation that transfers private data between Principals.

This operation is constrained by attribute management principle 2, limiting the distribution of private data to Principals of the correct Trait.

$$BA = \{(a,t) \mid \exists p((t,p) \in TA \wedge (a,p) \in MATCH)\} \tag{12}$$

Using an Authorization token to access a service. This models the use of an authorization token to invoke a service on an existing Transaction. Of course, data may be returned to the Principal that invokes this service. This requires an additional constraint to ensure privacy: the only bindings to the Transaction must be from Private Attributes that are either private to the Principal that invoked the service or have the same Trait as the Principal that invoked the service.

$$SA = \{(t,p) \mid \forall a((a,t) \in BA \Rightarrow [(a,p) \in PRIV) \vee (a,p) \in MATCH])\} \tag{13}$$

Public Data. To complete the graph it is necessary to record data flows that involve public data. Any item of public data can influence a transaction:

$$PA = D \times T \tag{14}$$

and data flows between public data items are not constrained:

$$PB = D \times D \tag{15}$$

[4] In a practical system, possession, or first use, of a token may confer access to a service, or there may be constraints on which Principals could make use of a token, either statically encoded in the access policy of the service or dynamically encoded in the state of the Transaction. These additional constraints are beyond the scope of this paper.

Completing the model. The edge set of information flow paths in the system can now be constructed:

$$E = IS \cup TA \cup TB \cup CA \cup DA \cup BA \cup SA \cup PA \cup PB \quad (16)$$

2.3 The Privacy Proposition

Informally, the privacy proposition is:

Any flow of information from a Private Attribute to a Principal is either from the Principal's own Private Attributes, or from a Private Attribute of a Trait that the Principal is allowed to process.

A formal account of this proposition and its proof is given in Appendix A. This demonstrates that the system has the property that no service provider is able to reconstruct the private data associated with another Principal by invoking any sequence of system services.

2.4 Summary of Constraints

This analysis clarifies the constraints that are required in a system to prevent aggregation of personal data. The constraints embodied in the model are:

1. A Principal must be assigned a single Trait (Eq. 2).
2. Each Private Attribute is a member of a single Trait (Eq. 3).
3. A Principal has an identified set of Private Attributes (Eq. 6).
4. Authorization tokens must be opaque identifiers that do not include private information (Eq. 10).
5. Private Attributes provided to a Principal as part of an authorization token, or otherwise, must match the Principal's Trait (Eq. 12).
6. Any data returned to a Principal from a Transaction must originate from either that Principal's Private Attributes, from Private Attributes that match the trait of the Principal, or from non-private data (Eq. 13).

These constraints mirror the privacy principles exactly; the last two (5,6) are important because they provide a more detailed formulation of the second principle. The first of these (5) is a simple statement of principle 2 (only provide attributes to principals with appropriate trait); the second (6) proves to be subtler:

- The 'Transaction' is a record of information flow into service state, and so this places a requirement on service providers to know when state has originated from private data.
- A data item that originates from private data may be returned to the original owner of that private data, or to any Principal of the correct trait.

3. USING THE PRINCPLES

The foregoing demonstrates that comprehensive attribute protection requires unlinkable protocols, information flow trust in services, system-wide knowledge of service traits, and agreements about how attributes are grouped into traits. However, if attribute management principles are followed when business processes are decomposed into services, then some of these constraints (such as knowledge of the trait of a service) can be encoded in the design, rather than requiring operational mechanisms. Space precludes a full discussion of implementation issues, but a further example will illustrate this process.

A common concern in mobile computing is location privacy – how users are able to obtain services based on their location, while avoiding personal tracking. The attribute-management solution is to query services by providing the user's location, but no further information. The issue of unlinkable temporary pseudonyms has also been considered in this context [17] but researchers have not dealt with the problem that further personal attributes are needed to utilize services after they have been located.

Consider the case of a roaming user who wishes to print a document. The user requires a print service to locate a nearby printer and manage printing. The document resides on a workgroup server, to which the user must provide authentication information before access to the file is granted.

In this case it is straightforward to partition the user's personal attributes (location and workgroup information) into two separate traits, and assign one to the print system and the other to the file server. The primitive protocol elements used in the analysis (see 2.1) are sufficient to outline the process:

- The user presents a workgroup authentication attribute to the file server and obtains an opaque authorization token that confers access to the specified file.
- The user provides location co-ordinates to the print service, and obtains a reference to the nearest printer.
- The user presents the authorization token to the printer, which is able to retrieve the file and print it.

This outline description avoids the protocol details: how a user establishes temporary unlinkable pseudonyms with the services in order to carry out the transactions, suitably opaque forms of authorization tokens, and the use of an attribute authority to authenticate the workgroup attribute. However, it does demonstrate how the attribute management principles can be used to influence process design, and the importance focusing on the whole process chain, not just a single service interaction.

4. CONCLUSIONS

The extent that personal attributes can be linked determines the extent that private data can be profiled; this is of fundamental importance to privacy, and this viewpoint is consistent with the principles of purpose and consent contained in the Data Protection standards.

This paper has investigated the threat that users' private attributes may be directly aggregated into personal profiles, and shows that it is possible to avoid this problem if services are designed to meet *attribute management principles* (1.4). The principles group private attributes into *traits* and ensure that no service needs attributes from more than one trait.

The analysis of these principles shows that they can be applied in service-based systems that support the distribution of authentication and authorization tokens [18], and a worked example demonstrates their practical use in the decomposition of a business process into services.

The constraints derived in the analysis provide a single framework for system level privacy that motivates the need for established mechanisms, such as unlinkable protocols, as well as additional concerns arising from direct attribute aggregation.

The analysis and proof shows that if the management principles are observed then the desired property of unlinkability is upheld in the system as a whole. The relative robustness or fragility of different attribute distribution policies in the face of a collusion attack is still an open question, but the principles described here are believed to be robust, because they would force many services to collude before a user profile could be reconstructed.

REFERENCES

[1] *On the protection of individuals with regard to the processing of personal data and on the free movement of such data*, in *European Parliament and of the Council*. 1995.

[2] *The Data Protection Act 1988*, in *United Kingdom*. 1998.

[3] *Secretary's Advisory Committee on Automated Personal Data Systems, Records, Computers, and the Rights of Citizens viii*, U.S. Dep't. of Health, Education and Welfare, July 1973. http://www.epic.org/privacy/hew1973report/foreword.htm

[4] D. G. Johnson and K. W. Miller, The Ties that Bind: Connections, Comet Cursors, and Consent. *ACM SIGCAS Computers and Society*. **31**(1): p. 12 - 16 (2001)

[5] H. Chivers, J. A. Clark, and S. Stepney. Smart Devices and Software Agents: the Basic of Good Behaviour, in Proceedings of *The first International Conference on Security in Pervasive Computing*, Boppard, Germany. LNCS vol 2802. Springer-Verlag (2003)

[6] M. Erdos and S. Cantor, *Shibboleth Architecture*, Internet2, 8 October, 2001. http://middleware.internet2.edu/shibboleth/

[7] V. Benjumea, J. Lopez, J. A. Montenegro, and J. M. Troya. A First Approach to Provide

Anonymity in Attribute Certificates, in Proceedings of *Public Key Cryptography – PKC 2004: 7th International Workshop on Theory and Practice in Public Key Cryptography*, Singapore. LNCS vol 2047. Springer Verlag (2004)
[8] S. Holtmanns. Privacy in a Mobile Environment, in Proceedings of *13th International Workshop on Database and Expert Systems Applications (DEXA'02)*, Aix-en-Provence, France. IEEE Computer Society (2002)
[9] *Platform for Privacy Preferences (P3P) Project*, W3C, http://www.w3.org/P3P/
[10] H. M. Choldin, Government Statistics: The Conflict Between Research and Privacy. *Demography*. **25**(1): p. 145-154 (1988)
[11] K. A. Wallace, Anonymity. *Ethics and Information technology*. **1**(1): p. 21-31 (1998)
[12] D. Chaum, Security without identification: Transaction Systems to Make big brother obsolete. *Communications of the ACM*. **28**(10): p. 1030-1044 (1985)
[13] J. Camenisch, J. M. Piveteau, and M. Stadler. Fair blind signatures, in Proceedings of *Advances in Cryptology - EUROCRYPT '95, International Conference on the Theory and Application of Cryptographic Techniques*, Saint-Malo, France. Lecture Notes in Computer Science vol 921. Springer Verlag (1995)
[14] D. Chaum, Untraceable Electronic Mail, Return Address, and Digital Pseudonyms. *Communications of the ACM*. **24**(2): p. 1030-1044 (1981)
[15] T. Okamoto and K. Ohta. Universal Electronic Cash, in Proceedings of *Advances in Cryptology - CRYPTO '91*. LNCS vol 576. Springer Verlag (1991)
[16] J. M. Spivey, *The Z notation: A Reference Manual*. Prentice Hall International Series in Computer Science, ed. C.A.R.Hoare. 1989: Prentice Hall.
[17] A. R. Beresford and F. Stajano, Location Privacy in Pervasive Computing. *IEEE Pervasive Computing*. **2**(1): p. 46-455 (2003)
[18] *Security Services Use Cases and Requirements, Consensus draft 1*, Organization for the Advancement of Structured Information Standards (OASIS), draft specification 30 May 2001. http://www.oasis-open.org/committees/security/

APPENDIX A: PROOF OF THE PRIVACY PROPOSITION

Section 2.3 defines the privacy proposition as: *Any flow of information from a Private Attribute to a Principal is either from the Principal's own Private Attributes, or from a Private Attribute of a Trait that the Principal is allowed to process.*

$$\text{PRIVATE\_FLOW} = \text{PRIV} \cup \text{MATCH} \tag{17}$$

Proof. The method is to enumerate all possible paths from A to P in the graph, and show that this set of paths is a subset of PRIVATE_FLOW.

The set of all possible paths is the set of possible relational compositions of the edge set:

$$\text{PATHS} = \text{E} \circ \text{E} \circ \text{E} \circ \text{E} \circ \text{E}...... \tag{18}$$

The possible paths in this graph can be enumerated straightforwardly by inspection of their types, assuming the base classes in the model are disjoint:

$$\text{PATHS} = \text{PRIV} \cup (\text{BA} \circ \text{TA}) \cup (\text{BA} \circ \text{SA}) \tag{19}$$

The three sets whose union is PATHS are considered separately and each is shown to be a subset of PRIVATE_FLOW:

PRIV

PRIV occurs in (17) as a subset of PRIVATE_FLOW.

BA∘TA

Expanding the definition of composition, then further expanding BA:

$$\begin{aligned} BA \circ TA &= \{(a, p) \mid \exists t((a, t) \in BA \wedge (t, p) \in TA)\} \\ &= \{(a, p) \mid \exists t(\exists x[(t, x) \in TA \wedge (a, x) \in MATCH] \wedge (t, p) \in TA)\} \end{aligned} \tag{20}$$

Moving the quantifier for x out; then since (t,x) and (t,p) are in TA, and TA is a function we can conclude that x=p, eliminate x by substitution and remove one of the conjoined TA membership predicates:

$$= \{(a, p) \mid \exists t((t, p) \in TA \wedge (a, p) \in MATCH)\} \tag{21}$$

Moving quantifiers in and re-arranging:

$$= \{(a, p) \mid \exists t((t, p) \in TA) \wedge ((a, p) \in MATCH)\} \tag{22}$$

Since an element of this conjunction is MATCH, we can conclude that *BA∘TA* is a subset of MATCH and hence, from (17) a subset of PRIVATE_FLOW.

BA∘SA

Expanding the definition of composition, then further expanding SA:

$$\begin{aligned} BA \circ SA &= \{(a, p) \mid \exists t((a, t) \in BA \wedge (t, p) \in SA)\} \\ &= \{(a, p) \mid \exists t((a, t) \in BA \wedge [(a, t) \in BA \Rightarrow ((a, p) \in PRIV) \vee (a, p) \in MATCH)]\} \end{aligned} \tag{23}$$

Expanding the implication [...] and distributing the conjunction across the resulting expression:

$$\begin{aligned} &= \{(a, p) \mid \exists t([(a, t) \in BA \wedge \neg(a, t) \in BA] \vee \\ &[(a, t) \in BA \wedge (a, t) \in BA \wedge ((a, p) \in PRIV \vee (a, p) \in MATCH)])\} \end{aligned} \tag{24}$$

The left hand side of the disjunction can be eliminated (false), moving the quantifier in and eliminating one of the conjoined BA membership predicates:

$$= \{(a, p) \mid [(a, p) \in PRIV \vee (a, p) \in MATCH] \wedge \exists t((a, t) \in BA)\} \tag{25}$$

Since an element of this conjunction is (PRIV v MATCH), we can conclude from (17) that *BA∘SA* is a subset of PRIVATE_FLOW.

Conclusion

Each of the three sets *PRIV*, *BA∘TA* and *BA∘SA* are subsets of PRIVATE_FLOW; their union PATHS (19) is therefore also a subset of PRIVATE_FLOW. ***QED***

LOCAL MANAGEMENT OF CREDITS AND DEBITS IN MOBILE AD HOC NETWORKS*

Fabio Martinelli, Marinella Petrocchi, and Anna Vaccarelli
Istituto di Informatica e Telematica - CNR - Pisa, Italy
{ fabio.martinelli,marinella.petrocchi,anna.vaccarelli } @iit.cnr.it

Abstract Nodes in mobile ad hoc networks often need the help of others in order to have their packets delivered to their destination. However, nodes may not be governed by a single authority and need not share a common goal. Thus, a *selfish* node may prefer to save resources for its own communication, rather than to forward packets for other nodes. We suggest to collect information about the forwarding of packets in the network in a decentralized manner. Through reception of acknowledgments, a node can update a local repository, on which the node can rely to judge the behavior of the other nodes. We define a secure structure for the acknowledgments and the rules for updating the local repository. Also, we discuss a solution to achieve a univocal identification of a node in MANET environments.

Keywords: Mobile Ad Hoc Networks (MANETs), Selfishness

1. Introduction

Unlike traditional mobile networks, ad hoc networks do not rely on any wired infrastructure. Instead, the network is kept connected by the mobile hosts. In order to make a mobile network functional, the nodes need to be self-organized, in such a way that a message is delivered from a source to a destination through a set of intermediate nodes. The deployment of ad hoc networks for civilian applications is taking a footing. In such applications, the nodes are not governed by a single authority and need not share a common goal (the contrary could be the case in emergency and military applications). Thus, cooperative behaviors, such as forwarding each other's packets, cannot be easily assumed. The single nodes could prefer to save battery life for their own communication, rather than to forward packets for other nodes. Such an attitude is denoted in the recent literature as *selfishness* of the node. Simulation results (see, *e.g.*, (Michiardi and Molva, 2002b)) have recently pointed out that

*Work partially supported by the MIUR project: "Strumenti, Ambienti e Applicazioni Innovative per la Società dell'Informazione", sottoprogetto SP1: Reti INTERNET: "efficienza, integrazione e sicurezza"; by the CSP project: SeTAPS II; by the Quality of Protection (QoP) project: CREATE-NET.

a selfish behavior can be as harmful, in terms of the network throughput, as a malicious one.

There is a growing interest in the research community for detecting and preventing selfish behavior, and promoting cooperation between nodes, (see, *e.g.*, (Buchegger and Boudec, 2002; Buttyan and Hubaux, 2002; Marti et al., 2000; Michiardi and Molva, 2002a; Salem et al., 2003; Zhong et al., 2003)). Here, we propose an infrastructure for a local management of credits (*i.e.*, a measure of how many packets node A has forwarded for node B) and debits (*i.e.*, a measure of how many packets node B has forwarded for node A). Each node maintains this information in a local repository that we call *credit table*, on which the node can rely to judge the past behavior of the other nodes in the network. More specifically, we define rules for the table initialization, its maintenance, and secure acknowledgments testifying the actual forwarding of packets in the network.

MANETs are prone to the following security threat: a node could be tempted to discard its initial identity and re-enter the network in disguise in environments where i) users are punished for their selfish behavior, or ii) new users are *a priori* granted to have an initial amount of packets forwarded. We investigate solutions to achieve a univocal relation between a physical device and the identity it claims at its first steps in the network.

We propose to use network-layer acknowledgments (additional data in routing protocols specifications like (Johnson et al., 2001)) to provide to the packet source an authenticated proof that the packet has been delivered to its destination. We specify the structure for the acknowledgment request and the corresponding acknowledgment. Then, we introduce a mechanism that amortizes the signaling of "occurred delivery" over blocks of *n* data packets, thus reducing the communication overhead on the way back from destination to source. Further, we deal with some kind of attacks to which our scenario is prone.

Finally, in the model we have developed, if node A behaves well in forwarding packets for node B, then it can exploit this correct behavior only with B (meaning that A may rely on routes including B for sending its packets). Intuitively, systems based on such a rule can get stuck. Then we introduce the notion of credits *transferring*, according to which A may ask B to transfer, in a secure way, its credits to some other nodes.

The remainder of the paper is organized as follows: the next section illustrates related work in the area. In Section 3, we summarize the basic operation of the Dynamic Source Routing protocol (DSR), on which we rely at routing level. In Section 4 we define the trust setup of the network and the adversary model. Section 5 is dedicated to design the structure of the *credit table*. Then, we introduce the notion of credit *transferring* and we conclude the paper.

2. Related Work

We discuss here some work related to secure on demand routing protocols and cooperation enforcement in mobile ad hoc networks.

So called –on demand routing protocols– are those routing protocols in which a node tries to discover a route only when it has a packet to send.

Among on demand routing protocols, the Dynamic Source Routing protocol (DSR (Johnson et al., 2001)) is a protocol providing self-organization in configuring routing topologies for mobile wireless networks. It consists of two main phases, Route Discovery, the mechanism by which a source node, that does not have in its *Route Cache* the route to some destination yet, initiates to find a route, and Route Maintenance, the mechanism by which the source node detects, while sending a packet to some destination, if the route has been broken.

Hu *et al.* propose Ariadne, (Hu et al., 2002), securing a basic version of DSR. Ariadne provides: i) source authentication at the target's side; ii) authentication of each entry of the discovered path at the source's side; iii) integrity of the discovered path.

In (Zhou and Haas, 1999), the authors highlight peculiarities of ad hoc networks to fight against possible misbehaviors. Since routing protocols like DSR can return multiple routes, a node could exploit this *redundancy* to switch to an alternative route when the primary one has been broken because of a misbehavior.

A reputation system may be used in ad hoc networks to provide incentives in order to forward messages, *e.g.*, see (Buchegger and Boudec, 2002; Marti et al., 2000; Michiardi and Molva, 2002a). Both (Buchegger and Boudec, 2002) and (Marti et al., 2000) assume a network layer based on DSR. In (Marti et al., 2000), the authors consider complementing DSR with a watchdog mechanism to identify the misbehaving nodes, plus a path-rater mechanism to build new routes avoiding those nodes. Even if they show it is possible to keep the throughput of the network over a certain threshold even in presence of misbehaving nodes, the last are still allowed to send and receive packets. In (Buchegger and Boudec, 2002), the authors choose to act in a similar manner. They propose the CONFIDANT protocol, in which DSR is fortified by a neighborhood monitoring[1] and a trust manager which sends and receives alarm messages to and from other trust managers. A reputation system maintains a table listing ratings for all nodes and a path manager changes the route when the ratings for some nodes fall under a certain threshold. Hence, misbehaving nodes are totally isolated from the rest of the network.

We base our work on a (secure) DSR, like (Buchegger and Boudec, 2002; Marti et al., 2000) for MANETs. Similar to (Marti et al., 2000), our nodes do not exchange information with each other and they locally maintain history about their past behavior. Contrary to (Marti et al., 2000), we achieve information through cryptographic and acknowledgment mechanisms, whereas (Marti et al., 2000) assumes wireless interfaces that support promiscuous mode oper-

[1] In broadcast mediums, hosts are able to listen to messages that are not addressed to them. In particular, neighboring nodes are able to listen to their next-hop node transmissions.

ation. When this mode is enabled, a node can listen in on a neighbor's traffic. Thus, when A forwards a packet to B, A can overhear if B, in its turn, forwards the packet. Hence, (Marti et al., 2000) relies on first-hand information (*e.g.*, experienced and observed forwarding behavior of neighbors). Instead, we rely on trusted second-hand information, close to the approach of (Buchegger and Boudec, 2002), but we do not directly punish misbehaved nodes, rather we distinguish the well-behaved ones. Further, we focus on cryptographic solutions to handle the security of the information about the attitude of the nodes w.r.t. forwarding or dropping packets.

Michiardi and Molva, (Michiardi and Molva, 2002a), analyze enforcement of cooperation in game theoretical terms. The authors introduce the concept of redemption of nodes, *i.e.*, a misbehaving node starts well-behaving can be re-integrated in the network. The work in (Urpi et al., 2003) develops a formal model, based on game theory too, that captures features of MANETs like node mobility and selfishness. The paper provides a general model to describe cooperation enforcement policies.

Another possibility to provide incentives is to award well-behaving nodes with credits. (Buttyan and Hubaux, 2002) introduces a virtual currency called *nuglets*, by which a node is being paid when it forwards packets. Also, the node is forced to pay nuglets to send its own packets. With a pure selfish behavior, the node will soon finish its money and will not be able to send packets. In order to avoid the possibility that a node arbitrarily increases its own nuglets, a tamper-proof security module is required at each node.

The approach in (Buttyan and Hubaux, 2002) may appear close to our approach. As shown in Section 5, our packet source increases a debit counter for B upon receiving a proof that B has actually forwarded the source's packets. On the other hand, (Buttyan and Hubaux, 2002)'s philosophy is different from ours since our money is not physically gained by B, rather we rely on the fact that the source reasonably returns the favor to B for subsequent communication. Further, we do not put constraints to the node's capability to send packets. For this reason, and for the fact that each node will base its behavior on the data locally maintained, we do not need a tamper-proof module at each node. Within our framework, the credits that we gain cannot be spent with all nodes in the network, but only with those nodes for which we have forwarded something. On the contrary, *nuglets* can be spent for sending packets over all the available routes. We try to fill this gap by introducing the notion of credit *transferring*.

An award-based technique has been recently proposed also in (Zhong et al., 2003), where the authors rely on a central authority. Basically, when a node receives a message, it keeps a receipt for that message. Then, the node reports to the authority all the collected receipts. The authority evaluates the receipts and, consequently, it assigns charges and credits. The system does not need tamper-proof modules. (Zhong et al., 2003) presents similarities with our work because it considers secure receipts to testify the correct packet delivery. However, we rely on a central infrastructure only when a node enters the network, in order to bootstrap trust. Indeed, our solution exactly tries to avoid the necessity of such a central authority during the whole lifecycle of the community. We propose a self-organized credit management.

We ought to cite relevant work related to enforce cooperation between nodes belonging to other scenarios. Indeed, besides pure ad hoc networks, so called multi-hop cellular networks are getting a footing too. They combine features of both cellular and mobile ad hoc networks. Basically, they are cellular networks where there is the possibility of peer to peer or relayed multi-hop connections. Mobile hosts communicate with a wired infrastructure by means of wireless technology. A peculiarity is that communication between a base station and a mobile station may be relayed by other mobile stations. As novel work on co-operation in multi-hop cellular networks, we cite the approach of (Salem et al., 2003). Here, all communication between mobile hosts are required to pass through a base station, that actually acts as an authority for the distribution of symmetric primitives for securing data. Further, the base station is responsible for charging the initiator of a communication and for awarding the forwarding nodes.

Note that a multi-hop cellular network scenario allows (Salem et al., 2003) to exploit a base station either for the distribution of secret keys, thus exploiting symmetric cryptography between the base station and the nodes, and for charging and awarding nodes. Thus, (Salem et al., 2003) nicely addresses a scenario where a central authority is given for free.

(Lamparter et al., 2003) proposes another award-based mechanism for motivating cooperation in what the authors call *stub* ad hoc networks, *i.e.,* mobile networks with access to the Internet. Again, an external third party authenticates the nodes involved in a communication and it assigns charges and credits.

3. DSR

DSR (Dynamic Source Routing, (Johnson et al., 2001)) is an on-demand routing protocol designed to be used in mobile ad hoc networks. It consists of two main phases, Route Discovery, *i.e.,* the mechanism by which a source node initiates to find a route, and Route Maintenance, the mechanism by which the source node detects, while sending a packet to some destination, if the route has been broken.

The initiator of Route Discovery sends a Route Request message as a local broadcast specifying the Discovery's target. Each node receiving the request appends to the request its own IP address, unless it has recently seen that request, then it re-broadcasts the request. When the target receives the request, it creates a Route Reply message containing the list of addresses and sends it back to the initiator.

Route Maintenance monitors the reliability of a route. Detection of link breaks is often provided at no cost, when the routing protocol in use relies on a Medium Access Control protocol such as 802.11 (of the IEEE Computer Society, 1999), that provides link-layer acknowledgments. In this case, to test the reachability of the next-hop node, the previous-hop node waits for the reception of a link-layer acknowledgment (ACK). A limited number of retransmissions of the same packet is due, then, if the node does not receive link-layer ACKs from its next-hop neighbor, it sends a Route Error message back to the source, notifying it of a link break.

Instead of using link-layer acknowledgments, a node can explicitly require a network-layer acknowledgment to the next-hop neighbor (Johnson et al., 2001). The acknowledgment request is added as an optional part in the DSR header. In Section 5, we will propose to exploit network-layer ACKs to convey information about the actual forwarding of packets in the route. Though these ACKs were born with the intent of detecting link failures, we will exploit them to update information that each node locally maintains. We will suitably modify the acknowledgment mechanism, such that the nodes will be able to prove to have forwarded packets along a certain route.

Hereafter, it is understood that we rely on link layer ACKs at Medium Access Control level to detect link failures, while network-layer ACKs are used to convey information about the forwarding of packets. Further, we assume bidirectional communication on every link, *i.e.,* if node A is able to transmit to node B, then B is able to transmit to A.

4. Trust Setup

Before deployment, each node in the network generates a pair of public/private keys. A correct use of asymmetric cryptography requires to authenticate in a secure manner the association between the public keys and the identities with which they are associated. Public key certificates are a very well-known solutions to manage the matter. In frameworks where certificates validate the nodes at stake, we get into the issue of defining to which identifier (*e.g.,* node's identifier, IP address, MAC address, *etc.*) a public key must be associated. Indeed, an user could be tempted to discard its initial identity (hence requiring a new certificate, tied to a new identity) when its rating falls below a certain threshold. In reputation systems where misbehaving nodes are punished according to their reputation ratings, *e.g.,* by being isolated from the rest of the network, a way for the node to re-enter the network is to start from the beginning in disguise. Thus, the key point for MANETs is not only bootstrapping authentication of each node, *e.g.,* by establishing an authenticated link between a node's attribute and a public key, but also to avoid the delivery of two, or more, certificates that link different identifiers to the same device.

Location-Limited Channels (LLCs), out-of-band channels to bootstrap authentication in wireless networks, were first introduced in (Stajano and Anderson, 1999) and successively inherited by (Balfanz et al., 2002). In the former work, the *Resurrecting Duckling* protocol sets up a relationship between two devices, by exchanging a secret key over an LLC established through *physical contact.* In the latter, a pre-authentication phase has been considered, where mobile hosts exchange data that will then be used for subsequent authentication of the parties at stake, *e.g.,* the parties may commit to their public keys over LLCs. LLCs must support: i) *demonstrative identification, i.e.,* identification based on physical context (*e.g.,* operators must be able to visibly control which devices are communicating with each other during a transmission); ii) *authenticity, i.e.,* it is not feasible, at least with high probability, that a host transmits over these channels without being detected.

We provide the network with an infrastructure of authorities and LLCs s.t. a certificate is delivered over the LLC to an user that has requested for it over the LLC. By exploiting LLC features like physical contact, (Stajano and Anderson, 1999), – or demonstrative identification and authenticity, (Balfanz et al., 2002) – a device is able to obtain a certificate only upon communicating under, a visible monitoring, a univocal credential (hereafter, UC). Such a credential could be either the serial number or the MAC address physically assigned to that device. Although a MAC address can be forged at software level, here we require its physical acquisition. The released certificate associates a public key (acquired by the authority together with UC) with the hash value of UC and it is signed by the private key of the authority.

By virtue of the media over which data are sent, a credential can be achieved by an authority in an unforgeable way. Thus, we extend the use of LLCs, originally introduced for pre-authentication between devices that successively communicate with each other. We propose them to assign unique certificates to mobile devices, thus precluding a device from re-certifying with a new UC.

One may comment that in the environment under investigation an approach based on a Certification Authority is not adequate, given the fully distributed and self-organizing topology of mobile ad hoc networks. Note that assumptions relying on central facilities intrinsically exist in the literature. As an example, *nuglets* in (Buchegger and Boudec, 2002) are universally known as valid by the community, and a tamper-proof module is required at each node. This makes it reasonable to think about an initial bootstrapping of the required infrastructure. Further, note that the use of the authority is here limited to an initial phase, in which bootstrapping of some required features is achieved, while other schemes, *e.g.,* (Lamparter et al., 2003; Zhong et al., 2003), rely on a central facility for the whole network lifecycle.

Identities in digital certificates. Although in standard X.509 based PKIs the same CA does not knowingly issue certificates to different entities under the same distinguished name, *i.e.,* all the valid certificates related to the same distinguished name are bound to the same entity, it could be possible for one entity to obtain several certificates, whose validity periods possibly overlap, validating different public keys under different pseudonyms. However, in many applications, there is the need for a third party to identify certificates that are bound to the same entity. Uncertainties in taking a decision are, for example, when: i) different pseudonyms are used by the same entity; ii) certificates issued by different CAs present a coincidence of names in the distinguished name field. Steps towards a possible solution are in (Pinkas and Gindin, 2004) (released on January, 2004, it will expire on July, 2004), where the concept of *Permanent Identifier* PI has been defined. PI is assigned to an entity by an Assigner Authority, and any certificate including the same identifier refers to the same entity, whatever the distinguished name may be. Since organizations can create links between different certificates through PIs, privacy problems can arise. Privacy issues are actually taken into account in (Jong-Wook and Polk, 2003) (released on October, 2003, it has expired on April, 2004; as declared by the authors, it should be considered as a work in progress — the same holds for (Pinkas and Gindin, 2004)), where the authors propose the notion of *Protected Identification Information, i.e.,* a commitment to PI.

Here, we consider a scenario with similarities to the above-depicted one. In particular, in our scenario there should be, at any time, only one valid certificate related to a certain device. (Actually, one may consider key rollover features for the renewal of certificates. We do not deal with key rollover in the current work. We assume here the lifetime of the network under consideration to be shorter than the lifetime of all the certificates at stake.)

Thus, we do not only need to find a credential *cr* peculiar to device *dv*, thus allowing a univocal association *cr*–*dv*, but also we need to assure that *dv*, at any time, does not possess more than one valid UC. We remark that this requirement is due since devices may easily use pseudonyms and IP addresses may be assigned by any mechanism (*e.g.,* through DHCP for dynamic assignment).

We rely on some physical attribute of the devices at stake (*e.g.,* the serial number), unforgeable since acquired by the authority through LLCs. At any time, the authority is responsible for the existence of one valid certificate related to a certain UC. Note that UCs do not appear in the certificate as a plaintext, hence our scheme may preserve privacy of the device at stake.

Finally, some words about open issues we do not deal with in this paper. Digital certificates have a validity period, after that they expire. One may also explicitly ask the certificate issuer to revoke the certificate, when, for instance, the user's private key is lost or compromised. In our framework, in case the private key is stolen, the responsibility for the thief's actions could fall on the original user. Indeed, the certificate binds the public key corresponding to the stolen private key to a UC that unequivocally identifies the original user. Dealing with expiration and explicit requests for revocation is actually a part of our ongoing research.

Adversary model. According to (Michiardi and Molva, 2003), "a selfish node does not directly intend to damage other nodes [...] by disrupting routing information [...] but it simply does not cooperate to the basic network functioning". Routing disruption attacks are those attacks, (Hu et al., 2002), where an adversary can route packets in a dysfunctional way, *e.g.,* it may attempt to make a suboptimal route to be chosen, for example a longer one. On the other hand, some authors assume that a selfish node may have also an active, malicious behavior, located somewhere between a non-cooperative behavior and a misbehavior aiming at damaging the others. As an example, in a reputation system providing awards, like the one in (Buttyan and Hubaux, 2002), a tamper-proof module is required at each node to prevent the node itself from intentionally increasing its nuglet counter.

The above considerations lead us to assume the following: a selfish node could not cooperate to the basic network functioning (*e.g.*, packet forwarding) and it could also illegally act in order to obtain benefits for sending its own packets. Suppose an adversary adds virtual nodes to a route which it belongs to, and suppose furthermore the adversary *owns* those added virtual nodes, then, it could consequently take the credit for the correct behavior of these nodes. Hence, it appears necessary to supply the network with protocols guaranteeing authenticity and integrity of control routing packets. To this aim, one may assume at routing level a secure version of DSR, like Ariadne (Hu et al., 2002). In our architecture all nodes have their cryptographic pair of keys certified before entering the network. Thus, we assume a secure Route Discovery based on Ariadne in its digital signature version (*i.e.*, Route Request is composed by nested signatures of IP addresses). We further assume the following extension: node i, receiving and processing a Route Request, appends its digital certificate $Cert^i$ to the request. Thus, Route Reply back to the source contains a certificate list, and each node receiving Route Reply is required to cache the list. Finally, node i, taking part in Route Discovery, appends to the request the hash of its univocal identifier, $h(UC_i)$.

Route Requests presenting more than one signature verifiable with the same public key should be marked as invalid requests and discarded. Further, there must be a correspondence between each fingerprint $h(UC_i)$ certified in $Cert^i$ and the one in the signed request.

A final remark: a certificate is validated by verifying its digital signature through the public key of the authority that has released the certificate. We assume that such public key is transmitted through the LLC.

5. The Credit Table

A table called the *credit table* (CT) is maintained at each node's side. Rows in the table consist of triples (*h(UC)*, *# debs*, *# creds*), where $h(UC)$ is the hash value of its univocal identifier, and *# creds* and *# debs* are the current values of the credits and debits counter related to that node.

The entity who maintains the table, say node A, quantifies the good behavior of the node corresponding to *h(UC)*, say node B, w.r.t. B's past attitude to forward packets for A. From a complementary point of view, node B, that maintains in its turn memory about its behavior w.r.t. A, quantifies how much A can be indebted to B, *i.e.,* until when B can run the risk to forward packets for A. To limit the damages to forward packets for selfish nodes that do not return the favor, we give an upper bound over which it is not possible to help a node. We set this value to a default value $gap > 0$, equal for all nodes when they enter the network. Potentially, the entity who maintains a table can assign different values for *gap* to different entries in its table. For example, after deployment, a node *A* can set n different values $gap_1, \ldots, gap_n$, according to the perception *A* has about $node_1, \ldots, node_n$'s behavior (the latter being entries in *A*'s table). Provided that node *B* behaves correctly, it forwards packets for node *A* if *creds* – *debs* $\leq$ *gap*, where *debs* and *creds* are the value of the debits/credits counters related to *A* in *B*'s table.

B spends the earned credit *creds* at *A*'s side when it starts sending packets along a route including *A*. From another point of view, suppose *B* needs to send packets to destination *D*: it either can recover an established path from its route cache or starts DSR Route Discovery, possibly returning several paths. In any case, by maintaining history of the past behavior of the network, *B* could choose the more *convenient* route (in terms of the nodes belonging to the route) rather than the shortest one.

CT Initialization. *S* asks for Route Discovery the first time it needs to send packets to destination *D*. The hash values of the univocal identifiers of the nodes in the returned path are the first entries in *S*'s table. For all entries, the initial value assigned to both *debs* and *creds* is zero.

A CT table is initialized also by nodes belonging to a discovered path. Hence, a node forwarding a Route Reply message back to the source initializes its table by inserting those nodes listed in the path list, source included.

CT Maintenance. CT Maintenance is the mechanism by which the nodes update their CT. There could be two cases: 1) the node is the packet source *S*. In this case, updating the table happens once an authenticated proof has been received which testifies that the packet has been delivered to its destination. The authenticated proof is contained in a network-layer acknowledgment. When the source receives the acknowledgment, it increases by one the *debs* field correspondent to the identifiers of all the nodes constituting the current route. Thus, *debs* gives a measure, at *S*'s side, of how many packets a certain node has forwarded for *S*. 2) The node belongs to the route from source *S* to destination *D*. Upon forwarding a packet, the node increases by one the *creds* field for *S*. Thus, the *creds* counter maintains information about how many packets the node has forwarded for *S*. Before forwarding a packet, the node checks if the difference of *creds* and *debs* related to *S* is greater (or equal) than the default value *gap* (or the value gap_S that the node has assigned to *S*). If so, the node forwards the packet for *S* (unless the node is a selfish one), otherwise it drops the packet.

We do not need a tamper-proof security module at each node, because the information recorded in a node's CT does not influence the rest of the network.

5.1 Authentication of data packets.

In the following, we consider a simple path from node S to node D through intermediate nodes A, B and C. We call route S-A-B-C-D Route 1.

In (Salem et al., 2003), the authors consider two kind of attacks to which a mobile ad hoc environment is prone. The first attack is when an intermediate node, say A, exploits a sub-route of Route 1, *e.g.*, A-B-C, to send its own packets. A may claim that those packets come from S and intermediate nodes B and C will charge S upon forwarding the packets. The second attack is the free riding attack. A may append (or substitute) its own payloads to the data packets transmitted from S to D over Route 1. The forged payloads may be consumed by C, that colludes with A, and B will charge S[2].

The above-mentioned attacks may be solved by exploiting part of a mechanism originally developed to sign digital streams, (Gennaro and Rohatgi, 2001). Let us suppose that S is to send blocks of *n* data packets to D. The construction exploits the technique of embedding the hash of the following packet in the current packet. Bootstrapping authentication is obtained by applying an initial digital signature, in combination with hash chaining. p_i be the i-th data packet sent by S (packet header plus meaningful payload). Then, the high-level formalization is as follows (we omit to explicitly denote the intermediate nodes A, B, C):

$$\begin{array}{llllll} 0) & S & \rightarrow & D & : p'_0 : & \{h(p'_1)\}_{pk_S^{-1}} \\ i) & S & \rightarrow & D & : p'_i : & p_i, h(p'_{i+1}) \quad i = 1, \ldots, n-1 \\ n) & S & \rightarrow & D & : p'_n : & p_n \end{array}$$

By doing so, source authentication is provided. Then, an intermediate node neither can append, or substitute, meaningful payloads to the data in the packet, since it should be able to forge digital signatures and hash functions, nor can claim its own transmissions to come from S, since it does not know the private key pk_S^{-1} [3]. Finally, this technique is applied on the whole packet, thus preserving integrity both of the data and of the packet header. Note that that construction assures authenticity to the ACK request option too.

Structure of network-layer ACKs and ACKs requests. Instead of requiring one ACK for every single packet arrived to its destination, we expect one ACK for every single block of *n* packets. This reduces the communication overhead on the way back from D to S.

To this aim, we propose the ACK request option in the first data packet header to have the following structure:

$$\text{ACK Req Opt: } << type, len, id, SAddr, DAddr >>$$

where *type* specifies this is an acknowledgment request option, *len* is the length of the option, *id* is the identifier of the packet to be acknowledged. We set *id* = *n*, *i.e.,* the number of packets for which an acknowledgment is required, starting from this data packet. *SAddr* is the address of the node requesting the acknowledgment[4] and must be set to $(IP_S, h(UC_S))$. *DAddr* is the address

[2]Note that possible solutions to these attacks are beyond the scope of secure ad hoc routing protocols like Ariadne. Indeed, they address the authenticity of routing control packets, but not the one of data packets.

[3]As is common in security protocol analysis, we assume that digital signatures and hash functions cannot be forged, and moreover that it is not possible for an adversary to guess secrets of other participants.

[4]Extension already implemented in routing protocols specification like (Johnson et al., 2001).

of the node that should acknowledge the reception of n packets and must be set to $(IP_D, h(UC_D))$[5]. An acknowledgment request option must be ignored by all the intermediate nodes and must be processed only by D. If D correctly receives all the *n* packets for which ACK has been requested, it processes the request by sending back to *SAddr* an authenticated acknowledgment, whose structure is the following:

$$\text{ACK Opt: } << \{type, len, id, SAddr, DAddr, path\}_{pk_D^{-1}} >>$$

where *type* specifies this is an acknowledgment option, *len* is the length of the option, *id* = *n* is the number of packets that are acknowledged as received. *SAddr* is the address of the node originating the acknowledgment, *i.e.,* $(IP_D, h(UC_D))$. *DAddr* is the address of the node to which the acknowledgment is to be delivered, *i.e.,* $(IP_S, h(UC_S))$. With respect to routing protocols specification such as (Johnson et al., 2001), we have added the extension *path, i.e.,* the sequence of addresses as in the DSR Source Route Option in the header of the received packets. Here, *path* $=(IP_A, h(UC_A)), (IP_B, h(UC_B)), (IP_C, h(UC_C))$.

Since ACKs have smaller size than control and data packets, we assume that the nodes co-operate in sending ACKs back to the source. Further, given that S does not update its CT until it receives the proof that the packets have been delivered to their destination, it appears reasonable to assume that the intermediate nodes, that have already forwarded the packets, will cooperate in forwarding back to S the ACK.

If a node stops forwarding packets within a block, D never acquires the last packet, and it does not send back the ACK. As a consequence, the well-behaved nodes are never awarded by S. Possible patches to this drawback are: i) when D stops receiving packets, it notifies the anomaly to S, by sending an alert message (possibly over multiple routes); ii) an upper bound gap to the block size may be fixed. Thus, the intermediate nodes will not forward more than gap packets (*i.e.,* the limit we gave at the beginning of this section).

Like control and data packets, ACKs may be lost because of link breaks. We deal with this matter as follows: provided that D has in its Route Cache multiple routes to S, ACKs can be sent over all the available routes to S. Again, we assume to send (and forward) ACKs to be less power consuming than sending (and forwarding) data packets.

5.2 On the transfer of credits.

In the model we have presented, credits gained by node X can be *spent* only with the node for which X has forwarded something, say A. Intuitively, systems based on such rules can get stuck. We consider an established route

[5] The last field can be included as additional data in the Acknowledgment Request option in routing protocols specification like (Johnson et al., 2001).

A-B-X-C-D from source A to destination D. We know that if an intermediate node, say X, behaves correctly in forwarding packets for A, then it can reasonably rely on A for subsequent transmissions originated by X, when these transmissions involve routes including A. On the other hand, suppose X starts sending packets through route X-Y-W-Z and furthermore suppose that condition $creds - debs \leq gap_C$ is not fulfilled either for Y, or W, or both of them. In this case, X appears unable to correctly deliver packets to its destination.

Thus, we propose the notion of credits *transferring*, according to which X may rely on nodes not involved in the current route, say R, but likely willing to forward packets for X, for transfer their credits to the nodes in R. In particular, X will collect information regarding the nodes, in R, that are debtors to the nodes in X table for which it holds $creds - debs \leq 0$, meaning that X has made more favors to those nodes than they have made to X.

Credit transferring protocol. We consider three entities, namely: X, willing to send n packets over route R; A $\notin$ R, that is a X *first-hand debtor* (*i.e.*, A might accept to forward a certain number of packets for X); B $\in$ R, that is a X *second-hand debtor* (*i.e.*, B might accept to forward a certain number of packets for A).

$$
\begin{array}{llcll}
1) & X & \rightarrow & B & : \{\text{X fhd list}, X, B, n, nonce_X\}_{pk_X^{-1}} \\
2) & B & \rightarrow & X & : \{A, B, X, m, nonce_X\}_{pk_B^{-1}} \quad m \leq n \\
3) & X & \rightarrow & A & : \{\{A, B, X, m, nonce_X\}_{pk_B^{-1}}\}_{pk_X^{-1}} \\
4) & A & \rightarrow & X & : \{nonce_X, yes\}_{pk_A^{-1}} \\
5) & X & \rightarrow & B & : \{\{nonce_X, yes\}_{pk_A^{-1}}\}_{pk_X^{-1}}
\end{array}
$$

The messages are signed by the private key of the sender. We assume that a special tag is contained in each message, to determine the message's step in the protocol. In message 1, X asks B if it agrees to accept a transfer of n credits from a node belonging to the list of X first-hand debtors. In particular, B should indicate who, among the nodes in the list, is its creditor. To maintain, in part, the user's privacy, items in the list should be hash values of the X first-hand debtors. The recipient of message 1 first computes the hash of the identifiers of the nodes to which it owes something, then it compares the hashes. Clearly, all the nodes processing message 1 may perform the same test, but, if they do not know those identifiers, X first-hand debtors remain unknown.

B indicates node A as a possible candidate for credit transferring (message 2). Through message 3, X asks A to transfer $m \leq n$ debits to B. A notifies the request acceptance to B (message 4). X notifies the credit transferring acceptance by forwarding message 4.

Provided that the protocol's participants behave correctly, they update their CT tables upon the reception of the messages. Updating CT tables is as reported in the scheme. In particular, X should refresh its table, as shown in Table # 1, upon receiving message 4 (meaning: X will not consider A as its debtor anymore, at least as far as m packets are concerned). In its turn, A refreshes its table, as shown in Table # 2, upon receiving a receipt that message 4 has been delivered to destination X. We rely on ACKs to convey receipts.

Upon reception of message 5, B will update its table as shown in Table # 3 (this is how we formalize the credit transferring operation). What appears after the updating is that in the past A has forwarded for B less packets than the packets A actually has forwarded, while X has forwarded for B more packets than the forwarded ones.

When m packets have finally reached their destination, not only X expects an acknowledgement, but also A. If A receives this proof, it updates its table as shown in Table # 4, meaning that A will not consider B as its debtor anymore.

Tables # 5 and # 6 show X and B updates, respectively, upon transmission of m packets. These standard updates follow the rules listed in Section 5.

A credit transferring protocol should be invoked in particular situations, *e.g.*, if the network under investigation supports high levels of mobility. We thus assume that the nodes cooperate in forwarding protocol messages and ACKs tied to a credit transferring, in order to maintain the basic network functioning, whereas the network could get stuck.

6. Conclusions

We have proposed to manage information about the forwarding behavior of the nodes in mobile ad hoc networks. Cryptography makes the information deduced by each node more reliable. Furthermore, we have proposed a mechanism to transfer the knowledge between different nodes. The novelty, w.r.t. previous mechanisms, is the avoidance of a central authority, the special stress on secure communication as well as on mechanisms to avoid that a user drops its identity. We are currently working on simulating the network performance to validate our approach. As future work, we plan to investigate new forms of

	debs	*creds*
id_A	-	creds-m
id_B	-	creds+m
other IDs	-	-

X table # 1

	debs	*creds*
id_X	debs-m	-
other IDs	-	-

A table # 2

	debs	*creds*
id_A	debs-m	-
id_X	debs+m	-
other IDs	-	-

B table # 3

Credit transferring

	debs	*creds*
id_B	-	creds-m
other IDs	-	-

A table # 4

	debs	*creds*
id_B	debs+m	-
other IDs	-	-

X table # 5

	debs	*creds*
id_X	-	creds + m
other IDs	-	-

B table # 6

credit transferring and routing protocols, based on the information gathered by users, as well as certificate expiration and key rollover issues.

References

Balfanz, D., Smetters, D., Stewart, P., and Wong, H. C. (2002). Talking to Strangers: Authentication in Ad-Hoc Wireless Networks. In *Proc. of NDSS'02*. The Internet Society.

Buchegger, S. and Boudec, J. L. (2002). Performance Analysis of the CONFIDANT Protocol. Cooperation Of Nodes – Fairness In Dynamic Ad-hoc Networks. In *Proc. of ACM MobiHoc'02*.

Buttyan, L. and Hubaux, J. (2002). Stimulating Cooperation in Self-Organizing Mobile Ad Hoc Networks. *ACM/Kluwer Mobile Networks and Applications (MONET)*, 8(5).

Gennaro, R. and Rohatgi, P. (2001). How to Sign Digital Streams. *Information and Computation*, 165(1):100–116.

Hu, Y., Perrig, A., and Johnson, D. (2002). Ariadne: A secure on-demand routing protocol for ad hoc networks. In *Proceedings of the Eighth ACM International Conference on Mobile Computing and Networking (Mobicom 2002)*.

Johnson, D., Maltz, D., and Broch, J. (Addison-Wesley, 2001). DSR The Dynamic Source Routing Protocol for Multihop Wireless Ad Hoc Networks. *Ad Hoc Networking, chapter 5*, pages 139–172.

Jong-Wook, P. and Polk, T. (Internet Draft, October 2003). Internet X.509 Public Key Infrastructure Subject Identification Method SIM.

Lamparter, B., Plaggemeier, M., and Westhoff, D. (2003). About the Impact of Co-operation Approaches for Ad Hoc Networks. In *Proc. of ACM MobiHoc'03*.

Marti, S., Giuli, T., Lai, K., and Baker, M. (2000). Mitigating Routing Misbehaviour in Mobile Ad Hoc Networks. In *Proc. of MobiCom'00*, pages 255–265. ACM.

Michiardi, P. and Molva, R. (2002a). Core: A Collaborative Reputation Mechanism to Enforce Node Cooperation in Mobile Ad Hoc Networks. In *Proc. of CMS'02*.

Michiardi, P. and Molva, R. (2002b). Simulation-based Analysis of Security Exposures in Mobile Ad Hoc Networks. In *Proc. of European Wireless'02*.

Michiardi, P. and Molva, R. (2003). A Game Theoretical Approach to Evaluate Cooperation Enforcement Mechanisms in Mobile Ad hoc Networks. In *Proc. of WiOpt'03*.

of the IEEE Computer Society, L. M. S. C. (1999). Wireless LAN Medium Access Control (MAC) and Physical Layer (PHY) Specifications. In *IEEE Standard 802.11, 1999 Edition*.

Pinkas, D. and Gindin, T. (Internet Draft, January 2004). Internet X.509 Public Key Infrastructure Permanent Identifier.

Salem, N. B., Buttyan, L., Hubaux, J., and Jakobsson, M. (2003). A Charging and Rewarding Scheme for Packet Forwarding in Multi-hop Cellular Networks. In *Proc. of ACM MobiHoc'03*.

Stajano, F. and Anderson, R. (1999). The Resurrecting Duckling: Security Issues for Ad-Hoc Wireless Networks. In *Proc. of 7th Security Protocols Workshop*, volume LNCS 1796, pages 172–194.

Urpi, A., Bonuccelli, M., and Giordano, S. (2003). Modelling Cooperation in Mobile Ad-hoc Networks: a Formal Description of Selfishness. In *Proc. of WiOpt'03*.

Zhong, S., Chen, J., and Yang, Y. (2003). Sprite: a Simple, Cheat-Proof, Credit-Based System for Mobile Ad-Hoc Networks. In *Proc. of IEEE Infocom'03*.

Zhou, L. and Haas, Z. (1999). Securing Ad Hoc Networks. *IEEE Network*, 13(6):24–30.

HOW SECURE ARE CURRENT MOBILE OPERATING SYSTEMS?

Tobias Murmann, Heiko Rossnagel
Chair of Mobile Commerce and Multilateral Security
Johann Wolfgang Goethe-University Frankfurt
D-60054 Frankfurt / Main, Germany
www.whatismobile.de

Abstract: There are numerous initiatives to use mobile devices as so-called "trusted pocket signers" to produce electronic signatures. The actual signature is generated by means of a conventional signature card. The mobile device serves as the card reader, storage device for the document to be signed and as a display for the signature application. The operating system used on the mobile device has thus a pivotal importance to ensure the integrity and accountability of the electronic signature. Also mobile devices are used to provide mobile workers with access to the corporate backend. We examined the currently available mobile operating systems in regard to their security and conclude that not a single one is secure enough for "trusted" signing and only partially for secure backend access. We show two possible ways of how to make mobile devices more secure and possibly to enable something close to "what you see is what you sign".

Key words: Mobile Operating Systems, Trusted Devices

1. INTRODUCTION

Mobile devices are becoming ever more capable and are able to open up a broader range of applications in professional environments due to their increasing functionalities. Personal Digital Assistants (PDAs) and Smartphones allow users to access sensitive personal data at any time and any place, making it possible to increase productivity. In the case of mobile devices carrying sensitive data like patient data, customer lists and address data, amongst others, the security of these data must be ensured.

Corporations are using mobile devices to enable their mobile workforce to get access to their backend. Since this company data can be very confidential the access to the backend must be secure. The WiTness project sponsored by the European Union [WiTness2004] aims to provide secure backend access by means of GSM technology. Figure 1 shows an application scenario where a "pervasive salesman" has secure, corporate-controlled access to all data available to him in the corporate information system. Access is controlled by a security module based on a SIM with additional security functionality.

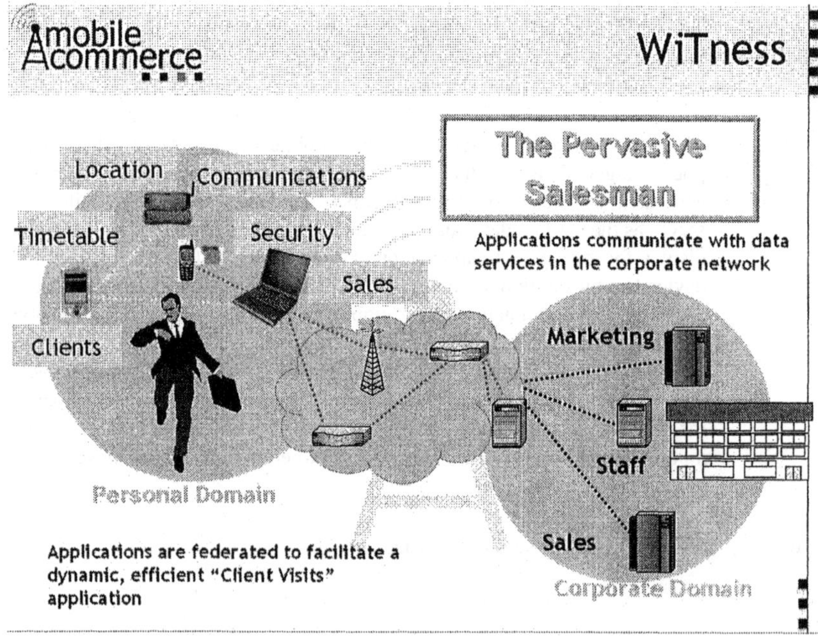

Figure 1: WiTness Pervasive Salesman Scenario [WiTness2004]

But even if the communication and access to the backend are secured, the mobile device itself remains open to possible attacks. If corporate data is stored on the device an attacker could try to circumvent the access control mechanisms of the device in order to get access to the stored data.

There are also some initiatives using mobile devices as so-called "trusted pocket signers" to produce electronic signatures [MobTra2004]. The actual signature is generated by means of a conventional signature card (according to the EC-Directive [EC_esig1999]). The mobile device serves as the card reader, storage device for the document to be signed and as a display for the signature application. Therefore, it must be ensured that the data shown on the display is identical with the data signed by the signature card (WYSIWYS)[1]. The operating system used on the mobile device has thus a pivotal importance to ensure the integrity and accountability of the digital signature.

If the authorization mechanisms, memory protection, process generation and separation or protection of files in an operating system are flawed, an attacker may gain access to the different internal processes. He might take advantage of this situation to generate forged signatures.

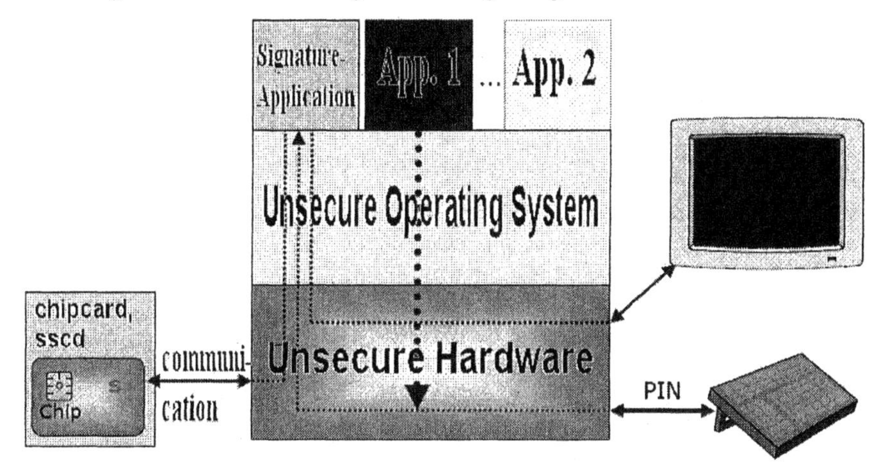

Figure 2: Manipulated digital signature [Federr2003]

Figure 2 illustrates that application 1 as a malicious program can intercept the PIN, for example. An even considerably higher risk exists, however, if the malicious application changes the data to be signed after they are displayed to the user. Due to the virtually unrestricted hardware access, a malicious program is able to manipulate all data transmitted to the signature application before the actual signature takes place.

We examine the current available mobile operating systems in regard to their suitability for both scenarios. Using the mobile device as a trusted pocket signer poses the hardest security requirements (especially in regard to accountability and integrity). From a business perspective the confidentiality of the corporate data seems to be the most important protection goal.

In section 2, operating systems that are currently available on the market are examined, and some important security flaws are pointed out. Section 3 presents a glance at the future and examines how these problems can be

[1] What You See Is What You Sign

solved by means of software or hardware solutions. In section 4, the results obtained are summarized.

2. SECURITY ANALYSIS OF CURRENT MOBILE OS

2.1 PocketPC

PocketPC [Pocket2004] does not provide the possibility to encrypt data. Even the internal communication is not secured. Due to its design, PocketPC neither separates memory blocks nor applications effectively from each other. Each application can adjust its priorities, terminate other applications, access their memory or prevent the switchover into the power-save mode.

Passwords can be deactivated by the user and are frequently deactivated in the standard setting. Also, an attacker can easily take out the external storage medium from the device and steal the data that is stored there. Even worse is the possibility to port malware onto the PDA in this way. This malware could later fake a signature as shown above.

Fake dialogs are possible because of malware. But even an uninfected PDA with PocketPC allows fake dialogs. As the Microsoft operating system supports Active X and Java, these can be used to create fake dialogs.

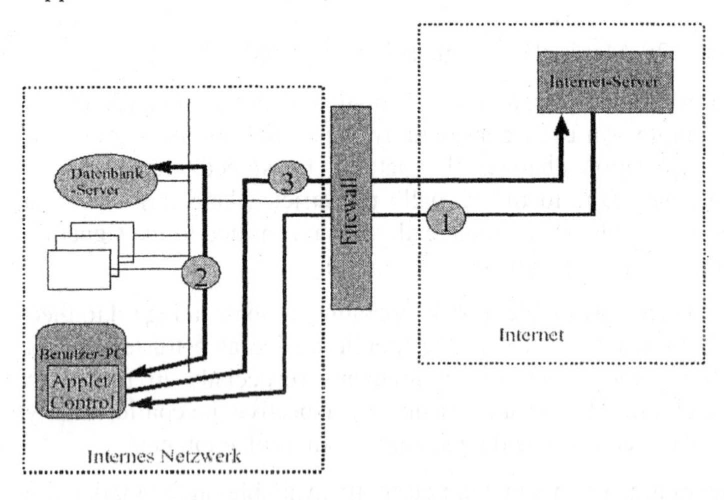

Figure 3: Mobile code attack scenario [FoxHor1991]

1. The user loads the applet (Java) or control (ActiveX) from a web server, which is then executed on the customer's mobile device.

2. The applet/control makes use of the owner's authorizations to gain access to the company's database, and copies data onto the mobile device.
3. The applet/control sends the data obtained back to the Internet server.

In case of a Java applet, the so-called sandbox restricts the applet's access to the hardware and software. However, the user may have granted the applet too many rights, or an attacker may use one of the many security gaps in the Java virtual machine. The user's security may be protected by a code-signing mechanism, with which the origin of programs can be certified. However, with this mechanism, only the origin of a program can be determined, but the actual contents can be harmful. But since the administration of certificates is not possible with PocketPC, any form of mobile code must be deactivated in the setting.

There is a theoretic possibility of hidden backdoors in PocketPC, as the source code is not open. A protection from buffer overflows and against the manipulation of the DMA functionality cannot be provided by means of additional software. Manipulated programs are able to act with all user authorizations, as there is no distribution of rights. PocketPC 2002 exhibits a large number of security gaps which cannot be closed completely by means of additional security software, such as PDA Secure [PDASe2004] or PDA Defense [PDADe2004]. Due to these security risks, PocketPC cannot be used as an operating system for a "trusted" pocket signer. Even for the scenario of the WiTness Pervasive Salesman in Figure 1, PocketPC should not be used. The impossibility of deactivating or bypassing passwords is an essential feature for this scenario. Furthermore, certificate management is necessary. Certificate management can't even be reached with additional software, which shows that PocketPC is only secure enough for private usage.

2.2 PalmOS

Like PocketPC, PalmOS [Palm2004] does not have an effective distribution of rights and separation of processes. There is no secure path between the applications and the kernel, and the communication is vulnerable. Furthermore, the user, as with all operating systems, cannot check if the status of the device is secure. This could be achieved by means of an LED, for example, which indicates if the PDA is in a secure stadium after examination. A more detailed description will be given in section 3.

If an attacker gains possession of the activated device, he can synchronize it with any PC and install malware. Passwords, too, are protected unsatisfactorily in PalmOS. As the source code is not open in PalmOS either, there is a possibility of hidden backdoors. Mobile code can be executed by means of Java on the mobile device so that the "mobile code attack scenario", as shown in Figure 2, applies as well. Palm does not support a certificate management system either so that a manipulated certificate would not be recognized.

Direct memory access is supported by PalmOS through the support of ARM and DragonBall processors.

A manipulated program has the possibility to act with all user authorizations. Just as for PocketPC, security software, such as PDA Secure or PDA Defense, is available. But even if these are applied, there are still security risks that do not make it possible to employ PalmOS as a secure operating system for electronic signatures.

PalmOS shows similar security holes as PocketPC 2002. Without additional software there is no possibility to secure the passwords. Further more there is no certificate management. This points out that PalmOS, like PocketPC, is not secure enough for the Pervasive Salesman Scenario. Due to these risks, PalmOS like PocketPC cannot be used as an operating system for a "trusted" pocket signer.

2.3 Symbian

Symbian [Symbian2004] as an operating system provides better protection than PalmOS and PocketPC 2002. The device can be administered in the corporate network by means of an access control list. By using this list, certain contents can be protected from being accessed by other device management servers so that the data can only be synchronized with a certain server.

So far, no major security gaps are known for the operating system. However, with the Nokia Wintesla maintenance program [UCable2003], far-reaching interventions in the mobile device are possible, even when it is blocked. The attacker obtains full access to all setup options of the device, can unblock it with the knowledge gained and has full access to the stored data. Any security claims for Nokia devices are thus reduced to absurdity.

Mobile code and thus fake dialogs are possible due to the support of Java. In contrast to PalmOS and PocketPC, certificate management is installed as a protection against forged certificates. But the user cannot check the security status of the device and has hardly any possibility to install additional security software on the device.

Symbian devices are thus not suited to generate qualified signatures, as there are security gaps, such as a lack of process separation, and especially since there are tools that are able to bypass any security instruments in Symbian. Without the problem of the Wintesla Tool, Symbian provides more security features than PalmOS or PocketPC. With the features of the access control list and the support of certificate management Symbian supports the scenario of the Pervasive Salesman. But even with the better protection of the saved data, Symbian is by far not secure enough for the "trusted pocket signers" scenario.

2.4 Linux

The Linux operating system provides the user with the largest number of security functions from the operating systems presented so far. Due to the possibility of determining permissions for processes, data, etc., a better protection of the data against misuse is ensured. However, there are still numerous security gaps, such as the DMA functionality, which has to be deactivated manually, or the possibility of performing synchronizations without authentication. Furthermore, there are viruses and worms, even if not directly for mobile Linux distributions. It is clear, however, that these are endangered as well, and protection, for example, by means of rights distribution and against buffer overflows is not sufficient. In addition, virtually no additional software is available for Linux-operated devices so that an additional protection cannot be installed. Also, there are too few Linux devices, and changing from the existing operating system to Linux is time-consuming and risky.

The SUSE distribution in combination with the IBM server was thus only graded EAL2 by the German Federal Office of Security in Information Technology [BSI2003]. PDAs with a distribution built on the standard kernel therefore cannot generate sufficiently secure signatures that would make them legally equivalent to the hand-written signature.

Linux provides the best security features for mobile devices. But as described above, Linux could not provide a totally secure area for a "trusted pocket signer". This is pointed out by the decision of the BSI [BSI2003]. But with the implementation of many security features, Linux is the most secure conventional operating system and supports the Pervasive Salesman scenario.

3. POSSIBLE SOLUTIONS

The two following suggestions for a solution are in their development stages and can presently only be used to a limited extent. Nonetheless, they will provide a better protection of the PC and/or mobile device in the future. The objective of these approaches is to protect the internal processes by means of a strict distribution of permissions in the lowest layers. Only by a system-wide separation of memory, access and input/output rights for processes and applications can a system be protected against any kind of malicious programs. By not giving malicious programs all user rights as in current systems, the solutions presented seek to minimize the risk of damage. Above all, the user for the first time has the possibility to check if the computer is in a secure state and if he is communicating securely with the kernel. This is not possible in current systems.

3.1 Perseus

Perseus is an open source project at Saarland University [Perseu2004]. It is aimed at developing a small microkernel as a secure platform. In addition, the user interface shows the user securely what status the system is in, without a malicious program being able to manipulate it. Generally, a kernel is responsible for the administration of the device, files, memory and processes and is loaded directly after booting. The Perseus kernel is aimed at protecting security-critical applications by isolating the individual processes from each other. Perseus is based on the approach that a normal operating system runs like an application, and therefore the Perseus kernel lies below the operating system in the layer architecture. Only by being embedded below the operating system, which is still needed, can Perseus permit isolated processes to take place system-wide between the applications. Isolated processes are not possible for applications within the standard operating system, however, but only between the individual "secure applications" and the Perseus operating system.

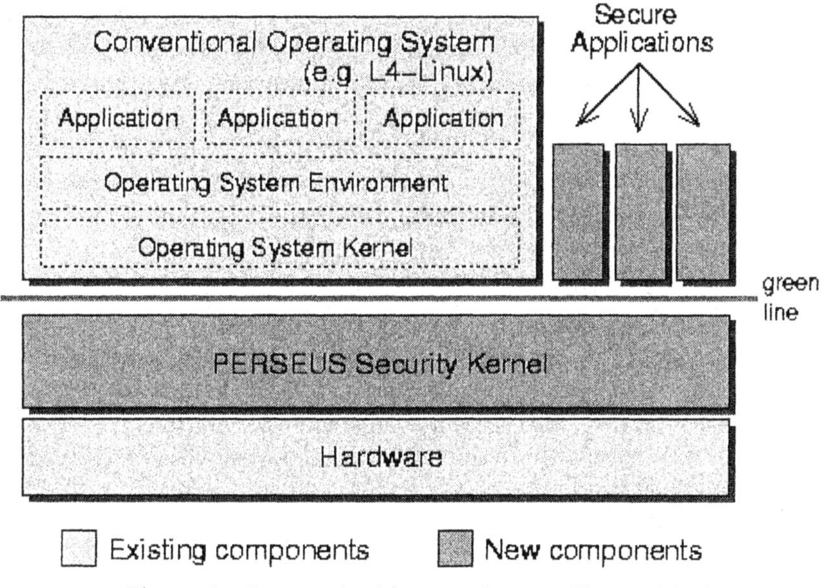

Figure 4: System Architecture Perseus [Perseu2004]

In the Perseus prototype, the trustworthy user interface reserves a line in the upper section of the screen that is permanently under the control of the security kernel.

As the line or LED is under the sole control of Perseus, it cannot be misused by a compromised operating system. If the display indicates that the user is communicating with the Perseus kernel, the control of the display and keyboard solely lies with the security kernel.

3.2 Trusted Platform Module

The "Trusted Platform Module" (TPM) was specified by the "Trusted Computing Group (TCG)", formerly "Trusted Computing Platform Alliance (TCPA)" [TCPA2004].

The TCG hardware consists of two tamper resistant modules called TPM and CRTM (Core Root of Trust for Measurement). Both of them will only be of use if an operating system is used that supports them. Currently there are two operating systems being developed that will support TCG hardware. Microsoft is developing a security technology called NGSCB (Next Generation Secure Computing Base) that will be included in the Longhorn operating system and there are also initiatives to develop a Linux distribution that supports the TCG security modules [MaSmMaWi2003].

The TPM hardware module can be regarded as an extended smart card on which secrets inside and outside of the TPM can be produced and stored [Pearso2002]. These secrets are symmetric and asymmetric keys that are used to ensure the trustworthiness of files, signing of data and the authentication of third parties on the platform. Furthermore, hash values are examined to identify the trustworthy hardware and software components and are stored in data integrity registers. For TPM to be active its hardware must be switched on and the software activated.

For each component (BIOS, OS-Loader and Operating System) a hash value is generated and transmitted to the TPM when the system is started. These values are stored in the "platform configuration register". It is then examined if the currently established hash values are identical with those stored on the TPM. If this is the case, the user can assume that the components and/or the data stored on them have not been manipulated, as otherwise the hash value would have changed and the system or the software would have informed the user. This way an authentication chain is established starting with the CRTM.

The operating system can then build a trusted space (i.e. the "nexus" of NGSCB) for security critical applications in which the applications are separated from each other, and any access from the outside into the "trusted space" is prevented. Uncertified programs, such as a virus or Trojan Horses do not have access to the trusted space.

4. CONCLUSION

The mobile operating systems available today are not suited to produce legally binding electronic signatures. None of the operating systems support secure input/output of the data. In addition, there are still a large number of open security gaps in these operating systems.

The producers of operating systems will have to implement the solutions offered with Perseus and the TCG in future versions or develop comparable solutions. Only then will it be possible to use mobile devices to a larger extent than now, and also employ them in security critical areas.

Until then, the use of mobile devices will continue to be connected with enormous security risks and will require careful consideration. Above all, however, the use of additional software, such as PDA Defense, is highly recommended at the moment, as this eliminates at least a large part of the security risks. The use of a large amount of security software, however, is too demanding for the average user, causes additional costs and is connected with high administrative effort.

REFERENCES

[BSI2003] Bundesamt für Sicherheit in der Informationstechnik (2003): "BSI-DSZ-CC-0216-2003" at: http://www.bsi.bund.de/zertifiz/zert/reporte/0216a.pdf

[EU_esig1999] DIRECTIVE 1999/93/EC OF THE EUROPEAN PARLIAMENT AND OF THE COUNCIL of 13 December 1999 on a Community framework for electronic signatures

[Federr2003] H. Fedderath: Digitale Signatur und Public Key Infrastruktur, http://www-sec.uni-regensburg.de/security/5PKI.pdf

[FoxHor1991] Fox, D.; Horster, P. (1999): "Datenschutz und Datensicherheit" in DuD, Verlag, Braunschweig, p. 194

[MaSmMaWi2003] R. MacDonald, S. Smith, J. Marchesini, O. Wild: Bear: An Open-Source Virtual Secure Coprocessor based on TCPA, http://www.cs.dartmouth.edu/~sws/papers/msmw03.pdf

[MobTra2004] Mobile Electronic Transactions http://www.mobiletransaction.org/index.html

[Palm2004] Palm Website, http://www.palm.com

[PDASe2004] PDASecure – The encryption software, http://www.pdasecure.de/

[PDADe2004] PDA Defens Website, http://www.pdadefense.com/

[Pearso2002] Pearson, S., et al. (2002): "Trusted Computing Platforms - TCPA Technology in context", Prentice Hall PT., New Jersey, p. 5

[Perseu2004] B.Pfitzmann, C. Stüble: PERSEUS: A Quick Open-Source Path to Secure Electronic Signatures, http://www.perseus-os.org/

[Pocket2004] Windows Mobile – based Pocket PCs, http://www.microsoft.com/windowsmobile/products/pocketpc/default.mspx

[Symbian2004] Symbian OS – the mobile operating system, http://www.symbian.com

[TCPA2004] TCPA – Trusted Computing Platform Alliance, http://www.trustedcomputing.org/home

[UCable2003] WinTesla v.5.31 Nokia Service Software for Windows, http://ucables.com/nokia/service/wintesla.html

[WiTness2004] European IST Project „Wireless Trust for Mobile Business“ (WiTness), www.wireless-trust.org

AN OVERVIEW OF SECURITY ISSUES AND TECHNIQUES IN MOBILE AGENTS

Mousa Alfalayleh and Ljiljana Brankovic
The School of Electrical Engineering and Computer Science, The University of Newcastle, Newcastle, NSW 2308, Australia. E-mail: {mousa, lbrankov}@cs.newcastle.edu.au

Abstract: Mobile agents are programs that travel autonomously through a computer network in order to perform some computation or gather information on behalf of a human user or an application. In the last several years, mobile agents have found numerous applications including e-commerce. In most applications, the security of mobile agents is of the utmost importance. This paper gives an overview of the main security issues related to the mobile agent paradigm. These issues include security threats, requirements, and techniques for keeping the mobile agent platform and the agent itself secure against each other.

Key words: Security, Mobile agents, Mobile code, Malicious host, Electronic commerce.

1. INTRODUCTION

During the last several years, we have witnessed fundamental changes in distributed and client-server computer systems. In the past, software applications were bound to particular nodes in computer networks. This reality has changed with the appearance of mobile agents [1], that is, programs that act in a computer network on behalf of a human user or an application. Agents can travel autonomously among different nodes in the network, in order to perform some computation or gather information [2]. In this paradigm, clients do not need to have a network connection established while their agents are performing operations on different servers. As such, they provide an appealing alternative to the client-server architecture for many applications [3].

The applications of mobile agent technology are abundant and include electronic commerce, personal assistance, distributed information search and retrieval, monitoring, network management [4], real-time control, building middleware services, military command and control [5], and parallel processing. The promises made by this technology can hardly be overstated. There are numerous advantages of using the mobile agent paradigm rather than conventional paradigms such as client-server based technologies. Using a mobile agent paradigm reduces network usage [2], dynamically updates server interfaces, improves fault tolerance [6], introduces concurrency [2], and assists operating in heterogeneous environments [4].

On the other hand, mobile agent technology has some limitations, primarily in the area of security. These limitations have raised many concerns about the practical utilisation of mobile agents. Current research efforts in the area of mobile agent security adopt two different points of view. Firstly, from the platform perspective, we need to protect the host from malicious mobile agents such as viruses and Trojan horses that are visiting it and consuming its resources. Secondly, from the mobile agent point of view, we need to protect the agent from malicious hosts. Both points of view have attracted much research effort. This paper gives an overview of the main solutions that have been described in the literature to keep the mobile agent platform and the agent itself protected from each other.

The paper is organized as follows. Section 2 deals with the security issues related to the mobile agent paradigm such as security threats and requirements. Section 3 gives an overview of the main solutions for keeping a mobile agent platform secure against a malicious mobile agent. Similarly, Section 4 presents a set of solutions for ensuring the security of mobile agents against illegitimate platforms. Finally, Section 5 gives some concluding remarks.

2. SECURITY ISSUES IN THE MOBILE AGENT PARADIGM

The mobile agent paradigm appeals to many specialists working in different applications. This is especially true for e-commerce applications, including stock markets and electronic auctions. Such applications involve dealing with vast amounts of money and thus users will hesitate to use mobile agents unless they feel that they are secure and can be trusted. Therefore, the security of mobile agents is an important issue that has triggered much research effort in order to find a suitable solution.

One of the most valuable characteristics of mobile agents is their mobility that enables them to travel autonomously through the network. However, it is precisely because of this property that mobile agents are exposed to different types of attacks. We next present these attacks, together with those that are launched by agents to harm platforms.

Unauthorized Access. Malicious mobile agents can try to access the services and resources of the platform without adequate permissions. In order to thwart this attack, a mobile agent platform must have a security policy specifying the access rules applicable to various agents, and a mechanism to enforce the policy.

Masquerading. In this attack, a malicious agent assumes the identity of another agent in order to gain access to platform resources and services, or simply to cause mischief or even serious damage to the platform. Likewise, a platform can claim the identity of another platform in order to gain access to the mobile agent data. In both cases, the malicious agent or platform will not receive any blame for its potentially detrimental actions. Instead, the unsuspecting agent or platform whose identity was misused will be held responsible [2,4].

Denial of Service. A malicious platform can cause harm to a visiting mobile agent by ignoring the agent's request for services and resources that are available on the platform, by terminating the agent without notification, or by assigning continuous tasks to the agent so that it will never reach its goal. Likewise, a malicious agent may attempt to consume the resources of the platform, such as disk space or processing time, or delete important files or even the whole hard disk contents, thus causing harm to the platform and launching a denial of service attack against other visiting agents [2,4].

Annoyance attack. Examples of this attack include opening many windows on the platform computer or making the computer beep repeatedly [2]. Such attacks may not represent a very serious problem to the platform, however they still need to be prevented.

Eavesdropping. In this attack, a malicious platform monitors the behavior of a mobile agent in order to extract sensitive information from it. This is typically used when the mobile agent code and data are encrypted. Monitoring may include the identity of the entities that mobile agent is communicating with, and the types of services requested by the mobile agent [2,4].

Alteration. In the alteration attack, a malicious platform tries to modify mobile agent information, by performing an insertion, deletion and/or alteration to the agent's code, data, and execution state. Modifying the mobile agent execution code and state may result in the agent performing harmful actions to other platforms, including the agent's home platform [2,4].

We next explore the different security requirements that the mobile agent paradigm needs to satisfy.

Confidentiality. It is important to ensure that the information carried by a mobile agent or stored on a platform is accessible only to authorized parties. This is also the case for the communication among mobile agent paradigm components.

Integrity. It is essential to protect the mobile agent's code, state, and data from being modified by unauthorized parties. This can be achieved either by preventing or by detecting unauthorized modifications.

Availability. Platforms typically face a huge demand for services and data. In the case that a platform cannot meet mobile agents' demands, it should notify them in advance. Additionally, a platform must be able to afford a certain level of fault-tolerance and fault-recovery from unpredicted software and hardware failures [4].

Accountability. Platforms need to establish audit logs to keep track of all visiting mobile agents' actions in order to keep them accountable for their actions. Audit logs are also necessary when the platform needs to recuperate from a security penetration or a system failure.

Anonymity. As mentioned above, platforms need to keep track of mobile agents' actions for accountability purposes. However, platforms also have to balance between their needs for audit logs and mobile agents' needs to keep their actions private [4].

In the next two sections we present the existing techniques for protecting agents and platforms. These techniques fall into two categories: Prevention and detection. Prevention techniques are aimed at making it impossible for platforms and agents to successfully perform an attack. For example, a tamper-proof device can be used to execute an agent in a physically sealed environment. However, in the literature the term "prevention mechanism" is often used to denote a technique that makes it impossible to modify an agent in a meaningful way [26]. Examples of such techniques include "Environmental Key Generation" and "Computing with Encrypted Functions". On the other hand, detection techniques aim at detecting the attacks. The "Co-Operating Agents" technique and "Execution Tracing" belong to this category.

3. SECURITY OF PLATFORMS

The primary issue in the security of mobile agent systems is to protect mobile agent platforms against malicious attacks launched by the agents. This section presents a set of detection and prevention techniques for keeping the platform secure against a malicious mobile agent.

3.1 Sandboxing

Sandboxing [7] is a software technique used to protect mobile agent platform from malicious mobile agents. In an execution environment (platform), local code is executed with full permission and has access to crucial system resources. On the other hand, remote code, such as mobile agents and downloadable applets, is executed inside a restricted area called a "sandbox" [10,11]. Restriction affects certain code operations [9] such as interacting with the local file system, opening a network connection, accessing system properties on the local system, and invoking programs on the local system. This ensures that a malicious mobile agent cannot cause any harm to the execution environment that is running it. A Sandboxing mechanism enforces a fixed security policy for the execution of the remote code. The policy specifies the rules and restrictions that mobile agent code should confirm to. A mechanism is said to be secure if it properly implements a policy that is free of flaws and inconsistencies [8].

The most common implementation of Sandboxing is in the Java interpreter inside Java-enabled web browsers. A Java interpreter contains three main security components: ClassLoader, Verifier, and Security Manager [8,11,12,13,16]. The ClassLoader converts remote code into data structures that can be added to the local class hierarchy. Thus every remote class has a subtype of the ClassLoader class associated with it [8]. Before the remote code is loaded, the Verifier performs a set of security checks on it in order to guarantee that only legitimate Java code is executed [12,13]. The remote code should be a valid virtual machine code, and it should not overflow or underflow the stack, or use registers improperly [8,16]. Additionally, remote classes cannot overwrite local names and their operations are checked by the Security Manager before the execution. For example, in JDK 1.0.x, classes are labelled as local and remote classes. Local classes perform their operations without any restrictions while remote classes should first surrender to a checking process that implements the platform security policy. This is implemented within the Security Manager. If a remote class passes the verification, then it will be granted certain privileges to access system resources and continue executing its code. Otherwise, a security exception will be raised [8,11,12,13,16].

A problem with the Sandboxing technique is that a failure in any of the three above mentioned interrelated security parts may lead to a security violation. Suppose that a remote class is wrongly classified as a local class. Then this class will enjoy all the privileges of a local class. Consequently, the security policy may be violated [8]. A downside of the Sandboxing technique is that it increases the execution time of legitimate remote code [7] but this can be overcome by combining Code Signing and Sandboxing, as will be explained later.

3.2 Code Signing

The "Code Signing" technique ensures the integrity of the code downloaded from the Internet. It enables the platform to verify that the code has not been modified since it was signed by its creator. Code Signing cannot reveal what the code can do or guarantee that the code is in fact safe to run [14,15].

Code Signing makes use of a digital signature and one-way hash function. A well-known implementation of code signing is Microsoft Authenticode, which is typically used for signing code such as ActiveX controls and Java applets [15].

Code Signing enables the verification of the code producer's identity but it does not guarantee that they are trustworthy. The platform that runs mobile code maintains a list of trusted entities and checks the code against the list. If the code producer is on the list, it is assumed that they are trustworthy and that the code is safe. The code is then treated as local code and is given full privileges; otherwise the code will not run at all. This is known as a "black-and-white" policy [8,16], as it only allows the platform to label programs as completely trusted or completely untrusted.

There are two main drawbacks of the Code Signing approach. Firstly, this technique assumes that all the entities on the trusted list are trustworthy and that they are incorruptible. Mobile code from such a producer is granted full privileges. If the mobile agent is malicious, it can use those privileges not only to directly cause harm to the executing platform but also to open a door for other malicious agents by changing the acceptance policy on the platform. Moreover, the affects of the malicious agent attack may only occur later, which makes it impossible to establish a connection between the attack and the attacker [8]. Such attacks are referred to as "delayed attacks". Secondly, this technique is overly restrictive towards agents that are coming from untrustworthy entities, as they do not run at all. The approach that combines Code Signing and Sandboxing described in the next section alleviates this drawback.

3.3 Code Signing and Sandboxing Combined

Java JDK 1.1 combines the advantages of both Code Signing and Sandboxing. If the code consumer trusts the signer of the code, then the code will run as if it were local code, that is, with full privileges being granted to it. On the other hand, if the code consumer does not trust the signer of the code then the code will run inside a Sandbox as in JDK1.0 [17,21]. The main advantage of this approach is that it enables the execution of the mobile code produced by untrustworthy entities. However, this method still suffers from the same drawback as Code Signing, that is, malicious code that is deemed trustworthy can cause damage and even change the acceptance policy.

The security policy is the set of rules for granting programs permission to access various platform resources. The "black-and-white" policy only allows the platform to label programs as completely trusted or untrusted, as is the case in JDK1.1. The combination of Code Signing and Sandboxing implemented in JDK 1.2 (Java 2) incorporates fine-grained access control and follows a "shades-of-grey" policy. This policy is more flexible than the "black-and-white" policy, as it allows a user to assign any degree of partial trust to a code, rather than just "trusted" and "untrusted" [16,17]. There is a whole spectrum of privileges that can be granted to the code. In JDK1.2 all code is subjected to the same security policy, regardless of being labelled as local or remote. The run-time system partitions code into individual groups called protection domains in such a way that all programs inside the same domain are granted the same set of permissions. The end-user can authorize certain protection domains to access the majority of resources that are available at the executing host while other protection domains may be restricted to the Sandbox environment. In between these two, there are different subsets of privileges that can be granted to different protection domains, based on whether they are local or remote, authorised or not, and even based on the key that is used for the signature [16,17,18]. Although this scheme is much more flexible than the one in JDK 1.1, it still suffers from the same problem, that an end user can grant full privileges to malicious mobile code, jeopardising the security of the executing platform.

3.4 Proof-Carrying Code

Lee and Necula [19] introduced the *Proof-Carrying Code* (PCC) technique in which the code producer is required to provide a formal proof that the code complies with the security policy of the code consumer. The code producer sends the code together with the formal safety proof, sometimes called machine-checkable proof, to the code consumer. Upon receipt, the code consumer checks and verifies the safety proof of the incoming code by using a simple and fast proof checker. Depending on the result of the proof validation process, the code is proclaimed safe and consequently executed without any further checking, or it is rejected [4,19,21,22]. PCC guarantees the safety of the incoming code providing that there is no flaw in the verification-condition generator, the logical axioms, the typing rules, and the proof-checker [20].

PCC is considered to be “self-certifying”, because no cryptography or trusted third party is required. It involves low-cost static program checking after which the program can be executed without any expensive run-time checking. In addition, PCC is considered “tamper-proof” as any modification done to the code or the proof will be detected. These advantages make the Proof Carrying Code technique useful not only for mobile agents but also for other applications such as active networks and extensible operating systems [19,22].

Proof Carrying Code also has some limitations, which need to be dealt with before it can become widely used. The main problem with PCC is the proof generation, and there is a lot of research on how to automate the proof generation process. For example, a certifying compiler can automatically generate the proof through the process of compilation [19,23]. Unfortunately, at present many proofs still have to be done by hand [21]. Other limitations of the PCC technique include the potential size of the proof and the time consumed in the proof-validation process [19].

3.5 State Appraisal

While a mobile agent is roaming among agent platforms, it typically carries the following information: code, static data, collected data, and execution state. The execution state is dynamic data created during the execution of the agent at each platform and used as input to the computations performed on the next platform. The state includes a program counter, registers, local environment, control stack, and store. The state of a mobile agent changes during its execution on a platform. Farmer et al [25] introduced the “State Appraisal” technique to ensure that an agent has not become malicious or modified as a result of its state alterations at an untrustworthy platform.

In this technique the author, who creates the mobile agent, produces a state appraisal function. This function calculates the maximum set of safe permissions that the agent could request from the host platform, depending on the agent’s current state. In other words, the author needs to anticipate possible harmful modifications to the agent’s state and to counteract them within the appraisal function. Similarly, the sender, who sends the agent to act on his behalf, produces another state appraisal function that determines the set of permissions to be requested by the agent, depending on its current state and on the task to be completed. Subsequently, the sender packages the code with these state appraisal functions. If both the author and the sender sign the agent, their appraisal functions will be protected against malicious modifications. Upon receipt, the target platform checks and verifies the correct state of the incoming agent. Depending on the result of the verification process, the platform can determine what privileges should be granted to this incoming agent given its current state. Clearly, when the author and the sender fail to anticipate certain attacks, they cannot include them in the appraisal functions and provide the necessary protection [4,24,25].

In addition to ensuring that an agent has not become malicious during its itinerary, the State Appraisal may also be used to disarm a maliciously altered agent [25]. Another advantage of this technique is that it provides a flexible way for an agent to request permissions depending on its current state and on the task that it needs to do on that particular platform [24,25]. The main problem with this technique is that it is not easy to formulate appropriate security properties for the mobile agent and to obtain a state appraisal function that guarantees those properties [24].

3.6 Path Histories

When an agent travels through a multi-hop itinerary, it visits many platforms that are not all trusted to the same extent. The newly visited platform may benefit from the answers to the following questions: Where has the agent been? How likely is it that the agent has been converted to a malicious one during its trip? To enable the platform to answer these questions, a mobile agent should maintain an authenticable record of the previously visited platforms during its travel life. Using this history, the platform makes the decision whether to run the agent and what level of trust, services, resources and privileges should be granted to the agent [4,26,27]. The list of the platforms visited previously by the agent is the basis of trust that the execution platform has in the agent. Typically, it is harder to maintain trust in agents that have previously visited a huge number of platforms. Likewise, it is harder to trust the agent whose travel path is unknown in advance, for example the agent that is searching for new information and creates its travel path dynamically [27].

The "Path History" is constructed in the following way. Each visited platform in the mobile agent's travel life adds a signed record to the Path History. This record should contain the current platform's identity together with the identity of the next platform to be visited in the mobile agent's travel path. Moreover, in order to prevent tampering, each platform should include the previous record in the message digest that it is signing [4]. After executing the agent, the current platform should send the agent together with the complete Path History to the next platform. Depending on the information in the Path History, the new platform can decide whether to run the agent and what privileges should be granted to the agent. The main problem with the Path History technique is that the cost of the path verification process increases with the path history [4,26,27]. Constructing algorithms for Path History evaluation is an interesting research area [27].

4. SECURITY OF MOBILE AGENTS

In the previous section, we presented several techniques for protecting mobile agent platforms against malicious mobile agents. On the other hand, mobile agents themselves are exposed to various threats by the platforms they visit.

4.1 Co-Operating Agents

In order to improve the security of mobile agents against the attacks that are launched by the malicious platforms, the Co-Operating Agent technique [28,29,4] distributes critical tasks of a single mobile agent between two co-operating agents. Each of the two co-operating agents executes the tasks in one of two disjoint sets of platforms. The co-operating agents share the same data and exchange information in a secret way. The Co-Operating Agent technique reduces the possibility of the shared data being pilfered by a single host. Each agent records and verifies the route of its co-operating agent [28,29]. Co-Operating Agents can be used to perform e-commerce tasks or protocols such as the authorization of negotiation, bidding, auction, electronic payment, etc [29,30].

When the agent travels from one platform to another, it uses an authenticated communication channel to pass information to its co-operating agent. The information includes details about the agent's itinerary such as the last platform visited by the agent, the current platform, and the next platform to be visited. The peer agent takes a suitable action when anything wrong occurs, e.g., a platform sends the agent to a wrong destination, or claims to have received the agent from an incorrect source. However, this technique has some drawbacks. One of them is the cost of setting up the authenticated communication channel for each migration. Another drawback is that in the case of a co-operating agent being killed, it is difficult for its peer to decide which platform is responsible [4,28,29].

It is worth noting that an assumption made in the Co-Operating Agent technique, is that only a small percentage of platforms are in fact malicious and that it is not very likely that both agents will encounter such a host. However, care should be taken that the two sets of platforms assigned to the two agents are indeed disjoint, that is, that they never encounter the same host. This method can easily be extended to more than two co-operating agents.

4.2 Execution Tracing

Execution Tracing enables detection of any possible misbehavior by a platform, that is, improper modification of the mobile agent code, state, and execution flow. This technique is based on cryptographic traces that are collected during an agent's execution at different platforms. Traces are logs of the actions performed by a mobile agent during its lifetime. Execution Tracing enables an agent's owner to check the agent's execution history and see if it contains any unauthorized modifications done by a malicious platform. Each trace contains identifiers of all the statements performed on a particular platform. In the case that some of the statements require information from the external execution environment, the trace must also contain a digital signature of the platform. Such statements are known as "black" statements. On the other hand, the statements that only use the values of the agent's internal variables are called "white" statements [31,32].

The Execution Tracing technique assumes that all the involved parties own a public and private key that can be used for digital signatures, in order to identify involved parties. Different parties, such as users and platform owners, communicate by using signed messages. A platform that receives the agent and agrees to execute it produces the associated trace during the agent's execution. The message that an execution platform attaches to the mobile agent typically contains information such as the unique identifier of the message, the identity of the sender, the timestamp, the fingerprint of the trace, the final state and the trusted third party (which could later be used to resolve disputes). Later, the owner of the agent may suspect that a certain platform cheated while executing the agent. If this is the case, the owner will ask the suspicious platform to reproduce the trace. Finally, the agent's owner validates the execution of the agent by comparing the fingerprint of the reproduced trace against the fingerprint of the trace that is originally supplied by the suspicious platform [31].

In addition to detection of any modification of the agent performed by a malicious platform, Execution Tracing also provides a means to protect a legitimate platform against a malicious agent by obtaining the related traces from the involved parties. Execution Tracing has some limitations, such as the potential large size and number of logs to be retained. Another limitation of this technique is that the owner platform needs to wait until it obtains suspicious results in order to run the verification process. Also, this technique is considered to be too difficult to use in the case of multi-threaded agents [31,32].

A new version of the Execution Tracing technique, proposed by Tan and Moreau [32,33], modifies the original technique by assigning the trace verification process to a trusted third party, the verification server, instead of depending on the agent's owner.

When a mobile agent travels to a new platform during its itinerary, a copy of the agent is submitted to a corresponding verification server. The visited platform receives the agent and produces the associated execution trace. Before the agent's migration from the current platform to a new one, the current platform forwards the trace to a corresponding verification server. The verification server simulates the execution of the agent on the platform by using the corresponding execution trace and the agent's copy. The simulation process is repeated for every platform in the agent's path by the corresponding verification server, until the agent is sent back to its home platform. Tan and Moreau [32] provided a detailed protocol of message exchanges, as well as the formal modeling and verification of the protocol.

Execution Tracing with a verification server does not wait until a suspicion is raised in order to run the verification process. The verification here is compulsory and this is an advantage over the original Execution Tracing technique where the verification process is triggered only by suspicious results [32]. However, Execution Tracing with a verification server still suffers from the same limitation as the original technique, that is, the need to retain a potentially large size and number of logs. Additionally, each platform chooses a verification server and that might encourage and facilitate a possible malicious collaboration between a platform and the server.

4.3 Environmental Key Generation

Riordan and Schneier [34] designed the Environmental Key Generation technique to be used when a platform wants to communicate with another platform by sending it a message, yet it only wants the receiving platform to obtain the message if some environmental condition is satisfied. This can be achieved by sending a mobile agent carrying an encrypted message. The encrypted message may include some data and/or executable code. Neither can the mobile agent precisely predict its own execution at the receiver platform, nor can the platform foresee the incoming agent task. The agent will wait at the receiving platform for some environmental condition to occur. The environmental condition could be, for example, matching a certain search string. When the environmental condition is met, an activation key is generated in order to decrypt the enciphered message that the mobile agent is carrying. Without meeting the environmental condition, the agent is unable to decrypt its own message [34].

The activation key, which is used to decrypt the agent's message, could be hidden inside a fixed data channel. If this data channel is, for example, a file system, then the activation key could be hidden in a file or could be the hash of a certain file name. On the other hand, if the data channel is a mail message, the activation key could be a string inside this message or a hash of the message [34].

Environmental Key Generation may suit some applications other than mobile agents (some of which may even be malicious) including blind search engines, logic bombs, directed viruses, and remote alarms [34]. Tschudin [35] exploited the idea of Environmental Key Generation for the purpose of the programmed death of a mobile service, that is, the self-destruction of a mobile service when it is no longer required [35]. However, this technique has some limitations. The receiving platform could act maliciously against the incoming agent. When the environmental condition is met and the activation key is generated, the platform could modify the agent to perform a different function, for example, to print out the executable code instead of running it [4]. Another limitation of the technique is that the platform may consider it unsafe to execute an encrypted code that is attached to a mobile agent, as it could be, for example, a virus.

4.4 Non-Interactive Computing with Encrypted Functions

This technique represents a software solution for protecting a mobile agent from a malicious executing platform during its itinerary. This is a cryptographic solution to achieve integrity and privacy of the mobile agent. Protecting integrity means that the mobile agent is made safe against tampering by a malicious platform. Achieving privacy means that the mobile agent can conceal its program (code) when it is executed remotely in an untrusted environment. In addition to this, a mobile agent can safely compute cryptographic primitives on a remote platform by using this approach. An example of cryptographic primitives is a digital signature or encryption.

This technique is based on executing a program embodying an encrypted function on a mobile agent platform. It also ensures that the platform does not learn anything substantial about the encrypted function. Abadi and Feigenbaum [38] suggested the initial version of this technique. Their solution was interactive and required several rounds of message exchange with the agent's home platform. However, the interactive solution does not suit the mobile agent scenario, as agents operate autonomously without much interaction with their home platform.

Sander and Tschudin [36,37] suggested a non-interactive solution, which is suitable for the mobile agent paradigm. In their solution, the home platform has an algorithm to compute a function f. The target platform has an input x and can provide a service to the home platform by computing $f(x)$. However, the home platform doesn't want the target platform to learn anything about the function f. The home platform launches the operation by encrypting the function f to get $E(f)$, and then it implements $E(f)$ using the program $P(E(f))$. The home platform embeds the program $P(E(f))$ within the mobile agent and sends it to the target platform for execution. The target platform receives the agent and runs it. This includes executing $P(E(f))$ at x to produce $P(E(f))(x)$. Then, the target platform sends the agent back to its home platform. The home platform extracts the result from the agent and then decrypts it to get $f(x)$.

This solution enables the owner of the agent to execute encrypted programs over untrusted platforms. The executing platforms do not need to decrypt programs before running them. Assume that f is an encryption algorithm or a signature algorithm that contains an embedded key within it. That means that the agent has the ability to encrypt information or sign it without revealing anything about the value of the key being used.

The main challenge in this technique is to find a way to apply it to an arbitrary function f. At the moment the only classes of functions for which a suitable encryption is known are polynomial and rational functions [36,38]. Although this technique protects the mobile agent's integrity and privacy, it is vulnerable to certain attacks such as denial of service and replay attacks [36].

4.5 Obfuscated Code

Obfuscation is a technique in which the mobile code producer enforces the security policy by applying a behavior-preserving transformation to the code before it sends it to run on different platforms that are trusted to various degrees [39]. Obfuscation aims to protect the code from being analysed and understood by the host. Consequently, the host should not be able to modify the mobile code's behavior or expose sensitive information that is hidden inside the code such as a secret key, credit card number, or bidding limits [39].

Typically, the transformation procedure that is used to generate the obfuscated code aims to make the obfuscated code very hard to understand or analyse by malicious parties. There are different useful obfuscating transformations [40,43,44]. Layout Obfuscation tries to remove or modify some information in the code, such as comments and debugging information, without affecting the executable part of the code. Data Obfuscation concentrates on obfuscating the data and data structures in the code without modifying the code itself. Control Obfuscation tries to alter the control flow in the code without modifying the computing part of the code. Preventive

Obfuscation concentrates on protecting the code from decompilators and debuggers.

Hohl [41] suggested using the Obfuscation technique to obtain a time-limited black box agent that can be executed safely on a malicious platform for a certain period of time but not forever. D'Anna et al [39] pointed out that Obfuscation could delay, but not prevent the attacks on agent via reverse engineering. They also argue that an attacker with enough computational resources, such as enough time, can always deobfuscate the code. Barak et al [42] studied the theoretical limits of Obfuscation techniques and showed that in general achieving completely secure Obfuscation is impossible.

In addition to protecting a mobile agent, Obfuscation can also be used for other applications such as protecting digital watermarking, enforcement of software licensing, and protecting protocols from spoofing [39,40]. As far as the performance is concerned, some Obfuscation techniques reduce the size of the code and thus speed up its execution (Layout and Data Obfuscation), while others achieve the opposite (Control Obfuscation) [43]. Obfuscation is considered resistant to impersonation and denial of service attacks [40]. The main challenge in this technique is to make it easy to apply in practice.

4.6 Partial Result Encapsulation

Partial Result Encapsulation (PRE) is a detection technique that aims to discover any possible security breaches on an agent during its execution at different platforms. PRE is used to encapsulate the results of agent execution at each visited platform in its travel path. The encapsulated information is later used to verify that the agent was not attacked by a malicious platform. The verification process can be done when the agent returns to its home platform or at certain intermediate points in its itinerary.

The PRE technique has different implementations. In certain scenarios, the agent itself performs the encapsulation, while in others the platform does it. To meet certain security requirements such as integrity, accountability, and privacy of the agent, PRE makes use of different cryptographic primitives, such as encryption, digital signatures, authentication codes, and hash functions.

To ensure the confidentiality of its results, the agent encrypts the results by using the public key of its originator to produce small pieces of ciphertext that are decrypted later at the agent's home platform using the corresponding private key. This is one scenario of PRE where the agent itself does the encapsulation process. The agent uses a special implementation of encryption called "Sliding Encryption" that was suggested by Young and Yung [45]. *Sliding Encryption* encrypts small amounts of data within a larger block and thus obtains small pieces of ciphertext. Sliding Encryption is particularly suitable for certain application where storage space is valuable such as smartcards [46].

Yee [47] suggested “Partial Result Authentication Code” (PRAC), where again the agent does the encapsulation of the results. However, the agent’s originator also takes part in this scenario by providing the agent with a list of secret keys before launching it. For each visited platform in an agent’s itinerary, there is an associated secret key. When an agent finishes an execution at a certain platform in its itinerary, it summarizes the results of its execution in a message for the home platform, which could be sent either immediately or later. In order to produce the PRAC, the agent uses the associated secret key for the current platform to compute a Message Authentication Code (MAC), which is encapsulated together with the message to produce PRAC. It is important to note that the agent erases the used secret key of the current visited platform before its migration to the next platform. Destroying the secret key ensures the “forward integrity” of the encapsulation results. *Forward integrity* [47] guarantees that no platform to be visited in the future is able to modify any results from the previously visited platforms, as there is no secret key to compute the PRAC for these results. Only the agent’s originator has a copy of all used secret keys and thus can verify the encapsulated results. The result verification enables the originator to detect any modification (tampering) of the agent’s results. Yee [47] suggested that the results could also be encrypted using the originator’s public key, in order to guarantee both privacy and integrity.

Karjoth et al [48] proposed a “strong forward integrity”, which, in addition to forward integrity, also requires that the visited platform cannot later modify its own results. Karjoth et al’s approach depends on the visited platform doing the encapsulation process instead of the agent doing it. The visited platform encrypts the agent’s results by using the originator’s public key to ensure the confidentiality of the results. Then the visited platform uses its private key to digitally sign the encrypted results together with a hash chain. The hash chain links the results from the previous platform with the identity of the next platform to be visited. This prevents the platform from changing its results later and thus ensures strong forward integrity [48].

5. CONCLUSION

The mobile agent system is a very promising paradigm that has already established its presence in many applications including e-commerce and distributed information search and retrieval. At the same time, this technology has introduced some very serious security problems and emphasized some existing security issues. It is more difficult to ensure security in the mobile agent paradigm than in some other technologies where hardware solutions are practical.

In this paper we surveyed the main issues in the security of mobile agents. We considered both the mobile agent and the agent platform points of view, and reconfirmed that it is much more difficult to ensure the security of mobile agents than the security of agent platforms. We discussed the security threats and requirements that need to be met in order to alleviate those threats.

We presented the most important techniques for providing security in mobile agent systems. Some of those techniques, for example Sandboxing, have been used for a long time and are well understood. On the other hand, some other techniques, such as Computing with Encrypted Function are still at the theoretical level and are not yet widely used in practice. None of the existing techniques provides an optimal solution for all scenarios. For example, Sandboxing provides a high level of security but is overly restrictive as only a very few applications can operate in such a constrained environment. However, a combination of various techniques may yield powerful solutions. For example, in Java 2 Sandboxing has been used in combination with fine-grained access control and Code Signing. In any case, more research is needed in order to warrant sufficient trust in mobile agent technology by a wide range of users.

REFERENCES

[1] J. White, "Mobile Agents White Paper," General Magic Inc., 1996.

[2] N. Karnik, "Security in Mobile Agent systems," Ph.D. Dissertation, Department of Computer Science, University of Minnesota, Oct. 1998.

[3] S. Fischmeister, "Building Secure Mobile Agents: The Supervisor-Worker Framework," Diploma Thesis, Technical University of Vienna, Feb. 2000.

[4] W. Jansen and T. Karygiannis, "Mobile Agent Security," NIST Special Publication 800-19, National Institute of Standard and Technology, 2000.

[5] S. McGrath, D. Chac n, and K. Whitebread, "Intelligent Mobile Agents in Military Command and Control," Advanced Technology Laboratories, New Jersey.

[6] G. P. Picco, "Mobile Agents: An Introduction", Journal of Microprocessors and Microsystems, (25):65, 2001.

[7] R. Wahbe, S. Lucco, T. E. Anderson, and S. L. Graham, "Efficient software-based fault isolation," In Proceedings of the 14th ACM Symposium on Operating Systems Principles, pages 203--216, Dec. 1993.

[8] D. Rubin and D. E. Geer, "Mobile code security," IEEE Internet Computing, 1998.

[9] D. Chess, J. Morar, "Is Java still secure?," IBM T.J. Watson Research Center, NY, 1998.

[10] L. Gong, "Java Security Architecture (JDK1.2)," Technical Report, Sun Microsystems, Inc., 901 San Antonio Road, Palo Alto, California 94303, U.S.A, 1998.

[11] Li Gong,"Secure java class loading," IEEE Internet Computing, pages 56-61, 1998.

[12] M. Hauswirth, C. Kerer, and R. Kurmanowytsch, "A secure execution framework for Java," In Proceedings of the 7th ACM conference on computer and communications security (CCS 2000), pages 43--52, Athens, Greece, Nov. 2000.

[13] L. Gong, M. Mueller, H. Prafullchandra, and R. Schemers, "Going Beyond the Sandbox: An Overview of the New Security Architecture in the Java Development Kit 1.2," In Proceedings of the USENIX Symposium on Internet Technologies and Systems, Monterey, California, Dec. 1997.

[14] "Signed Code," (n.d.). Retrieved December 15, 2003, from James Madison University, IT Technical Services Web site: http://www.jmu.edu/computing/info-security/cngineering/issues/signedcode.shtml

[15] "Introduction to Code Signing," (n.d.). Retrieved December 15, 2003, from Microsoft Corporation, Microsoft Developer Network (MSDN) Web site: http://msdn.microsoft .com/library/default.asp?url=/workshop/security/authcode/intro_authenticode.asp

[16] Gary McGraw and Edward Felten (1996-9). *Securing JAVA* [Electronic version]. John Wiley and Sons. http://www.securingjava.com/

[17] M. Dageforde. (n.d.). "Security Features Overview," Retrieved December 21, 2003, from Sun Microsystems, Inc. The JavaTM Tutorial Web site: http://java.sun.com /docs/books/tutorial/security1.2 /overview/

[18] R. Levin (1998). "Security Grows Up: The Java 2 Platform," Retrieved December 21, 2003, from Sun Microsystems, Inc. Sun Developer Network (SDN) Web site: http://java.sun.com/features/1998/11/jdk.security.html

[19] P. Lee and G. Necula, "Research on Proof-Carrying Code on Mobile-Code Security," In Proceedings of the Workshop on Foundations of Mobile Code Security, 1997.

[20] A. Appel, "Foundational proof-carrying code," In Proceedings of the 16th Annual Symposium on Logic in Computer Science, pages 247-256. IEEE Computer Society Press, 2001.

[21] S. Loureiro, R. Molva, and Y. Roudier, "Mobile Code Security," Institut Eurecom, 2001.

[22] P. Lee. (n.d.), "Proof-carrying code," Retrieved December 28, 2003, from Web site: http://www-2.cs.cmu.edu/~petel/papers/pcc/pcc.html

[23] C. Colby, P. Lee, G. Necula, F. Blau, M. Plesko, and K. Cline, "A Certifying Compiler for Java," SIGPLAN Conference on Programming Language Design and Implementation. Vancouver B.C., 2000.

[24] V. Swarup, "Trust Appraisal and Secure Routing of Mobile Agents," DARPA Workshop on Foundations for Secure Mobile Code, Monterey, CA, USA, March 1997. Position Paper.

[25] W. M. Farmer, J. D. Guttman, and V. Swarup, "Security for mobile agents: Authentication and state appraisal," In Proceedings of the European Symposium on Research in Computer Security (ESORICS), pages 118--130, Sep. 1996.

[26] D. Chess, B. Grosof, C. Harrison, D. Levine, C. Parris and G. Tsudik, "Itinerant Agents for Mobile Computing," Technical Report, Oct. 1995, IBM T.J. Watson Research Center, NY.

[27] J. J. Ordille, "When Agents Roam, who Can You Trust?," Proceedings of the First Conference on Emerging Technologies and Applications in Communications, Portland, Oregon, May 1996.

[28] V. Roth, "Secure Recording of Itineraries Through Cooperating Agents," Proceedings of the ECOOP Workshop on Distributed Object Security and 4th Workshop on Mobile Object Systems: Secure Internet Mobile Computations, pages 147-154, INRIA, France, 1998.

[29] V. Roth, "Mutual protection of cooperating agents," In Secure Internet Programming: Security Issues for Mobile and Distributed Objects. J. Vitek and C. Jensen (Eds.), Springer Verlag, 1999.

[30] Y. Ye and X. Yi, "Coalition Signature Scheme in Multi-agent Systems," 2002.

[31] G. Vigna, "Cryptographic Traces for Mobile Agents," in: Giovanni Vigna (Ed.), Mobile Agent Security, LNCS 1419, 1998, Springer, pages 137-153.

[32] H. K. Tan and L. Moreau, "Extending Execution Tracing for Mobile Code Security," In K. Fischer and D. Hutter (Eds.), Proceedings of Second International Workshop on Security of Mobile MultiAgent Systems (SEMAS'2002), pages 51-59, Bologna, Italy.2002.

[33] H. K. Tan, L. Moreau, D. Cruickshank, and D. De Roure, "Certificates for Mobile Code Security," In Proceedings of The 17th ACM Symposium on Applied Computing (SAC'2002) --- Track on Agents, Interactions, Mobility and Systems, pages 76. 2002.

[34] J. Riordan and B. Schneier, "Environmental Key Generation Towards Clueless Agents," G. Vinga (Ed.), Mobile Agents and Security, Springer-Verlag, Lecture Notes in Computer Science No. 1419, 1998.

[35] C. Tschudin, "Apoptosis - the programmed death of distributed services," In Secure Internet Programming [14].

[36] T. Sander and C. Tschudin, "Protecting Mobile Agents Against Malicious Hosts," in G. Vinga (Ed.), Mobile Agents and Security, SpringerVerlag, Lecture Notes in Computer Science No. 1419, 1998.

[37] T. Sander and C. Tschudin, "Towards Mobile Cryptography," IEEE Symposium on Security and Privacy, pages 215-224, May 1998.

[38] M. Abadi and J. Feigenbau, "Secure circuit evaluation: a protocol based on hiding information from an oracle," Journal of Cryptology, vol. 2, 1990.

[39] L. D'Anna, B. Matt, A. Reisse, T. Van Vleck, S. Schwab, and P. LeBlanc, "Self-Protecting Mobile Agents Obfuscation Report," Report #03-015, Network Associates Laboratories, June 2003.

[40] G. Wroblewski, "General Method of Program Code Obfuscation," PhD Dissertation, Wroclaw University of Technology, Institute of Engineering Cybernetics, 2002, (under final revision).

[41] F. Hohl, "Time Limited Blackbox Security: Protecting Mobile Agents from Malicious Hosts," To appear in Mobile Agents and Security Book edited by Giovanni Vigna, published by Springer Verlag 1998.

[42] B. Barak, O. Goldreich, R. Impagliazzo, S. Rudich, A. Sahai, S. Vadhan, and K. Yang, "On the (Im)possibility of Obfuscating Programs," in Advances in Cryptology, Proceedings of Crypto'2001, Lecture Notes in Computer Science, Vol. 2139, pages 1-18.

[43] G. Hachez, "A Comparative Study of Software Protection Tools Suited for E-Commerce with Contributions to Software Watermarking and Smart Cards," Universite Catholique de Louvain, 2003.

[44] C. Collberg, C. Thomborson, and D. Low, "A taxonomy of obfuscating transformations," Technical Report 148, Department of Computer Science, University of Auckland, July 1997.

[45] A. Young and M. Yung, "Encryption Tools for Mobile Agents: Sliding Encryption," In: E. BIHAM (ed), Fast Software Encryption. Lecture Notes in Computer Science, no. 1267. Springer-Verlag, Germany, 1997.

[46] G. Karjoth and J. Posegga, "Mobile Agents and Telcos' Nightmares," *Annales des Télécommunications* Vol. 55, No. 7/8, 29-41, 2000.

[47] B. Yee, "A Sanctuary for Mobile Agents," DARPA Workshop on Foundations for Secure Mobile Code, Feb. 1997.
[48] G. Karjoth, N. Asokan, and C. Glc, "Protecting the Computation Results of Free-Roaming Agents," Second International Workshop on Mobile Agents, Stuttgart, Germany, Sep. 1998.

A SECURE CHANNEL PROTOCOL FOR MULTI-APPLICATION SMART CARDS BASED ON PUBLIC KEY CRYPTOGRAPHY

Konstantinos Markantonakis, Keith Mayes
Information Security Group Smart Card Centre, Royal Holloway, University of London, Egham, Surrey, TW20 0EX, United Kingdom, k.markantonakis@rhul.ac.uk, keith.mayes@rhul.ac.uk

Abstract: Smart card secure channel protocols based on public key cryptography are not widely utilised mainly due to processing overheads introduced in the underlying smart card microprocessors and the complexities introduced by the operation of a PKI infrastructure. In this paper we analyse the significance of public key secure channel protocols in multi-application smart cards. We believe that multi-application smart card technology (e.g. the GlobalPlatform smart card specification) should benefit more from the advantages of public key cryptography specifically for the initiation and maintenance of a secure channel. This paper introduces a public key based cryptographic protocol for secure entity authentication, data integrity and data confidentiality. The proposed secure channel protocol uses a combination of public key, secret key and the main idea behind the Diffie-Hellman key establishment protocols in order to achieve the desired goals.

Key words: Secure channel protocol, public key cryptography, Diffie-Hellman, GlobalPlatform, Java card, multi-application smart cards

1. INTRODUCTION

The recent introduction of multi-application smart cards has enabled cards to securely host multiple applications, dynamically and securely download or delete them at any point during the card's lifecycle. As a result, the complexity of the smart card operating system (SCOS) increased exponentially. Similarly, the complexity of the terminal applications increased significantly as new architectures [1, 2] emerged. Furthermore, as smart card technology evolves, the performance of smart card cryptographic algorithms improves and as new smart card applications are invented the benefits of public key cryptography are widely scrutinized.

Multi-application smart card technology can benefit from the use of public key cryptography both at the application level and in the SCOS level e.g. with the provision of secure channel protocols based on Public Key Infrastructures (PKI). Current versions of secure multi-application smart card standards [6] do not fully take into advantage the benefits of public key cryptography, specifically for the provision of a secure channel mechanism. The reasons range from the increased prices due to the additional processing power, up to the potentially limited performance of public key cryptographic primitives in the current generation of smart card microprocessors, or simply because there is no immediate need for such functionality.

The advantages and disadvantages of public key cryptography are widely documented in the academic literature [3, 4, 5]. In this paper we propose a public key secure channel protocol for smart cards. The protocol is based on the well known Diffie-Hellman key exchange protocol and it was designed by taking into account the processing and storage restrictions of current smart card microprocessors. Alongside with the protocol description we also provide a discussion on the operation and security requirements for its successful and efficient operation. We believe that as the number of smart card applications increases and the nature of smart card applications changes along with the differentiations on the operational requirements (e.g. dynamic application downloading and deletion), the demand for efficient smart card PKI will potentially increase.

The remainder of this paper is organised as follows. Firstly, we set up the scenery by elaborating more on the motivation behind the paper along with providing an overview of the main characteristics of a multi-application smart card standard, namely GlobalPlatform [6]. Subsequently, we highlight the main characteristics of the supporting public key infrastructure required for the successful operation of the protocol. Moving to the core idea of this paper we present the protocol details and architectural design. In order to provide a more complete coverage of the issues surrounding the implementation and operation of the proposed architecture we also provide a discussion around the security properties of the protocol by highlighting practical issues that imposed certain design decisions and directions for further research.

2. PUBLIC KEY SMART CARD SECURE CHANNEL PROTOCOLS AND THE REAL WORLD

In the following sections we provide an overview of limiting factors along with the driving forces behind the adoption of public key cryptography in multi-application smart card platforms. Similarly, we also highlight the main characteristics of a widely used multi-application smart card standard in order to provide a reference point, to the specifics of an existing architecture, along supporting the case for the existence of such a protocol.

Motivation

The advantages and disadvantages of public key cryptography have been a topic of discussion for many years. The significance of public key cryptography in smart cards, impose certain restrictions and complexities that are unique to smart card microprocessors and the nature of the infrastructures they operate.

A few years ago the main prohibiting factor for the utilization of public key cryptography in smart card microprocessors was the limited processing power of the underlying technology. However, following a number of significant improvements both at the hardware [24] and software level [20, 21, 22], the performance of public key cryptography in smart card microprocessors has improved significantly. Furthermore, the cost of a smart card microprocessor is not substantially influenced by the existence of the necessary public key functionality but rather from other factors (i.e. mainly the amount of memory).

The nature of smart card applications is also changing. Public key cryptography may be beneficial for the establishment of a secure channel when two unknown parties want to establish keys and protect subsequent communications. Such secure channels could be used for personalisation. Another use secure channels are post issuance operations, such as application/card management functions [6], protection of application or smart card operating system (SCOS) data [25].

Although the significance of public key cryptography in a smart card environment cannot be underestimated at the same time the drawbacks are not minimal. For example, a secure channel protocol designed specifically for smart cards has to be as lightweight as possible, depending of course on the underlying security and operational requirements. Furthermore, in order to improve the required performance and fulfil the security objectives a combination of cryptographic primitives and algorithms might be used. Finally, further constraints arise from the fact that often a public key based architecture requires the existence of a public key infrastructure (PKI) [26] for the management of identities, key and certificate management, etc.

Our proposed protocol aims to fulfil some of the aforementioned requirements. It is designed by keeping in mind the performance requirements and operational characteristics of smart card microprocessors. Although there is a plethora of public key cryptography secure channel protocols [3, 5, 33], most of them are not specifically designed by taking into account the specific characteristics of smart cards. For example, some cryptographic protocols although they offer more than adequate levels of security they do not keep in mind that smart card microprocessors have limited communication buffers, often ranging between 240-255 bytes. Therefore, if a protocol requires a large number of messages (e.g. key certificates) to be exchanged between the card and an off-card entity this will add to the communication and processing overheads [32]. Furthermore, the nature of a public key infrastructure requires the existence of cryptographic key certificates. For example, if a protocol requires regular checks in order to identify whether certificates are revoked or expired this might add to overall protocol security but on the other hand it will potentially complicate its mitigation in smart card environment.

The proposed solution does not claim to introduce a protocol based on new cryptographic techniques. Instead it is an implementation adaptation of existing cryptographic primitives and techniques which are carefully selected in order to be used in a smart card environment. Before moving into the details of the proposed architecture, we highlight the main characteristics of a multi-application smart card platform.

An Overview of GlobalPlatform Card Specification

In this section we highlight the main characteristics and the core components of the GlobalPlatform (GP) card specification [6], as a typical example of a multi-application smart card architecture that could benefit from the proposed protocol. Please note that among the main reasons behind the description of the GlobalPlatform architecture is that it provides the necessary functionality (e.g. secure storage of keys, key management, etc.) required by the protocol. However there are no restrictions or prerequisite for a specific type of smart card technology as the protocol could be utilised and implemented either at the application or at the (SCOS) [7, 8] level irrespectively of the characteristics of the underlying smart card microprocessor.

The GlobalPlatform smart card architecture comprises a number of on-card components that offer secure multi-application card management functionality at any given point during the card's lifecycle. Furthermore, the GlobalPlatform smart card architecture is closely coupled with the Java card [9] technology although there are no restrictions on its portability to other smart card platforms [10, 11].

The functionality provided by the underlying smart card management system includes the necessary mechanisms (e.g. secure channels [12]) that enable secure communication with the outside world. A secure channel is a mechanism that allows a card and an off-card entity to authenticate each other and establish session keys in order to protect the integrity and confidentiality of subsequent communications.

The GlobalPlatform card specification defines two protocols which are used to establish a secure channel. SCP01 is defined in Appendix D of the GlobalPlatform card specification as a symmetric key protocol that provides three levels of security (i.e. mutual authentication, integrity and data origin authentication, confidentiality). The details of the secure channel protocol (SCP02) can be found in Appendix E of the GlobalPlatform card specification. The two protocols use symmetric key cryptography for the authentication, establishment of session keys and protection of subsequent communication between the card and the outside world. While the existing protocols are mainly used for card content management purposes they can also be used by applications for secure communications. For example, secure communication between a card and an off-card entity is considered necessary whenever a sensitive operation (e.g. during cryptographic key exchanges) is about to be performed.

Another main component of GlobalPlatform is the notion of security domains. GlobalPlatform security domains are the on-card representatives of the card Issuer or an application provider. It is the security domains that allow Issuers to share control over selected portions of their card with approved partners. Additionally, security domains are responsible for cryptographic functions and key handling/separation functionality. In terms of communicating with the off-card entity in a secure way the security domains implement different secure channel protocols, as aforementioned. For the purpose of this paper, we will be using the notion of a security domain as a mechanism that will securely store keys and control access to the secure channel mechanisms.

The GlobalPlatform smart card specification is becoming the de-facto mechanism for secure application handling especially for Java cards [9] used in the GSM [28] and finance sectors [27]. There are currently ongoing discussions in order to enhance the functionality offered with the provision of additional secure channel protocols based on public key cryptography. In the following sections we present the main characteristics of the proposed protocol.

3. THE ARCHITECTURAL MODEL

In this section we highlight the main characteristics of a model for the use and operation of a public key cryptography smart card security protocol. Subsequently, we also define the main operational characteristics of the protocol.

Entities and Operation of the Model

The principal participants and relationships between participants are depicted in the following paragraphs. The main entities are off-card entities and smart cards. More specifically in a multi-application smart card usage scenario the entities that are likely to get involved in a communication session with the card are the Issuers and any Application Providers who have a business relationship with the Issuer.

For the purpose of this paper the establishment of a secure channel is divided into three sequential phases as defined in [6]:

- *Secure Channel Initiation* – when the card and the off-card entity have exchanged sufficient information enabling them to perform the required cryptographic functions. The Secure Channel Initiation phase also involved the authentication of the off-card entity by the card.
- *Secure Channel Operation* – following the exchange of card and off-card data the two entities will have the means to establish a secure channel based on recently established session keys.
- *Secure Channel Termination* – if at any stage during the operation of the secure channel either the card or the off-card entity determines that the messages received do not correspond to the expected messages or the messages do not carry the necessary cryptographic protection of expected fields then the secure channel should be terminated.

Therefore, for the purpose of this paper a secure channel is initiated either by the off-card entity using the appropriate Application Protocol Data Unit (APDU) command or by an on card entity (e.g. a Security Domain) directly when an APDU (that is cryptographically protected) is received.

Operational Characteristics

The established session keys are used for providing integrity and confidentiality on the exchanged messages. For this protocol the following requirements must be satisfied:

1. *C*, represents the smart card. Typically a sufficient tamper resistant device which is relatively difficult to compromise; it has access to a variety of cryptographic algorithms and a good random number generator. A multi-application smart card platform (e.g. GlobalPlatform) will provide significant functionality that will strengthen the overall concept of dynamic application management.
2. *H*, is a host defined as an off-card entity that requires establishing a secure channel with the smart card, application or smart card operating system (SCOS).

3. All entities share public values p and a, where p is a large prime number and a is an element of a large prime multiplicative order modulo p. We will write a^x for (a^x mod p) throughout.
4. Each card has a Diffie-Hellman key agreement key pair. More specifically, card C has private key agreement key y with corresponding public key a^y. The card's key pair can be either generated off-card by the issuer or the application provider and subsequently loaded onto the card, or it can be generated on-card (if the functionality is provided by the card). In either case the public key has to be certified by the corresponding off-card entity, i.e. the issuer or an application provider.
5. The host (H) has an RSA public encryption key, which is certified by the corresponding certification authority.
6. The card and the host share a symmetric cryptosystem and a key generation function (e.g. a one-way function) $f1(Z)$.
7. The card is capable of generating random numbers.
8. Each card (e.g. through a security domain) has a trusted copy of its owner's (e.g. certification authority, issuer or application provider) public certification key whose corresponding private key is used by the off-card entity for issuing certificates (i.e. for the Diffie-Hellman and RSA keys).

On top of these requirements the protocol should be able to fulfil the following requirements:

1. *Cheap to operate.* Its operation should not require the purchase of additional expensive smart card or host equipment.
2. *Fast.* Communication between the entities should take place with a minimal exchange of messages. Moreover the messages exchanged between the participants should minimise the use of unnecessary cryptographic operations (given the limited computational capabilities of smart cards).
3. *Efficient.* The system's operation should not restrict the normal participant's behaviour.
4. *Flexible.* It should also be able to accommodate the participant's requests for exchanging optional parameters.
5. *Secure.* It should be able to offer adequate levels of protection and follow the secure channel establishment steps as described above.

In the following section we present the architectural characteristics of the protocol.

Operational Assumptions

Given the number of the entities involved, there is clearly a need for a Public-Key Infrastructure (PKI) [29, 30] that assists these entities in managing their keys and supports the security functions of the proposed protocol.

The supporting functions of a PKI include key certification, authorisation of participating entities, and the ability of a participating entity to have multiple keys. For simplicity and in order to sustain the practicality of the overall architecture the description of the proposed infrastructure will provide examples linked with the GP architecture as described above. Furthermore, the details of the PKI infrastructure are not within the scope of this paper and we also assume that adequate key and entity management procedures are in place.

According to the proposed infrastructure, each participating off-card entity (being an Issuer or an Application Provider) has a key pair (namely certification key pair) which is used for the certification of other keys. The public key of this key pair is securely loaded on the card (e.g. in a security domain that represents the off-card entity on the card). The corresponding private key is used for the certification of RSA public encryption keys (which are used for the establishment of a secure channel). These certificates bind the included public key to the entity that is authorised to use this public key encryption key during the establishment of a secure session. As an alternative, the certification key pair might belong to a Certification Authority, which has a business relationship with the off-card entity.

Secure loading and replacement of these keys can take place by establishing a secure channel that will enable the secure transfer of keys to the card (e.g. by using the Put Key command as described in the GP specifications). Initial keys for the Issuer can be optionally hard-coded (e.g. masked in ROM) and used, during the personalisation phase, for the loading of the public certification keys. Loading of the public keys for Application Providers has to be done in a secure way (e.g. during the loading of the corresponding GP security domains or during the personalisation of these security domains). Following the loading of these certification keys, any public encryption key that belongs to an entity recognised by the security domain and is certified using the certification private key can be used for the establishment of a secure channel.

Given the proposed infrastructure, the card (or a security domain) is able to tell whether the key presented to it belongs to an entity that is authorised to establish a secure channel by verifying the certificate. For instance, if the certified key belongs to an Application Provider and is certified using the certification key loaded on the Application Provider's logical space in the card (e.g. a security domain) then the off-card entity is authorised to establish a secure session with one of the applications belonging to this Provider.

We summarise the notation used in the subsequent description of the protocol. This notation is an extended version of the notation defined in [5, 34]. Descriptions of the cryptographic algorithms appropriate for use in the protocols defined below can be found in [5, 35].

Table 1. Algorithms, Keys and Notation.

Notation	**Description**
Y||Z	Represents the concatenation of data items Y, Z in that order.
X→Y: C	Implies that entity X sends entity Y a message with contents C.
{X,Y,Z}	Implies that items within curly brackets are optional.
f1=h(Z)	IS the result of a collision resistant hash function such SHA-1 applied to the data Z.
E_K(Z)	Is the result of encipherment of data Z with a symmetric encipherment algorithm (e.g. AES or triple-DES) using key K.
PK_X(R)	Is the result of encipherment of data string R using a public key algorithm (e.g. RSA) with key X.
CSN	Represents the Card's Serial Number.
SK	Is a session key to be used for the subsequent cryptographic protection of a secure channel.
Rand_X	Is a random number generated by entity X (e.g. a Host or a Card).
Cert(X)	Represents a certificate on key X, e.g. X=Host_DH.
X_PEK	Represents entity's X Public Encryption Key, e.g. an RSA key.
X_SEK	Represents entity's X Secret Encryption Key, e.g. an RSA key.
X_DH	Represents entity's X Diffie-Hellman Public Key, e.g. Host_DH.

To strengthen the security provided by this scheme and considering that the off-card entity might use the certification key pair to certify keys not used by this protocol, certificates have to explicitly state that the certified keys are authorised to be used for the establishment of a secure channel. This explicit authorisation is granted when specified in one of the certificate extensions. Given an Issuer, who would typically have many certified keys for different purposes, there is clearly a need to protect the card from accidental or deliberate misuse of a key that is not authorised for this purpose. Therefore, the card should only use those keys that explicitly state in a dedicated extension that they can be used for communications with the card, and more specifically, for establishing a secure channel.

Apart from the off-card entities' RSA public encryption keys, the proposed protocol requires each card to have one or more Diffie-Hellman keys [12]. There are two options for the certification of these keys; either the card has a single key pair which is certified by the Issuer and shared among application (or security domains) that exist on the card, or each application (or security domain) has its own key pair certified by the entity it belongs to. The second option provides more flexibility as it allows the corresponding entity to specify the format based on their applications requirements. Given that none of these approaches introduce any risks to the security of the protocol it is up to the issuer's discretion to adopt either of these options. Please note that the infrastructure required for supporting the certification and verification of these keys or the certificate format [32] is beyond the scope of this paper.

4. A PUBLIC KEY SECURE CHANNEL SMART CARD PROTOCOL

In this section we present a technique that use well-established public key techniques for mutual authentication and key establishment between a smart card and an off-card entity based on the principles of the Diffie-Hellman key agreement protocol and a combination of symmetric and asymmetric cryptography.

The Protocol

The proposed protocol, which involves a host (off-card entity) H and a card C, consists of the following steps (please note that messages in curly brackets are considered as optional):

1. The host initiates the protocol by sending the following message to the card:

   H → C: Cert(Host_DH) || Rand_H || { Host_ID ||
   Request_Cert(Card_DH) ||
   Request_Cert(Card_PEK) ||
   Cert (Host_PEK)}

   where *{optional parameters}* is used by the host to inform the card on certain communication requirements (e.g. protecting certain card details and state whether the card has to return to the host the certificate on its Diffie-Hellman public key or just the certificate's identification number).

2. On receiving message (1) the card verifies the certificate *Cert(Host_DH)* using the preloaded public certification key of the corresponding off-card entity. If the certificate verification is successful and the entity is pre-authorised (e.g. if the entity possesses a security domain) then the card checks whether there are any optional parameters. If the are no problems with the message the card calculates *K, as* the output of a key generation function *f1* whose input is the shared Diffie-Hellman key α^{xy}, i.e. $K = f1(\alpha^{xy})$, it generates a pseudorandom number (Rand_C) and encrypts the two random numbers with key K. Subsequently, depending on the optional parameters it formulates the following message, which is optionally encrypted with the host public encryption key (Host_PEK):

   C → H E_K(Rand_H || Rand_C) { $PK_{HostPEK}$((Cert(Card_DH) || CSN) || Rand_H) }

   On receiving message (2) the host uses its private encryption key (Host_SEK) to decrypt the second part of the message. Subsequently, it verifies Cert(Card_DH) and ensures that the message comes from the required card (CSN). Subsequently, it generates key K (by using the card's Diffie-Hellman certificate) and decrypts the first part of the message in order to obtain the card's random number (Rand_C). Finally, it generates a new random value i.e. Rand_HB. The optional *session keys (SK)*, if sent to the card, will be used as the session keys for the established session. This is useful during card personalisation and card updates where the off-card system has pre-computed the messages to speed up the process. Note that if the off-card entity does not sent *session keys*, a key generating function can be utilised for the generation of session keys (which will be used to provide integrity and confidentiality for the exchanged messages). Finally, it sends the following response to the card:

   H → C E_K (Rand_C, {*SK*}, Rand_HB)

3. On receipt of the host's response the card decrypts the message and it verifies the content (i.e. the correct Rand_C); if no problems are encountered it uses the newly obtained session keys and sends the following response to the host:

C → H E_{SK}(Rand_HB, {optional parameters})

4. On receiving the message the host will use the previously established session keys in order to decrypt the message and obtain the previously sent random number (Rand_HB) along with any further optional card details.

If all the steps are successful the host and the card will use the established session keys (or the keys provided by the host in step two of the protocol) for the protection of exchanged messages throughout this session.

5. PROPERTIES AND SECURITY ANALYSIS

The proposed protocol provides mutual authentication and session key establishment between the communicating entities, i.e. an off-card entity and the card. The established session keys can be used to optionally provide integrity and message authentication as well as confidentiality on subsequent communications. Although the protocol is based on public key techniques it takes into account the restricted computing resources offered by a smart card (as briefly described in the previous sections). Therefore, the number of expensive computations (like the ones required by public key cryptography) are minimised to avoid processing overheads.

One of the factors that could affect the number of expensive computations was the choice of the Diffie-Hellman keys. Diffie-Hellman keys can be of two flavours; either long term, preferably certified, keys or just short term keys that are typically used for a single session. The card's Diffie-Hellman key pair is fixed in order to avoid the computational overhead required for the generation of a new key pair (a relatively computationally expensive operation for a smart card given that the card has this capability) for each session. However, there is nothing to prohibit a card to securely generate a new Diffie-Hellman key pair if operational security or application requirements impose this. On the other hand, it is assumed that the host possesses the computational resources for computing and storing a large number of key pairs. For that particular reason it uses a new key pair (for each communication), as opposed to a fixed certified one, so that to avoid one more certificate verification on the card. Note that the host can generate these keys in advance to avoid delays introduced by the generation of these keys during the establishment of a secure session.

What can go wrong?

Among the main issues surrounding the deployment and operation of a security protocol is the compromise of the scheme's private keys. If a card's

Diffie-Hellman key pair is compromised, it is the Issuer's decision whether to terminate or block this card, or simply update this card's Diffie-Hellman key pair. In the GP analogy if the key belongs to an Application Provider's security domain the Application Provider has to simply update this key by using the Put Key command.

If an off-card entity's (e.g. the Issuer or Certification Authority) RSA encryption key pair is compromised, the off-card entity has to perform the following actions in order to prevent further use of the compromised key by a malicious user:

1. The off-card entity has to generate a new certification key pair, which will replace the one used to certify the compromised key.
2. The off-card entity has to generate a new RSA encryption key pair and certify the public key of this key pair using the new private certification key. Note that if the issuer has issuer multiple certification keys, it then has the option not to generate a newly created key pair but to use an existing one.
3. All the cards that carry the old public certification key have to be updated with the new public key. As soon as the cards obtain the new certification key they will be able to reject certificates that were created using the compromised key.

Replacement of the certification key pair is also deemed necessary when RSA public encryption key certificates are due to expire to ensure that a key is not used beyond its expiration date. The off-card entity can use the above method to replace these keys.

An off-card entity, being the Issuer or an Application Provider, can have multiple RSA encryption key pairs to avoid unnecessary exposure of a single key. Given that the public key of this key pair is certified by a certification private key whose public counterpart is loaded on the card, the card will be able to verify this key and use it for the establishment of the secure channel. Off-card entities can also use multiple certification keys. In that case, however, the off-card entity has to have access to information that will assist it in the choice of the correct public encryption key certificate, prior to initiating the establishment of a secure channel. In the GP analogy (as defined in [6]) this information can be part of the security domain management data provided to the host as a response to the SELECT command.

Protocol Efficiency

At the very first instance it can be argued that the protocol is relatively heavy, especially when compared with corresponding symmetric key protocols. However, it is well established that the advantages that public key cryptography has to offer will have to be balanced with the anticipated processing and architectural overheads. Most of the publicly available smart card secure channel protocols are based on symmetric cryptography techniques, e.g. the GlobalPlatform ones. On the other hand a potential comparison with a number of public key secure channel protocols for devices with not some many communication and processing characteristics will not add a lot of value.

However, by taking into account the performance of cryptographic algorithms as defined in [31, 32] we can provide some indicative estimates on the performance of the cryptographic protocol, please refer to Table 2.

From Table 2 we can observe that cryptographic operations of the protocol can be completed in less than a second. Please note that this figure does not include the time spent by the SCOS to form the messages according to the protocol requirements and also to move any data from EEPROM to RAM and vice versa. Furthermore, it does not include any performance measurements for the transmission of APDUs as required by each step in the protocol. However, they give an indication as to how much time is spent in the cryptographic part of the protocol.

Table 2. Approximate Performance of the Cryptographic Protocol According to Theoretical Timings.

Operations	**Approximate Timings (ms)**
1. Two RSA signature verifications for the host certificate verification on the Host public, and Diffie-Hellman keys.	~2*160
2. A random generation (RandC).	~ 30
3. An RSA encryption for encrypting RandC, the card CSN and the key K1.	~160
4. A DH computation of a shared secret value α^{xy}	~300
5. A secret key encryption for the encryption of the card certificate cert (C-DH).	~10
6. A symmetric decryption.	~10
Totals:	**~830ms**

Furthermore, in order to successfully verify the actual performance details of the protocol we are currently, experimenting with its development in a Gemplus GemXpresso card (i.e. Java card Ver. 2.1 [18] and GP 2.1

platform [19]). We believe that in the final version of the paper we will also have obtained the required performance measurements which will be included as another section (i.e. performance measurements from a Java card implementation of the protocol) in the paper.

6. CONCLUSIONS

In this paper we have outlined the necessity and importance of using public key based cryptographic protocols for the establishment of secure channels in a multi-application smart card environment. Although public key protocols were not widely used in smart card microprocessors due to their limitations in processing power, recent technological improvements [14, 15] along with improvements in the operation of cryptographic algorithms [16, 17], make the whole idea more attractive and more feasible.

The core of this paper is dedicated in the development of secure channel establishment protocol that uses standardised public-key techniques (e.g. Diffie-Hellman) in order to provide mutual authentication and key establishment. The supporting infrastructure required to sustain the protocol's cryptographic operations is also defined. The proposed protocol, which benefits from the advantageous key management functionality provided by public key cryptography, can be utilised in a wide range of smart card microprocessors. It can be used both by the underlying SCOS and by smart card applications. More importantly, it can also be smoothly integrated in the architecture of existing multi-application smart card technologies as in the case of GP.

The future demands for public key smart card protocols will increase taking into account the needs and architectural/business models of various security sensitive applications. We are currently experimenting with the theoretical and practical implementation details around the design of public key secure channel protocols (e.g. based on elliptic curve cryptography) and also compare their performance with other existing protocols.

7. REFERENCES

1. PC/SC Workgroup. "Specifications for PC-ICC Interoperability". www.smartcardsys.com
2. OpenCard Consortium. "OpenCard Framework Specification OCF". www.opencard.org
3. B. Schneier. "Applied Cryptography", Second Edition, John Wiley & Sons, 1996.
4. W. Rankl, W. Effing. "Smart Card Handbook", John Willey and Sons, 1997.
5. A. Menezes, P. van Oorschot, S. Vanstone. "Handbook of Applied Cryptography", Boca Raton CRC Press, 1997.
6. Global Platform. "Open Platform Card Specification", Version 2.1. June 2001. http://www.globalplatform.org.

7. P.H. Hartel , E.K. de Jong Frz. "Smart Cards And Card Operating Systems", In J. Bartlett, editor, UNIFORUM' 96, pages 725-730, San-Francisco, California, Feb 1996. Uniforum, Santa Clara, California.
8. C. Markantonakis. "The Case For A Secure Multi-Application Smart Card Operating System", Springer-Verlag Lecture Notes in Computer Science Vol. 1396.
9. Javasoft. "Java Card Platform Specifications", Version 2.2, September 2002. http://java.sun.com/products/javacard/specs.html
10. Microsoft. "Windows for Smart Card". http://www.microsoft.com/HWDEV/TECH/input/smartcard/
11. MAOSCO. "MULTOS Reference Manual Ver 1.2". http://www.multos.com/
12. International Organization for Standardization. Genève, Switzerland. ISO/IEC 7816–4, Information technology—Identification cards—Integrated circuit(s) cards with contacts—Part 4: Interindustry commands for interchange, 1995.
13. W. Diffie, M. Hellman. "New Directions in Cryptography", IEEE Transactions on Information Theory, 22:644-654, 1976.
14. R. Ferreira, R. Malzahn, P. Marissen, J.-J. Quisquater and T. Wille. "FAME: a 3rd generation coprocessor for optimising public key cryptosystems in smart card applications", Smart Card Research and Advanced Applications – Cardis '96, Publ. Stichting Mathematisch Centrum, pp. 59-72, 1996.
15. T. Boogaerts, "Implementation of elliptic curves cryptosystems for smart cards", CARDIS 1998, 14-16th September 1998.
16. H. Handschuh, P. Paillier. "Smart Card Cryptoprocessors for Public Key Cryptography", In Third Smart Card Research and Advanced Application Conference – CARDIS'98, Lecture Notes in Computer Science, volume 1820, pages 372-379, Springer-Verlag, 2000.
17. L.C. Guillou, M. Ugon, J.J. Quisquater. "The Smart Card (A standardised Security Device Dedicated to Public Cryptology)", in G.J. Simmons, Ed., Contemporary Cryptology: The Science of Information Integrity, ISBN 0879422777.
18. Gemplus. GemXpressoRAD. Gemplus, 2003.
19. Giesecke & Devrient. StarSIM Developer Suite. G&D 2003.
20. J.S. Coron, M. Joye, D. Naccache, P. Paillier. "Universal padding schemes for RSA" In M. Yung, Ed., Advances in Cryptology - CRYPTO 2002, vol. 2442 of Lecture Notes in Computer Science, pp. 226-241, Springer-Verlag, 2002.
21. J.S. Coron, D. M'Ra hi, C. Tymen. "Fast generation of pairs (k,[k]P) for Koblitz elliptic curves" In S. Vaudenay and A.M. Youssef, Eds., Selected Areas in Cryptography, vol. 2259 of Lecture Notes in Computer Science, pp. 151-164, Springer-Verlag, 2001.
22. M. Joye, P. Paillier, S. Vaudenay. "Efficient Generation of Prime Numbers" In .K. Ko and C. Paar, Eds., Cryptographic Hardware and Embedded Systems – CHES 2000, vol. 1965 of Lecture Notes in Computer Science, pp. 340-354, Springer-Verlag, 2000.
23. R. Ferreira, R. Malzahn, P. Marissen, J.J. Quisquater, T. Wille. FAME: A 3rd generation coprocessor for optimising public key cryptosystems in smart card applications, In P. H. Hartel et al., editor(s), Smart Card Research and Advanced Applications – Cardis '96, pages 59-72, Springer-Verlag, 1996.
24. UCL. "A Smarter Chip for Smart cards". www.dice.ucl.ac.be/cascade, 1996.
25. K. Markantonakis. "Secure Log File Download Mechanisms for Smart Cards", Third Smart Card Research and Advanced Application Conference (CARDIS'98), September 14-16 1998, UCL Louvain-La-Neuve-Belgium, Lecture Notes in Computer Science, volume 1820, pages 285-304, Springer-Verlag, 2000.
26. ISO/IEC 11770-3. "Information Technology - Security Techniques - Key Management - Part 3: Mechanisms using asymmetric techniques", ISO 1999.
27. L.G. Wang. "Smart Visa and Java Technology", June 04, 2001. http://java.sun.com/features/2001/06/visa.html

28. 3GPP. "GSM 03.48 Digital Cellular Telecommunications System, SIM Toolkit Secure Messaging".http://www.3gpp.org/ftp/tsg_cn/WG4_protocollars/Temp/SMG%2323/TDocs/P-97-790.pdf
29. ISO/IEC 11770-1. "Information Technology - Security Techniques - Key Management - Part 1: Framework", 1996.
30. ITU-T X.509. "The Directory – Public key and Attribute Certificate Frameworks".
31. H. Handschuh, P. Paillier. "Smart Card Crypto-Coprocessors for Public-Key Cryptography", The Technical Newsletter RSA Laboratories, Vol 1, Number 1, Summer 1998.
32. K. Markantonakis. "Is the Performance of the Cryptographic Functions the Real Bottleneck?", IFIP TC11 16th International Conference on Information Security (IFIP/SEC'01), June 11-13, 2001, Paris, France, In "Trusted Information: The New Decade Challenge" , Kluwer Academic Publishers , ISBN 0-7923-7389-8, pages 77-92.
33. C. Boyd, A. Mathuria, "Protocols For Authentication and Key Establishment", Springer Verlag in Information Security and Cryptography, June 15, 2003.
34. "ISO/IEC 9798-1. Information Technology – Security Techniques – Entity Authentication – Part 1: General", 1997.
35. D.R Stinson, "Cryptography: Theory and Practice", CRC Press 1995.

MOBILE TRUST NEGOTIATION

Authentication and Authorization in Dynamic Mobile Networks

Timothy W. van der Horst, Tore Sundelin, Kent E. Seamons, and Charles D. Knutson
*Brigham Young University, Provo, Utah**

Abstract We examine several architectures for extending the nascent technology of automated trust negotiation to bring nonidentity-based authentication and authorization to mobile devices. We examine how the location of trust agents and secure repositories affects such a system. We also present an implementation of one of these models. This protocol leverages software proxies, autonomous trust agents, and secure repositories to allow portable devices from different security domains (i.e., with no pre-existing relationship) to establish trust and perform secure transactions. This proposed system is called surrogate trust negotiation as the sensitive and resource-intense tasks of authentication are performed vicariously for the mobile device by a surrogate trust agent.

Keywords: Trust negotiation, authentication, authorization, access control, mobile computing, proxy, software agent, credential repository

1. Introduction

Interpersonal transactions are often contingent upon relevant attributes of the involved parties (e.g., nationality, age, job title, financial resources, etc.). These transactions can be quite intricate and involved. In the digital world, such interactions have historically been viewed as static identity-based schemes, handled out-of-band using alternative means, or simply avoided. One proposed solution for this problem of real-time, attribute-based digital interactions is called *automated trust negotiation* [WSJ00, BS00, WYS+02] (see Section 2).

*This research was supported by funding from DARPA through AFRL contract number F33615-01-C-0336 and SSC-SD grant number N66001-01-1-8908, the National Science Foundation under grant no. CCR-0325951 and prime cooperative agreement no. IIS-0331707, and The Regents of the University of California.

Trust negotiation appears well-suited for a mobile environment because mobile devices usually operate outside their trusted domain and thus have a greater need to determine whether a stranger can be trusted. This application becomes particularly compelling in light of the proliferation of such devices, their associated usage models, and their intuitive contextualization as digital representatives of their respective users.

The development of such a system presents significant obstacles. Mobile devices, due to their size, ease of transportation, and high value, are both ideal targets for theft and prone to physical accidents which can lead to their demise. In addition, they can be easily lost. Trust negotiation relies upon elements of public key cryptography and policy compliance checking that are often excessively burdensome on mobile devices. Also, because mobile network topologies are often unpredictable, such a system must handle interactions between devices of mixed capabilities in varied infrastructure configurations. Limited resources, battery limitations, processing power, and connectivity also plague mobile devices.

We use the foundation of trust negotiation to examine an advanced authentication system compatible with the limited capabilities of many mobile computing devices, and present one solution to this problem. The goal of our system is to enable mobile devices to safely and efficiently perform sensitive transactions on behalf of their owners in circumstances in which this was previously not possible.

2. Trust Negotiation

Mobile trust negotiation is designed to support automated trust negotiation between strangers that meet in the physical world and desire to perform sensitive transactions between their mobile devices (PDA, cell phone, etc.). For example, suppose two military groups from separate nations meet on the battlefield while conducting joint operations. The commanders desire to authenticate and authorize each other in order to reliably share fresh information on enemy positions and tactics. During a natural disaster, emergency response personnel from local, state, and government agencies converge to the scene and desire to share information with authorized personnel. A consumer can complete an e-commerce transaction while in an airport and be assured that he is communicating with a trustworthy business.

Trust negotiation solves the problems associated with classical authentication and authorization schemes by allowing individuals outside a local security domain to safely access sensitive data and services [WSJ00, BS00, WYS+02]. It enables two parties to perform secure transactions by first establishing trust through a bilateral, iterative process of requesting and disclosing digital credentials and policies. Digital credentials are the electronic analogues of paper credentials, and may be used to verify such attributes as identifying information, licensing certifications, and association memberships. These credentials are digitally signed by an issuer and assert the veracity of certain attributes of the owner. The properties of public key cryptography guarantee that these credentials are both unforgeable and verifiable.

Along with credentials, trust negotiation relies on access control policies, which protect sensitive resources such as services, data, credentials, and even other policies from unauthorized access. By specifying the necessary credentials that a party must possess in order to access a specific resource, policies provide a means by which any user may be granted or refused access to a resource in real-time. Associating policies with particular resources allows trust negotiation to thrive in a dynamic environment in which users and resources are constantly changing. As both parties in a given transaction may have sensitive resources protected by applicable policies, trust negotiation often occurs with respective parties progressively fulfilling the other parties' policies while iteratively making policy-based credential requests of their own.

Trust negotiation has two main requirements in order to operate. First, a trust agent is needed to perform a negotiation on the user's behalf. Second, a secure repository is needed to store the sensitive information that is needed by the trust agent during the negotiation. This information includes, but is not limited to, credentials, private keys, and policies.

Trust agents are intelligent, autonomous software modules that can be used to establish trust on behalf of their owner with another trust agent. An agent makes use of access control polices to protect and manage its owner's credentials, policies, and keys during a negotiation. There are various configurations for a trust agent in a mobile environment. When the trust agent resides on the device, it is called a local agent. When it does not reside on the device, it is called a remote agent. TrustBuilder [WYS+02] is an existing implementation of a trust negotiation agent.

3. Secure Repositories

A secure repository is necessary to store the sensitive data used for trust negotiation. Repositories can be local or remote.

3.1 Local Repositories

A local repository, as its name indicates, is stored locally on the user's device. Many existing schemes, such as an encrypted file system or a set of encrypted files, can be used to store sensitive data locally. The encrypted storage can be protected by a password or biometric possessed by the user. There are several application specific methods, e.g., Window's EFS, as well as several widely deployed standards, such as PKCS#12, that could be used to achieve this result.

Another type of local repository stores the sensitive data in an encrypted form on a secure module that could be attached to the mobile device. An example of this is Sony's Memory Stick. Through the use of MagicGate [Ara00], a Memory Stick can store its contents in an encrypted form and only release them to someone that can successfully authenticate.

Another secure module that could be used with a mobile device is a smart card. Smart cards have several advantages over other local repositories. Access to the card is protected by a password or biometric. The private keys never have to exist outside of the card since all necessary processing can be done within the card. However, the space available on these cards is very limited. There is normally about 32KB of space for both an application and its data. It makes sense, therefore, that only the private keys should be stored on the smart card. Any other data could be stored in an encrypted form on the mobile device.

In order to compromise the user's sensitive information the mobile device, the smart card, and either the password or biometric used to access the card would all have to be compromised. This dilutes the risk of carrying sensitive information in a mobile environment. The physical attributes of the smart card lend itself to the protections of physical credentials while maintaining their digital protection properties as well.

A local repository provides several advantages. First, it requires no communication with remote devices. The user can also choose whether all or a subset of credentials should reside on the device. The user's sensitive information is always with him and available for use. Many existing, widely-tested systems are currently available.

Local repositories also have several disadvantages. One problem is synchronization. If a user has several mobile devices, he has to replicate his sensitive information on every device. This could be considered less secure, because there are more copies of the sensitive information and thus a greater possibility that one of the copies of the data would be compromised. When a credential expires, is revoked, or for any reason needs to be updated or removed, the changes would have to be replicated on every device that is possessed by the user. This could be a costly and time-consuming process. Also, since the repository is local, one must always be in possession of the repository when access to the sensitive information is desired.

3.2 Remote Repositories

A remote repository provides a central location for a user to store and manage his credentials. The remote repository could be administered by the user on a machine of his choosing or he could delegate that responsibility to a trusted third party to host it on his behalf.

Remote repositories can be divided into two different categories. Sandu et al. [SBG02] define these categories as virtual soft tokens and virtual smart cards. Virtual soft tokens are a network-based storage solution of sensitive credentials. Credentials are located on an online server and are stored in an encrypted form such that only the user may decrypt them. Since the server cannot decrypt the credentials, the user is in control of their disclosure. When the user desires to use his credentials, he can authenticate to the server and retrieve his encrypted credentials; he can then decrypt and use them. Ideally the credentials should be cleared from the device when the transaction that required them has completed. This would prevent undue exposure of the sensitive credentials and keys. An example of a virtual soft token is the MyProxy system [NTW01]. Another example is the proposed standard: Securely Available Credentials (SACRED) [AF01][GJN04][Far03]. This standard has the added benefit of application and device-independence.

In the virtual smart card paradigm, the remote repository acts like a smart card. There are, however, several subtle differences between these two solutions. In contrast to the physical card, the private key is never completely known to the virtual card. This is accomplished through the 3-key RSA algorithm. In this algorithm the private key is split into two-parts, the user and the virtual smart card each hold a part of the key. Through a shared signature scheme, the two parties can create a valid digital signature that neither side by itself could create. Virtual smart cards also have the benefit of instant revocation. Removal of the server-side component neutralizes a compromised user-side key. Unfortunately, not all RSA keys can be converted into the 3-key format and thus it is not plausible to move many existing certificates to this system.

NSD Security's Practical PKI [BYBS03] is an example of a virtual smart card. It uses Microsoft's Cryptographic API or PKCS #11 to make the credentials available to any application.

Remote repositories offer many advantages. Credentials are always up-to-date and are accessible from any location, even if the user does not have his mobile device with him. They have the added bonus of being application and device independent. Also, there is no sensitive information stored on the mobile device, so if the device is ever lost the credentials are not lost with it. Since the online repository is unable to decrypt the credentials stored there, the user controls their disclosure.

There are several disadvantages which plague remote repositories. They must be available at transaction time and thus create a dependence on a third party in order to complete the transaction. If the online repository is not accessible from where the mobile device is located, or is merely not accessible, it is useless. An online repository creates an additional communication overhead: each time a transaction requires credentials, the mobile device must interact with it.

3.3 Hybrid Repositories

Both local and remote repositories have their benefits and drawbacks. The local repositories have very little communication overhead, and do not require access to an online server at the time of the transaction. They also, however, require that the user bring the repository with them, and the propagation of updates in this model can become complicated. Remote repositories, on the other hand, always have up-to-date credentials and allow the user to access those credentials from any device of his choosing. Since the mobile device contains no sensitive credentials, when the device is lost, nothing but the device is lost. However, the communication overheard, accessibility, and availability issues can limit the effectiveness of online repositories.

A combination of these two systems could lead to the elimination of many of the drawbacks that are inherent in these two repositories. We propose that a virtual soft token be used with a physical smart card to accomplish this agglomeration.

The smart card would first authenticate the user, and then be used to authenticate to the online repository. A local repository of all or some of the sensitive credentials in the repository could then be created. For added security the local cache could be created such that only the smart card would be able to access the decrypted contents. The smart card could have the private keys preloaded, or it could receive the private keys directly in an encrypted form from the repository. A smart card could do the decryption of the sensitive credentials that are stored on the mobile device, or it could give the decryption key to the application that requires the credential. Both should be made available as an option.

A user should also be able to choose to go fully remote, fully local (a full copy still resides in the remote repository), or a mix of the two. This configurability would provide great flexibility to the user, which is essential due to the wide variety of situations that exist in the mobile environment. In any case, a user would require something he knows (his password) and something he has (his smart card).

There are several disadvantages that still exist in this model. Depending on the configuration, there could still be a communication overhead and availability/accessibility issues. There is also the cost of the additional hardware required, e.g., the smart card and smart card reader. The cost of this hardware, though, is rapidly decreasing. The additional hardware can be lost or stolen. Hopefully, since a smart card looks like a credit card, users will be able to treat it with similar regard and thus keep it safe, e.g., not leaving it attached to the mobile device.

4. Surrogate Trust Negotiation

We have created a *surrogate trust negotiation* prototype system that makes use of the ideas presented above. We adapted the trust negotiation agent, TrustBuilder, to negotiate trust on behalf of the user even if the user cannot directly communicate with it. This type of agent was chosen so that we could encompass the greatest range of mobile devices based on the resource requirements of a remote agent.

Although the hybrid repository discussed above shows promise for use in this environment, the creation of such a repository is left as future work. In the system presented below the trust agent maintains a local repository with the user's credentials. Even though the repository is local to the trust agent, it can be seen as a remote repository to the mobile device. This creates centralized storage that adds security and convenience to the system by avoiding the dangers of storing sensitive credentials on mobile devices and by allowing credential updates to be immediately accessible to all the user's devices. A user's mobile devices share a pre-existing relationship that enabled remote invocation of the trust agent. This relationship can be terminated by either side if the mobile device is compromised (see Section 4.2).

The mobile devices directly involved in the transaction are called *primary devices.* The requester of a transaction is referred to as the *client,* while the other device is the *server.* These designations, client and server, are not static as it is reasonable to assume that both will routinely switch roles as one requests a transaction from the other and vice versa. In surrogate trust negotiation, a *proxy* is any device that serves as an infrastructural intermediary between a primary device and its associated trust agent.

Figure 1 illustrates three general topologies that effectively categorize our usage models: *bilateral, unilateral,* and *intermittent* access to a wired infrastructure. *Bilateral* describes scenarios in which both primary de-

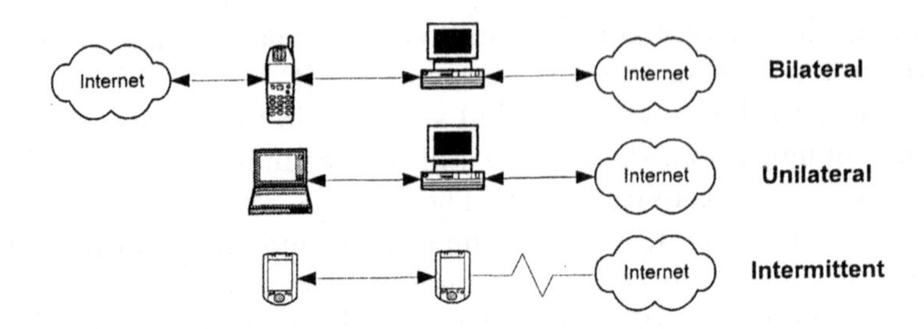

Figure 1. Topology Taxonomy.

vices have reliable, economical, and adequate bandwidth to the Internet. The next, *unilateral*, describes any situation in which only one device has a consistent connection with sufficient bandwidth. The final categorization, *intermittent*, depicts situations in which neither device has consistent access to a wired infrastructure. For clarity and brevity we will explore our system in terms of a unilateral topology only, though this system would work equally as well in the bilateral topology. In the unilateral topology one device will serve as a proxy to forward the negotiation request of the other device to its trust agent.

4.1 Networking Messages

Our surrogate trust system is designed for platform independence and operability with numerous networking protocols. This section presents a high-level discussion of the elements necessary to perform trust negotiation and establish secure communications for the transaction.

For simplicity, we will discuss the networking messages as occurring in three distinct phases: *transaction request*, *authorization*, and *transaction*. In the authorization phase, it is logical to further divide this phase into three sub-phases: *trust negotiation setup*, *trust negotiation*, and *trust negotiation response*. These phases and their composite messages appear in Figure 2.

An exchange begins with the transaction request phase, in which the client requests a transaction from the server. This is represented by the *Transaction Request* message, 1.1, in Figure 2. The trust negotiation setup phase begins when the server replies to the client and indicates that the requested transaction is protected and that trust negotiation must be used for authentication (shown as the *Trust Negotiation Request* message, 2.1). If the client is incapable of performing the trust negotiation protocol or chooses not to participate, this is communicated and the connection is broken. Otherwise, both devices then decide together

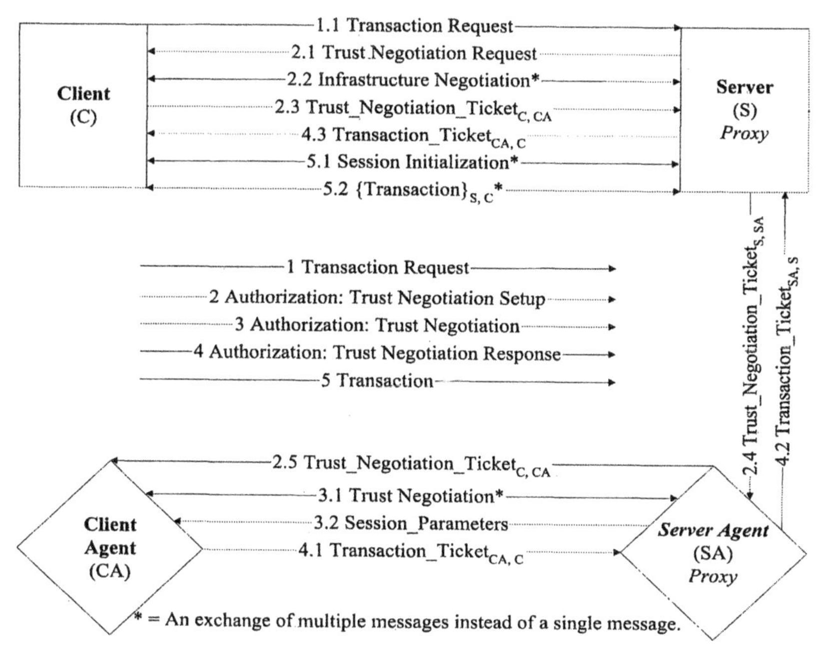

{payload}$_{X, Y}$ = A message payload that is formatted for the end-to-end connection from host x to host y.

Trust_Negotiation_Ticket$_{C, CA}$ = CA_ID | {Transaction_ID}$_{C, CA}$

Trust_Negotiation_Ticket$_{S, SA}$ = {Trust_Negotiation_Ticket$_{C, CA}$ | Trust_Negotiation_Role | Trans_ID}$_{S, SA}$

Session_Parameters = Sesssion_ID | Client_Write_Session_Key | Client_Authentication_Session_Key | Server_Write_Session_Key | Server_Authentication_Session_Key

Transaction_Ticket$_{CA, C}$ = {Trust_Negotiation_Result | Session_Paramters}$_{CA, C}$

Transaction_Ticket$_{SA, S}$ = {Transaction_Ticket$_{CA, C}$ | Trust_Negotiation_Result | Session_Paramters}$_{SA, S}$

Figure 2. Network Messages.

which has the best access to the Internet in order to serve as a proxy (shown as *Infrastructure Negotiation*, 2.2).

Following infrastructure negotiation, both client and server create a *Trust_Negotiation_Ticket* (2.3,2.4) that is sent to their respective trust agent. The ticket reliably notifies the trust agent that its associated primary device desires to participate in trust negotiation for a specific transaction. When the server acts as the proxy, the client sends a ticket to the server bundled with the location of the client's security agent. On the other hand, when the client serves as the proxy, the server creates a similar ticket but also includes an identifier for the requested transaction and its associated policy. The nature of trust negotiation tickets will be further discussed in Section 4.2.

Following the receipt of the appropriate trust negotiation ticket, the device that has been elected to function as the proxy connects to the server's trust agent and sends a message containing tickets from each primary device, 2.4. The server's agent examines the ticket from its respective primary host and verifies its request to negotiate trust. Following this confirmation, the server's agent connects to the client's agent and sends the appropriate trust negotiation ticket, 2.5. The client's agent will then likewise verify the validity of its ticket.

After both security agents have verified their associated primary devices' intentions, the trust negotiation portion of the authentication phase begins. Since the server is the device that is protecting the transaction, its security agent is responsible for initiating trust negotiation between the agents. As was briefly mentioned in Section 2, the server's security agent begins the process by disclosing policies and/or credentials to the client's agent, which then responds likewise. This bilateral exchange, 3.1, continues until the server's agent deems that the policy (included in the *Trust_Negotiation_Ticket*) governing the transaction has been satisfied or that the negotiation has failed. Factors that could contribute to a failure include the lack of necessary credentials, expired credentials, or the number of iterations exceeding a threshold.

Upon completion of a successful trust negotiation, the client and server trust agents establish the cryptographic key material (see Section 4.2) necessary to create a secure link for performing a transaction between the primary devices. This key exchange is denoted by the *Session_Parameters*, 3.2, message in Figure 2. Following this, the trust negotiation response portion of the authorization phase begins and this key material is sent back through the proxy to the respective primary devices in the form of *Transaction_Tickets* (4.1, 4.2, 4.3). If trust negotiation was successful, the primary devices decrypt these tickets and use the session parameters that they contain to initialize the secure link, which is depicted by the *SessionInitialization* exchange, 5.1. When channel initialization is complete, the server and client can securely perform the sensitive transaction, 5.2.

4.2 Security Provisions

There are three security goals necessary for our proposed system: integrity, authenticity, and confidentiality. The reasons for these goals are threefold. First, all are required to reliably initiate trust negotiation. Second, they ensure the safe delivery of key material to the primary devices following trust negotiation. Finally, they allow for a secure transaction between the primary devices following delivery of key material.

Another vulnerability to consider is that of a compromised mobile device. An ameliorating factor on the extent of potential damage is that the trust agent, the credentials, and keys reside on a physically secure server. These keys never leave this machine, and thus, even if one mobile device is compromised, these private keys as well as imprinted relationships with other devices remain secure. Furthermore, termination from the security agent's side of an end-to-end link is trivial if a user suspects a device has been compromised and re-initialization likewise in the case that the device is later recovered.

Cryptographic Tickets. Since the mobile devices may not be in direct communication with their trust agents, they must use another method to send reliable and confidential messages to their trust agents through a non-trusted third-party. This can be achieved using a cryptographic ticket, an encrypted container that holds data. These tickets are securely communicated between a mobile device and its associated trust agent because they are encrypted according to the pre-established relationship that was formed between these entities.

Our system uses two types of tickets. The *Trust_Negotiation_Ticket* is an instruction created by the primary devices to its trust agent to initiate or accept the request to initiate trust with another entity. *Transaction_Tickets* contain the result of the negotiation and, if successful, the *Session_Parameter* message which contains the keys necessary to form a secure channel between the primary devices.

Secure End-to-End Protocol. The key material that was generated by the trust agents on behalf of their primary devices is used to create two different kinds of keys: an authentication key, and a write key. Each side uses a unique key to encrypt messages and a different unique key to encrypt a message verification. This creates a total of four keys. Using these keys, a secure session is then initialized between the primary devices as specified by the selected transmission protocol. This exchange is depicted by the *SessionInitialization* messages in Figure 2.

Following session initialization, all transmitted messages will be formatted according to the security provisions of the selected transmission protocol. For example, IPSec's Encapsulating Security Payload (ESP) [Ken02] protocol is capable of providing all of our target characteristics (i.e., connectionless sessions, integrity, authenticity, and confidentiality). However, an actual implementation of the system can use any established protocol which fulfills our definition of an end-to-end link. In general, end-to-end messages will be formatted by wrapping the payload data with the necessary header information and then encrypting and authenticating the result. In Figure 2, messages formatted according to the end-to-end protocol are denoted by the syntax $\{\text{payload}\}_{sender,recipient}$.

Thus, using the procedure described above, the security characteristics of the implemented connectionless protocol, in this case ESP, can be leveraged to secure the communication channels. However, as the channel between trust agents is assumed to be secure by virtue of the utilized trust negotiation protocol (e.g., [HJM+02]), only the channels between the primary devices and between a primary device and its associated trust agent need adhere to our definition of an end-to-end link.

4.3 Implementation

We have implemented a surrogate trust negotiation prototype system [Sun03]. The hardware core of the prototype system was comprised of two WiFi-enabled iPAQ handhelds running Microsoft's Pocket PC operating system, which served as the primary devices. The physical and link layer of the primary channel was 802.11b. On top of this, basic TCP/IP sockets were used for communication between the primary devices. Both the server trust agent and client trust agent were run on Pentium 4 machines running Windows XP. The SOAP RPC protocol was used as a means of communication between negotiating trust agents as well as between primary devices and their respective trust agents.

5. Conclusions and Future Work

We have examined the role of secure repositories and trust agents in an architecture for enabling secure transactions between portable devices that have no pre-existing relationship. We have shown how the decision of the type of repository affects the safety of a user's sensitive information while in a mobile environment. Also, the choice of repository determines what types of mobile devices can benefit from this architecture.

We have outlined surrogate trust negotiation, a flexible model that effectively leverages the combined capabilities of network proxies, software agents, and secure repositories. This system also makes trust negotiation accessible to the greatest number of mobile devices since it shifts the resource-intensive task of authentication to a remote agent. The use of a local repository on this remote trust agent allowed us to obtain many of the desirable properties of a remote repository. Surrogate trust negotiation lays the foundation for the maturation of effective, new technology in the rapidly evolving research space of secure mobile transactions.

The system, however, is only suitable for the bilateral and unilateral topologies. We are currently working on a system that will satisfy the requirements for intermittently connected devices. The foremost problem in this topology is the inability to access a remote trust agent. Consequently, the resource-intensive task of authentication must be accomplished on the mobile device by a completely local trust agent. We are also working on a system that would provide the user with the flexibility to choose how and where the trust agent and repository will exist. This would involve creating a hybrid repository and trust agent capable of mixed degrees of locality and remoteness.

References

[AF01] A. Arsenault and S. Farrell. Securely Available Credentials – Requirements. *IETF Informational RFC 3157*, August 2001.

[Ara00] S. Araki. The Memory Stick. *IEEE Micro*, July-August 2000.

[BS00] Piero Bonatti and Pierangela Samarati. Regulating service access and information release on the web. In *Proceedings of the 7th ACM Conference on Computer and Communications Security (CCS-7)*, pages 134–143, Athens, Greece, November 2000. ACM Press.

[BYBS03] J. Basney, W. Yurcik, R. Bonilla, and A. Slagell. The Credential Wallet: A Classification of Credential Repositories Highlighting MyProxy. *Communication, Information and Internet Policy*, September 2003.

[Far03] S. Farrell. Securely Available Credentials Protocol. *IETF Internet Draft, draft-ietfcat-sacred-protocol-bss-09*, November 2003.

[GJN04] D. Gustafson, M. Just, and M. Nystrom. Securely Available Credentials (SACRED) – Credential Server Framework. *IETF Informational RFC 3760*, April 2004.

[HJM+02] A. Hess, J. Jacobson, H. Mills, R. Wamsley, K. Seamons, and B. Smith. Advanced Client/Server Authentication in TLS. *Network and Distributed System Security Symposium Conference Proceedings*, February 2002.

[Ken02] S. Kent. IP Encapsulating Security Payload (ESP). *IETF Standards Track RFC 2406*, July 2002.

[NTW01] J. Novotny, S. Tueke, and V. Welch. An Online Credential Repository for the Grid: MyProxy. *IEEE Symposium on High Performance Distributed Computing*, August 2001.

[SBG02] R. Sandhu, M. Bellare, and R. Ganesan. Password-Enabled PKI: Virtual Smart Cards versus Virtual Soft Tokens. *PKI Research Workshop*, April 2002.

[Sun03] Tore Sundelin. Surrogate Trust Negotiation. *M.S. Thesis, Computer Science Department, Brigham Young University*, July 2003.

[WSJ00] W. H. Winsborough, K. E. Seamons, and V. E. Jones. Automated Trust Negotiation. *DARPA Information Survivability Conference and Exposition*, January 2000.

[WYS+02] M. Winslett, T. Yu, K. E. Seamons, A. Hess, J. Jacobson, R. Jarvis, B. Smith, and L. Yu. Negotiating Trust on the Web. *IEEE Internet Computing*, November-December 2002.

WEAK CONTEXT ESTABLISHMENT PROCEDURE FOR MOBILITY AND MULTI-HOMING MANAGEMENT

Vesa Torvinen and Jukka Ylitalo
Ericsson Research, NomadicLab, Finland

Abstract: Trust establishment seems to be the most difficult problem in mobility and multi-homing management. Many protocol proposals assume the presence of some security infrastructure (e.g. a Public-Key Infrastructure). However, building such a global infrastructure has not taken place, maybe because it would be too expensive and difficult to deploy. In this paper, we introduce a security context establishment procedure that utilizes reverse hash chains, and does not require pre-existing security information. The procedure is known to be vulnerable to an active Man-in-the-Middle attack in the first message exchange, however, the procedure is efficient, and does not have inherent scalability problems.

Key words: security, mobility management, multi-homing management, and trust establishment

1. INTRODUCTION

Within the last couple of years, we have witnessed a lack of security awareness in many protocol design proposals. Even though many designers acknowledge the importance of considering security aspects right from the beginning, security is still far too often seen as an add-on, rather than an inherent part of the design process. The reason for the current situation is probably related to the complexity of current telecommunication and security protocols. Also, protocol designers are typically strongly discouraged from making their own security designs, which may alienate the designers from considering security related issues.

The situation is not much better from the security community point of view. There has been a lack of resources for doing security analysis in different application contexts. Furthermore, security requirements themselves may not have been realistic from a deployment point of view. Even though we may have "bullet-proof" security protocols, they may not be widely deployed.

In this paper, we study mobility and multi-homing management problems from a security point of view. We understand mobility management as a procedure in which the locator of an entity changes over time [cf. 21, 10]. Mobility mechanisms allow mobile nodes to remain reachable while moving around in the network. We assume that a mobile node changes its IP address every time it moves to a new link. Location changes are challenging especially for transport and higher-layer connections that should be maintained while moving around the network. Also, the protocol design should be resistant to various attacks, such as Denial-of-Service and re-direction attacks.

Multi-homing, on the other hand, comes very close to the mobility management problem. In this case, the node has several alternative access paths valid at the same time. Two entities may want to communicate via parallel paths at the same time especially if access paths are good for different types of traffic [cf. 1]. In multi-homing, the change of locators may be slower than in the mobility case (e.g. multi-homing may require re-numbering a site's address space), however, the problem of changing locators over time remains the same.

From a security point of view, we further develop the idea of "weak" security. Our goal is to develop a weak context establishment and update procedure that is reasonably secure against MitM, DoS and re-direction attacks, and that is not based on the use of public key cryptography. The procedure should be usable for mobility management and multi-homing. We also assume that the procedure does not need to take care of traffic confidentiality protection because there are other usable upper layer protocols available for this purpose.

The rest of the paper is organized as follows. The next section goes deeper into the security problems in the mobility and multi-homing context. The third section introduces the theoretical background to the security mechanisms we intend to use, i.e. reverse hash chains. Our generalized solution is presented in the fourth section, followed by a section utilizing the framework for multi-homing and local mobility management problems. Finally, we draw some conclusions based on our experience.

2. BACKGROUND

IP-based mobility, in which IP addresses are frequently changed, is challenging from an efficiency point of view. Each new network connection requires lots of processing, and message exchanges, e.g. network discovery, authorization, IP address configuration, router discovery, and mobility management procedures. Depending on the network and IP version, the cost of movement in terms of message count may be up to 16 messages. Multi-homing management has not been in the scope of mobility management protocols, but some recent development initiatives would like to look at both problems together [see e.g. 29]. In multi-homing, the frequency of location changes is typically assumed to be slower than in mobility but the primary management problems remain more or less the same.

There are different approaches for lowering the costs of movements, for example optimizing the procedures at different protocols layers [5, 11, 25, 13], or maintaining context information at the upper layer while isolating the changes to lower layers [e.g. 27, 4, 22, 7]. Local mobility management in different roaming scenarios has produced different architectural proposals, e.g. hierarchical structures of mobile anchor points [5, 25], or fast vertical handovers and context transfers between adjacent routers [13]. The shortcomings of these approaches are typically related to security. Most of the proposals require a Public-Key Infrastructure (PKI), and heavy IPsec processing even though there is no global key management infrastructure [18].

There has been recent interest in"opportunistic" or "weak" security procedures that are known to be vulnerable to active man-in-the-middle (MitM) attacks in the first message exchange, but which would still provide some security. In these approaches, the end-points are typically not authenticated in terms of knowing the real identities. Instead, the goal is to know that the entity remains the same during the communication. One example of such a procedure is a Diffie-Hellman key exchange using self-signed public key certificates [e.g. 23]. A benefit of this procedure is that deployments could start using Public-Key based cryptography even though key distribution and verification infrastructures did not exist. Another example of weak security is a procedure in which shared secrets or tokens are exchanged in clear text via two separate communication paths. For example, the MIPv6 return routability procedure assumes that attackers are not able to see messages in both paths, and consequently are not able to construct the secret [3, 10].

A lot of focus has been put on two kinds of attack, namely Denial-of-Service (DoS) attacks, and re-direction (or Distributed DoS, DDoS) attacks

[3]. DoS is typically prevented by delaying the phase when a state is created. The entity that initiates the communication is generally required to do most of the security processing before the responder gives much attention to him. The entity that responds to requests tries to remain stateless as late in the procedure as possible. Creating state too early opens a door for various DoS attacks. Another common method for DoS resistance is delaying the processing load. For example, public key operations are vulnerable to DoS attacks if the communication protocol requires lots of public key checking by the responder at the beginning. In most cases, protocols add computational load (e.g. by introducing cryptographic puzzles) to the initiator side.

Protection against re-direction attacks requires confirmation that there is really someone expecting a response at the source address, i.e. the attacker is not trying to re-direct the message flow to the victim's current location. It is generally not wise to trust blindly the location information. Quite often, communication protocols check that the communication peer is reachable at the source address, and is able to return some negotiation parameters from that address.

3. REVERSE HASH CHAINS

Our work is based on the simple, and well-known cryptographic construction called the "reverse hash chain" (or "hash chain" for short). [15] first introduced the method, and it has been applied in several areas, for example for public key certificate management [17], micro payments [24, 28], (anonymous) authentication [15, 8, 12], and micro mobility and routing protocols [26, 9]. Hash chains have also been deployed in a binary tree format [cf. 16, 28, 26, 9], however, in this paper we focus on the chain structures.

Technically speaking, a hash chain is a cryptographically generated list of inter-related data entities. It is practically impossible to calculate or otherwise figure out the next value in the chain even when you know the previous value. However, it is very easy to verify that some given value is the next value of a chain. A hash chain is a relatively secure method to be used in communication protocol designs when compared with other similar weak methods, such as the use of cookies, tokens or secret splitting.

A hash chain is created by recursively computing a hash function over a result of the same function. The initial argument for the first hash value computation is typically a large random number. The last generated value of the chain is called the "anchor" or "root" value. The hash values are revealed in reverse order starting from the anchor value. This technique is usually applied based on an assumption that only an authentic end-point knows the correct predecessor values of the chain.

Reverse hash chains can be used as keys in integrity protection and message origin authentication [cf. HMAC in 14]. However, the result is somewhat different from more typical message protection methods, such as shared secret based schemes. Firstly, anybody who is able to receive the subsequent messages is able to verify that the messages belong together. Secondly, message authentication with hash chain values needs to be delayed because the input value (the key) is not revealed until the next message. Even though the verification is delayed, this procedure can be used to verify that all subsequent messages come from the same entity as the first message if the hash chain is used to bind the messages together.

If two communicating entities want to use hash chains to protect their communication, they need to exchange anchor values. If the exchange is done without protection, a Man-in-the-Middle (MitM) attacker may replace the anchor value with its own hash chain. Note, however, that the use of hash chains makes the MitM attack much harder than if, for example, clear text passwords were used. With clear text passwords, the attacker can be passive, and just monitor the traffic to get the password, but with hash chains the attacker must be active right from the beginning in order to replace the anchor values.

A MitM attack can be mitigated by protecting the anchor value with a delayed message authentication code, and by sending the plain text anchor value and the message authentication code via different communication channels. In this case, the attacker must have access to both channels in order to perform the attack.

If the chains are short (which they should be in order keep the computational load low), there is a risk that a chain runs out of values. In this situation, the principles may need to re-negotiate new anchor values. However, it is also possible to link subsequent hash chains together into a longer chain by using the last value of one hash chain to protect the message carrying the anchor value of the next chain. For this reason, the length of the hash chains is not considered as a problem in this study.

4. FRAMEWORK

Our solution framework mimics the message structure of MIPv6 route optimization [10]. Context Establishment is used to establish state, to exchange the anchor values of reverse hash chains, and to initiate two locators. A Binding ModificAtion message updates location information, and it is only sent from an already verified location.

4.1 Context establishment

The context establishment (CE) exchange creates a state between an initiator (I) and a responder (R). The procedure uses the delayed authentication principle in which the initial message exchange is verified with the parameters included in the next message. The anchor values of the hash chains are agreed via two separate communication channels in order to make the MitM attack more difficult. The first round-trip of context establishment is designed to be stateless for the responder side. At the end of the exchange both initiator and responder have the anchor value of the other communication peer.

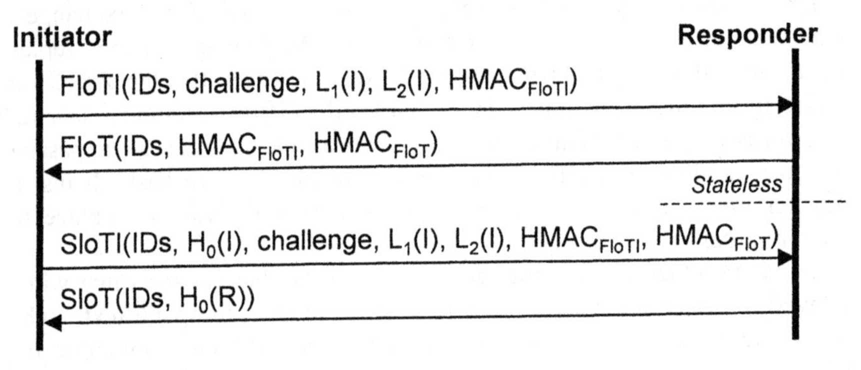

Figure 1: Context establishment

The initiator first sends the First Locator Test Init message, FloTI, to the responder via the first location L1(I). The FloTI message contains the identities of the initiator and responder (IDs), a challenge, location information L1(I) and L2(I), and a keyed hash, HMACFloTI. The HMACFloTI includes the anchor of a newly generated hash chain as a key, and it is computed over all other parameters in the message ("||"represents concatenation):

- HMACFloTI = {keyFloTI, messageFloTI}
- keyFloTI = H0(I)
- messageFloTI = IDs||challenge||L1(I)||L2(I)

Once the responder receives the FloTI message, it must check that the message has one of the locators as a source address. The responder must also check that it does not already have a context with the ID pair. If the context is not found, the responder continues with the negotiation. However, it does not want to establish a state because it is not able to verify the origin of the message. In order to remain stateless, the responder computes a temporary hash chain using the initiator's parameters in the FloTI message, and sends a First Locator Test message (FloT) to the initiator. The FloT message is protected with the anchor value of the responder hash chain. Note that the responder must be able to reconstruct the same hash chain based on the parameters that are present in the SloTI message in order to be stateless during the test of the first location (FloTI/FloT). This can be done securely, for example, by using a local secret as one input to the hash chain generation. Other useful input parameters are end-point identifiers, the challenge of the initiator, and the initiator's location information.

The keyed hash for the FloT message is computed using the anchor value as a key:

- HMACFloT = {keyFloT, messageFloT}
- keyFloT = H0(R)
- messageFloT = IDs|| HMACFloTI

The initiator replies to the FloT message with a Second Location Test Init message (SloTI). The SloTI message reveals the initiator's anchor value, and it is sent from the second location .

Again, the responder does not accept SloTI packets with an ID pair that already has a host pair-context. If the context is not found, the responder re-computes its own hash chain and verifies the message authentication codes (HMACFloTI and HMACFloT). The anchor value of the initiator hash chain binds the FloTI and SloTI messages together, and in this way the responder is able to verify that the messages are coming from the same entity. If the keyed hashes are valid, the responder creates the state, and replies with a Second Locator Test message (SloT) revealing its own anchor value.

The initiator verifies the keyed hash in the FloT message with the anchor value received in the SloT message, and finalizes its state.

From the responder's point of view, the context establishment is able to verify only the first location of the initiator. The responder cannot trust that the second location (L2(I)) is authentic until this locator is tested. For example, it is still possible that the initiator forges the source locator in the SloTI message (source address spoofing). In this case, the attacker never receives the SloT message, however, it may try to fool the responder to e.g. forward a media flow to a victim (re-direction attack).

Note also that the procedure includes some identity and security context information (marked as "IDs" in Figure 1), which is left open on purpose. Identities and/or security context names are a crucial part of the security of this framework. For example, naming a security context solely by IP addresses is not wise unless the ownership of the IP addresses can be confirmed by some other means [e.g. by the use of cryptographically generated addresses as specified in 3]. Otherwise, an attacker is able to "steal" the IP addresses from authorized parties. Allowing multiple contexts from/to the same IP address is a better strategy if IP address ownership cannot be verified. An attacker may still use a false IP address, however, the real user can also use it.

4.2 Binding modifications

Once the state has been completed, both entities may send to their peers an update message on the locator sets. The hash chains are used as keys in delayed message authentication, and consequently each locator update operation will require three messages. However, this is wise anyhow because of a potential re-direction attack, i.e. the new locator may be pointing to the victim's current location instead of the initiator's current location.

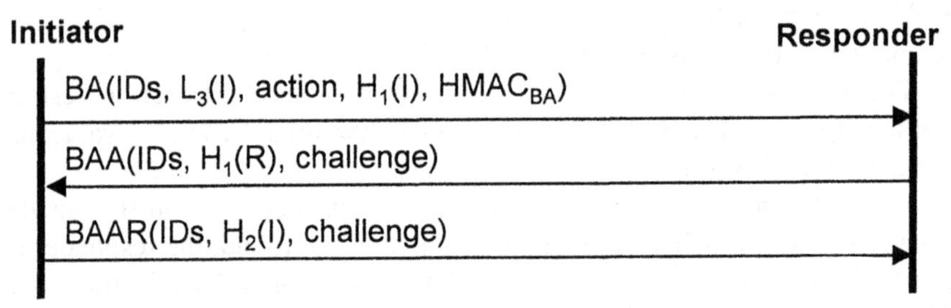

Figure 2: Binding ModificAtion

The Binding ModificAtion message (BA) includes the locator, which is about to be modified, e.g. locator "L3(I)" in the figure above. It also includes information about the action to be performed for this location, e.g. added as a new locator, or deleted because it is not in use anymore. Adding a message authentication code HMACBA protects the locator update;

- HMACBA = {keyBA, messageBA}
- keyBA = H2(I)
- messageBA = IDs||L3(I)||action

Once the responder receives the BA message, it verifies that the hash chain value H1(I) belongs to the initiator (this example assumes that the previously revealed hash chain value was the anchor, H0(I)). The responder replies with the Binding ModificAtion Acknowledgement message (BAA) to the received location. The BAA message includes the next value of the responder's hash chain, and a challenge. The challenge is returned back in the next message, and it is needed in order to avoid a re-direction attack.

The initiator verifies that the hash chain value H1(R) belongs to the responder. The Binding ModificAtion Acknowledgement Reply message

(BAAR) completes the locator update procedure, and it includes the next value of the initiator's hash chain, and the challenge from the BAA message. By returning the challenge, the initiator demonstrates that it really received the BAA message, and did not just wait for some time, and forward the BAAR message from some location (i.e. source address spoofing, re-direction attack).

The responder verifies the challenge and that the hash chain value H2(I) belongs to the initiator. The responder also verifies that all parameters in the original BA packet were unmodified using HMACBA. After successful verifications, the responder changes the state of locator L3(I) according to the requested action.

Even though we considered the length of the hash chain as a non-issue for this framework, it should be noted that the first message of Binding ModificAtions could be used for bootstrapping new hash chains. In this case, the BA and/or BAA message(s) includes also the anchor of the new hash chain. The anchor values must naturally be protected with HMAC using a value from an already existing hash chain as a key.

5. USE CASES

This section demonstrates the use of the framework in multi-homing and mobility contexts. Examples are not intended to be exhaustive protocol designs but rather act as simplified "proofs of concept". The first case example focuses on multi-homing, and the second on local mobility management. Note that the use cases cover two fundamentally different deployments of the framework, i.e. in the first example the communication paths are physically separate while in the second case the separation is logical.

5.1 Multi-homing management

In multi-homing management, the Multi-homing Node and some Responder have two physically separated communication paths – at least on the Multi-homing side. Communication paths may join close to the Responder. See figure 3.

Utilization of our framework is straight forward for this use case. HMAC values are exchanged via the first location (e.g. by piggybacking them in TCP SYN messages), and the clear text hash chain anchor values via the second location. Note, however, that there is no absolute need to finish the context establishment until the multi-homing node wants to start using the second location (if ever). This use case may cause two parallel context establishment procedures, and should be further studied.

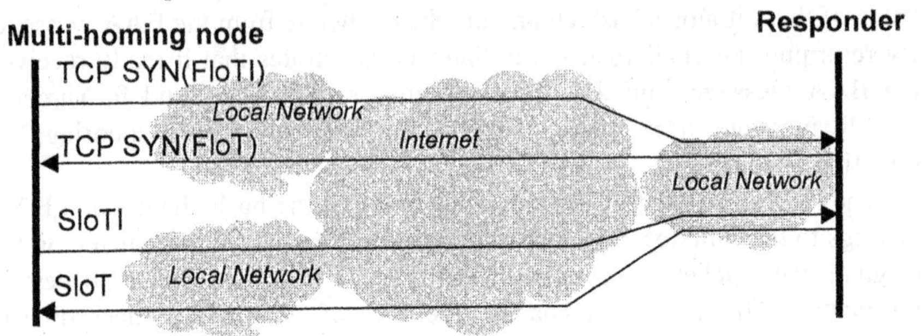

Figure 3: Context establishment in multi-homing context

An active MitM is able to change the hash chain anchor values from the context establishment close to the Responder. However, this is not weaker if compared to the use of IPsec in opportunistic mode, for example.

5.2 Local mobility management

As we stated before, security has been the biggest problem in developing efficient mobility management procedures. Most of the protocol proposals simply require the use of PKI in order to work in real-life roaming situations. Alternatively, the security associations must be configured manually.

Optimized mobility management proposals typically include some local mobility management entity (LME) in the visited/access network, e.g. a mobile anchor point in [25], or previous/next access router in [13]. Common for all these proposals is that mobile node (MN) needs to set security association with this entity.

The use of a LME does not remove the need for the MN to have a security association with the Home Agent (HA). Every time the MN changes its location, it must still update its new location with the HA – no matter if the new location is the real location of the MN, or the address of its LME. Once the MN is behind the LME, it does not need to update its location information while moving under the area of the LME. Binding Updates (BUs) are typically assumed to be sent to HAs using IPsec.

The use of our framework in this context requires the presence of two logically separated communication channels. Even though the MN and the LME do not have two physically separated communication channels, they do have two logical channels; one direct end-to-end path, and another path via the MN's HA (protected with IPsec between the MN and HA). Note also that the FloTI and SloTI messages are likely to arrive at the LME from different directions, especially if the LME is a "NAT-like" device.

The framework can be applied in this way: the FloTI and FloT messages are tunnelled via the HA using the HoTI/HoT message pair from the MIPv6 return routability procedure [10]. From the HA's point of view, the LME acts as the Correspondent Node (CN). The SloTI/SloT message pair can be exchanged directly between the MN and the LME without the MIPv6 return routability tunnelling. See figure 4.

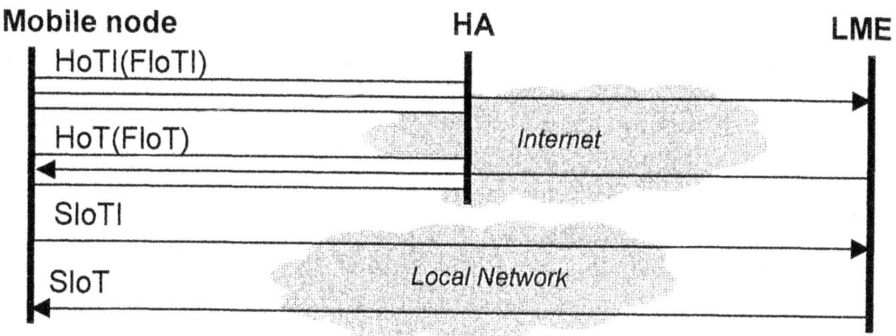

Figure 4: Local mobility management

Once the MN moves to a new location, it can send the Binding ModificAtion message to the LME. Note that the MN and the LME do not have any pre-configured security association, but they are able to create a weak one by relying on the hash chains and separate communication paths.

In theory, the context establishment could also be used in situations where the exchange messages are sent via two access routers (e.g. via the previous and next access routers). This scenario is more vulnerable to certain attacks because IPsec cannot be used, however, it could still be useful for some more limited use cases. For example, the use of this procedure could be secure enough to protect binding updates for ongoing upper layer sessions. An attacker acting as an access router may be able to temporarily hijack the session, however, there is nothing to prevent the MN from sending new binding updates to the CN via the HA. Also, the upper layer security procedures may still be used to protect the confidentiality of the communications.

6. CONCLUSION

In this paper, we have further developed the ideas related to "weak" or "opportunistic" security procedures in a mobile and multi-homing context.

Our exercise demonstrates that development of weak security protocols is possible, and that weak security seems to have some attractive properties especially from efficiency and effectiveness points of view.

In general, our security context establishment procedure is more secure than the return routability procedure in MIPv6 because our procedure requires an active MitM attacker to maintain reverse hash chains. Our procedure is also more efficient and scalable compared to existing protocols, and protocol proposals that mostly rely on PKI or manual keying.

We believe that weak security mechanisms may play an important role in mobility and multi-homing management in the near future. However, developing "forwards compatibility" with stronger security methods, such as PKI, HIP [e.g. 19] or cryptographically generated addresses [e.g. 2, 20], is not a bad idea assuming that these kinds of mechanisms may take over some day. Integration of a public key based method to our procedure can be easily done by adding public key information as part of the initial value of the hash chain operation. For example, signing some parameters from the context establishment, and revealing the signature later in the process could provide a nice migration path between these technologies.

7. REFERENCES

[1] Abley, J. Black, B. & Gill, B. Goals for IPv6 Site-Multihoming Architectures, Internet Engineering Task Force (IETF), RFC 3582, 2003.

[2] Aura, T. Cryptographically Generated Addresses (CGA), in Proceedings of 6th Information Security Conference (ISC'03), Bristol, UK, 2003.

[3] Aura, T. Roe, M. & Arkko. J. Security of Internet Location Management, in Asia-Pacific Computer Systems Architecture Conference, ACSAC'02, Monash University, Melbourne, Australia, February 2002.

[4] Campbell, A. Gomez, J. Kim S., Valko A. Wan, C. & Turanyi, Z. Design, implementation, and evaluation of Cellular IP, IEEE Personal Commun. Mag., Vol. 7, No. 4, pp. 42-49, 2000.

[5] Castelluccia, C. HMIPv6: A Hierarchical Mobile Ipv6 Proposal, ACM Mobile Computing and Communication Review (MC2R), Apr. 2000.

[6] Fischlin, M. Fast Verification of Hash Chains, to appear in the Proceedings of RSA Security 2004, Cryptographer's Track.

[7] Grilo, A. Estrela, P. & Numes, M. Terminal Independent Mobility for IP (TIMIP), IEEE Commun. Mag., Dec. 2001.

[8] Haller, N. The S/KEY One-Time Password System, Internet Engineering Task Force (IETF), RFC 1760, 1995.

[9] Hu, Y-C. Perring, A. & Johnson, D.B. Efficient Security Mechanisms for Routing Protocols, in Proceedings of Network & Distributed System Security Symposium 2003 (NDSS '03), February 6-7, San Diego, CA, pp. 57-73.

[10] Johnson, D. Perkins, C. and Arkko J. Mobility Support in IPv6, Internet Engineering Task Force (IETF), RFC 3775, 2004.

[11] Kempf, J. (editor) Problem Description: Reasons For Performing Context Transfers Between Nodes in an IP Access Network, Internet Engineering Task Force (IETF), RFC 3374, 2002.

[12] Kim, J. Provable Secure Anonymous Authentication Protocol based on Hash Chains, A Thesis for the Degree of Master of Science, Information and Communications University, South Korea, available: http://caislab.icu.ac.kr/pub/thesis/down/jskim.pdf, 2003.

[13] Koodli, R. (editor) Fast Handovers for Mobile IPv6, Internet Engineering Task Force (IETF), work in progress, draft-ietf-mipshop-fast-mipv6-01.txt, 2004.

[14] Krawczyk, H. Bellare, M. & Canetti, R. HMAC: Keyed-Hashing for Message Authentication, Internet Engineering Task Force (IETF), RFC 2104, 1997.

[15] Lamport, L. Password Authentication with Insecure Communication, Communications of ACM, Vol 24, No 11, pp. 770-772, 1981.

[16] Merkle, R. Secrecy, authentication, and public key systems, Ph.D. dissertation, Dept. of Electrical Engineering, Stanford University, 1979.

[17] Micali, S. Efficient Certificate Revocation, Technical Report, MIT/LCS/TM-542b, MIT Laboratory for Computer Science, 1996.

[18] Mink, S. Pahlke, F. Schafer, G. & Schiller, J. Towards Secure Mobility Support for IP Networks, in Proceedings of the IFIP International Conference on Communication Technologies (ICCT), Aug. 2000.

[19] Moskowitz, R. & Nikander, P. Host Identity Protocol Architecture, Internet Engineering Task Force (IETF), work in progress, draft-moskowitz-hip-arch-05.txt, 2004.

[20] O'Shea, G. & Roe, M. Child-proof authentication for MIPv6 (CAM), ACM SIGCOMM Computer Communication Review, Vol. 31, No 2, pp. 4-8, 2001.

[21] Perkins, C. IP Mobility Support, Internet Engineering Task Force (IETF), RFC 2002, 1996.

[22] Ramjee, R. Porta, T. Salgarelli, L. Thuel, S. & Varadhan, K. IP-based Acess Network Infrastructure for next Generation Wireless Data Networks, IEEE Personal Commun. Mag., Vol. 7, No. 4, 2000.

[23] Richardson, M. & Redelmeier, D. Opportunistic Encryption using The Internet Key Exchange (IKE), Internet Engineering Task Force (IETF), work in progress, draft-richardson-ipsec-opportunistic-15.txt, 2004.

[24] Rivest, R.L. & Shamir, A. PayWord and MicroMint--Two Simple Micropayment Schemes, CryptoBytes, volume 2, number 1 (RSA Laboratories, Spring 1996), pp. 7-11.

[25] Soliman, H. Castelluccia, C. El Malki, K. & Bellier L. Hierarchical Mobile IPv6 mobility management (HMIPv6), Internet Engineering Task Force (IETF), work in progress, draft-ietf-mipshop-hmipv6-01.txt, 2004.

[26] Tewari, H. & O'Mahony, D. Lightweight AAA for Cellular IP, in Proceedings of European Wireless 2002, February 25-28, 2002 – Florence, Italy, available in http://www.ing.unipi.it/ew2002/.

[27] Valko, A.G. Cellular IP: a new approach to Internet host mobility, ACM SIGCOMM Computer Communication Review, Vol. 29, Number 1, pp. 50-65, 1999.

[28] Yen, S. Ho L., Huang, C. Internet Micropayment Based on Unbalanced One-way Binary Tree, Proceedings of CrypTEC'99, Hong Kong, July, pp. 155-162.

[29] Ylitalo, J. Jokela, P. Wall, J. and Nikander, P. End-point Identifiers in Secure Multi-Homed Mobility", in Proceedings of the 6th International Conference On Principles Of Distributed Systems, Reims, France, December 11-13, pp. 17-28, 2002.

A GENERIC ARCHITECTURE FOR WEB APPLICATIONS TO SUPPORT THREAT ANALYSIS OF INFRASTRUCTURAL COMPONENTS

Lieven Desmet, Bart Jacobs, Frank Piessens, and Wouter Joosen
DistriNet Research Group, Katholieke Universiteit Leuven, Celestijnenlaan 200A, 3001 Leuven, Belgium

Abstract: In order to perform a useful threat analysis of a web application platform, some architectural assumptions about such applications must be made. This document describes a generic architecture for typical 3-tier web applications. It serves as the basis for analyzing the threats in the most important infrastructural components in that architecture, presented in the following papers.

Key words: Web applications, architectural overview, 3-tier model

1. MOTIVATION

Web applications are an interesting target for security attacks on the Internet. They are easily accessible through the HTTP-protocol, and often company-critical assets are part of the web application infrastructure. Moreover, while web applications infrastructures are fairly complex, basic technology for building web applications is easily accessible. Hence, web applications are often designed and built by developers with little or no distributed system security background. Therefore, useable guidelines for building secure web applications are highly useful.

This document describes a generic architecture of modern web applications, as commonly used in practice by Independent Software Vendors. Hereby, the most commonly used components within the infrastructure and their interactions are presented. The goal of this document is to define a common architectural view for web applications, which can be used to conduct a thorough threat analysis for each of the infrastructural components. Such an analysis will be presented in the following papers ([6. 7,8,9,10]), and will serve as the basis for a set of guidelines to support Independent Software Vendors in building secure web applications.

2. WEB APPLICATIONS

In the early days of the World Wide Web, web servers offered static content to end users visiting the website with a browser. But today, static web servers are more and more replaced by *web applications:* dynamic websites that use the browser as a user interface to a server-resident application. Typical examples of such web applications are e-commerce sites, or front-ends to business processes, databases or existing legacy systems.

A variety of technologies for building web applications exists today. Older technologies such as CGI (common gateway interface) provided a simple standardized interface between a web server and an existing application. The application was started on the web server for every dynamic request in order to process the request, introducing a big startup and shutdown overhead. In newer technologies such as Java Servlets, JSP and ASP.NET, dynamic requests are handled by components that can be plugged into the web server. The real processing work can be delegated to a separate application server, leading to better performance and manageability. Moreover, the application server can offer support for non-functional requirements of the application such as transactional behavior, synchronization, access control and so forth.

Because of these advantages and the widespread adoption of application servers in building complex web applications, only this last technology is considered in this document.

Web applications are distributed applications [11], using the HTTP transport protocol. The system architecture is a client-server model. Both the client (e.g. a rich client) and the server can take part in the processing of information, known as client side and server side processing.

In this paper, we distinguish between web *applications* and web *services*. Web services expose functionality through an XML-based messaging protocol (most often the SOAP protocol [13]), and are very often run on top of HTTP. Whereas web applications are intended to be used by end-users through a standard browser, web services are intended to support machine-to-machine communication over the Internet. Web services can be an important infrastructural component for building web applications.

3. ARCHITECTURAL OVERVIEW

Our generic web application architecture consists of a client at the end-user side, and a 3-tier processing server side (presentation tier, business tier and back-office tier) as shown in Figure 1. Firewalls can be placed between each tier to enable network perimeter security. Often, this architecture is simplified by omitting FW3 and/or FW2, and by implementing two or more tiers on the same machine. Also, in some deployments the authentication server is directly connected to the web server.

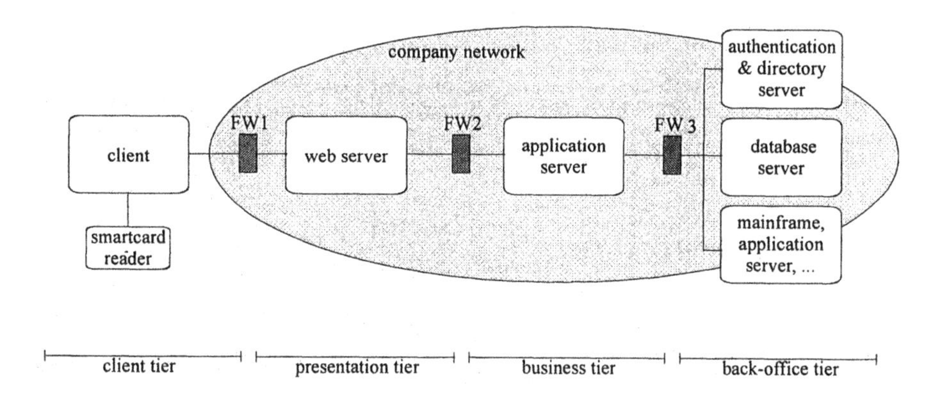

Figure 1. Architectural overview

3.1 Client tier:

Basically, the client tier consists of a recent web browser, possibly extended with client-side application components downloaded from the web server (such as Java Applets or .Net assemblies). In the latter case, the client is referred to as a rich client within this document. The client tier interacts with the web server through simple HTML over HTTP, or, in case of a rich client, the client can act as a web service entity and use SOAP over HTTP interactions with the web server.

Furthermore, the client can be equipped with a smart card reader to interface with a smart card or other security token. Such tokens can be used among others for authenticating the user and protecting the requests.

3.2 Presentation tier:

The presentation tier is responsible for formatting the processed information before returning it to the client, and for handling client requests by performing input validation and delegating them to the appropriate units within the business tier. Usually, the processed information is formatted using the markup languages HTML (in case of a client browser) or XML (in case of a rich client).

Infrastructural components within the presentation tier are typically the web server, sometimes accompanied by a web connector of the application server.

3.3 Business tier:

The business tier contains the application server. The application server implements the actual business logic. In order to achieve its functionality, several services can be provided to the application server from the back-office tier.

The web server from the presentation tier can interact with the application server by using remote procedure calls, web services or a proprietary application server protocol.

3.4 Back-office tier:

The back-office tier provides some basic services to the business tier, such as a database system and an authentication and directory service. The SQL query language is mostly used in requests towards the database system, and LDAP [14] in communication with the directory service. The communication protocol for the authentication service depends on the authentication system used (e.g. Kerberos [12]).

The back-office tier can also contain back-end systems including mainframes, wrapped legacy applications and interfaces to remote application servers.

The architecture presented here does not include some of the more advanced features of web applications, such as the dynamic discovery of services, business integration and associated trust relationships. These features are out of scope for this document, as this is typically not an Independent Software Vendor task.

4. A SIMPLE EXAMPLE

In this section, our architecture for web applications is mapped to actual technologies on Microsoft platforms. Each entity is assumed to be equipped with a recent version of Windows (for instance Windows XP on the client, and Windows Server 2003 on the servers). An architectural overview is illustrated in Figure 2.

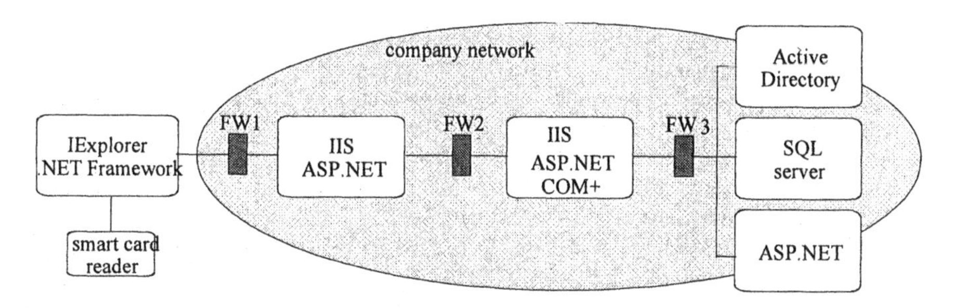

Figure 2. Architectural overview instantiated with Microsoft technologies

The client system has a recent version Internet Explorer and the .NET framework. The client interacts with the web server using simple HTML over HTTP or SOAP over HTTP. In the latter case, the client downloads and executes .NET assemblies within the browser. The client can use a smart card reader for authentication and encryption purposes.

The presentation tier hosts a web server running IIS and ASP.NET. The web server interacts with an application server in the business tier, using web services. The application server runs IIS, ASP.NET, COM+, ADSI, Visual Basic etc.

A directory server, a database server and a remote application server are located within the back-office tier. The directory server in a Microsoft environment is typically Active Directory. The business tier uses SQL to interact with the database server, running SQL Server. Connection to a remote application server or wrapped legacy application is done via SOAP.

5. ACKNOWLEDGEMENTS

This document is a result of the *Designing Secure Applications* (DeSecA) project, funded by Microsoft. Partners within this project are the Università Degli Studi Di Milano [1], the Technical University of Ilmenau [2], the University of Salford [3], and the COSIC [4] and DistriNet [5] research groups of the Katholieke Universiteit Leuven. Each of these partners performed a threat analysis on one particular infrastructural component or technology within the presented web architecture, focusing of course on the technologies provided by Microsoft. The results of these studies are reported in the following papers, respectively, for SQL server [6], ASP.NET [7], Active Directory [8], security tokens [9] and web services [10].

6. REFERENCES

1. Departemento di Informatica e Comunicazione, Univesità degli studi di Milano, Italy; url: http://www.dico.unimi.it
2. Technical University of Ilmenau, Research Group Multimedia Applications, Germany; url: http://www-ifmk.tu-ilmenau.de/mma
3. Information Systems Security Research Group, University of Salford, UK, url: http://sec.isi.salford.ac.uk/
4. COmputer Security and Industrial Cryptography (COSIC), Department Electrical engineering (ESAT), Katholieke Universiteit Leuven, Belgium; url: http://www.esat.kuleuven.ac.be/cosic/
5. DistriNet Research Group, Department of Computer Science, Katholieke Universiteit Leuven, Belgium url: http://www.cs.kuleuven.ac.be/cwis/research/distrinet/
6. E. Bertino, D. Bruschi, S. Franzoni, I. Nai-Fovino, and S. Valtolina. Threat modelling for SQL Servers. Eighth IFIP TC-6 TC-11 Conference on Communications and Multimedia Security (CMS 2004), September 2004, UK, pp189-201
7. R. Grimm and H. Eichstädt. Threat modelling for ASP.NET – Designing Secure Applications. Eighth IFIP TC-6 TC-11 Conference on Communications and Multimedia Security (CMS 2004), September 2004, UK, pp175-187
8. D. W. Chadwick. Threat Modelling for Active Directory. Eighth IFIP TC-6 TC-11 Conference on Communications and Multimedia Security (CMS 2004), September 2004, UK, pp203-
9. D. De Cock, K. Wouters, D. Schellekens, D. Singelee, and B. Preneel. Threat modelling for security tokens in web applications. Eighth IFIP TC-6 TC-11 Conference on Communications and Multimedia Security (CMS 2004), September 2004, UK, pp 213-223
10. L. Desmet, B. Jacobs, F. Piessens, and W. Joosen. Threat modelling for web services based web applications. Eighth IFIP TC-6 TC-11 Conference on Communications and Multimedia Security (CMS 2004), September 2004, UK, pp161-174
11. G. F. Coulouris, J. Dollimore and T. Kindberg. Distributed Systems: Concepts and Design, third edition. Addison-Wesley, 2001.
12. J. Kohl and C. Neuman. The Kerberos Network Authentication Service (V5), RFC 1510, September 1993, http://www.ietf.org/rfc/rfc1510.txt
13. W3C Note, SOAP: Simple Object Access Protocol 1.1, May 2000, http://www.w3.org/TR/2000/NOTE-SOAP-20000508/
14. M. Wahl, T. Howes, and S. Kille. Lightweight Directory Access Protocol (v3), RFC 2251, December 1997, http://www.ietf.org/rfc/rfc2251.txt
15. R. Housley, W. Ford, W. Polk, and D. Solo. Internet X.509 Public Key Infrastructure Certificate and CRL Profile, RFC 2459, January 1999, http://www.ietf.org/rfc/rfc2459.txt

THREAT MODELLING FOR WEB SERVICES BASED WEB APPLICATIONS

Lieven Desmet, Bart Jacobs, Frank Piessens, and Wouter Joosen
DistriNet Research Group, Katholieke Universiteit Leuven, Celestijnenlaan 200A, 3001 Leuven, Belgium

Abstract: Threat analysis of a web application can lead to a wide variety of identified threats. Some of these threats will be very specific to the application; others will be more related to the underlying infrastructural software, such as the web or application servers, the database, the directory server and so forth. This paper analyzes the threats that can be related to the use of web services technology in a web application. It is part of a series of papers, written by different academic teams, that each focus on one particular technological building block for web applications.

Key words: Threat analysis, web services, web applications

1. INTRODUCTION

Analyzing and modelling the potential threats that an application faces is an important step in the process of designing a secure application. Some of these threats are by nature very specific to the application, and one can only give quite general guidelines on how to identify such threats. But other threats are directly or indirectly related to the underlying platforms, technologies or programming languages. Hence, it makes sense to identify and document these technology-specific threats, and to provide guidelines to software vendors on how to mitigate the associated risks.

This paper reports on the results of such an analysis for the use of web services technology in web applications. It is part of a series of papers [1,2,3,4,5], written by different academic teams, that each focus on one particular technological building block for web applications. Each of these papers (including this one) starts from the generic architecture for web applications presented in [1].

2. WEB SERVICES

Web services are a more and more common building block in modern web applications. This section gives a short introduction to web services, and describes how they can be used in web applications.

2.1 Web services

A web service is essentially an XML-messaging based interface to some computing resource. The web services protocol stack consists of:

- Some transport layer protocol, typically HTTP.
- An XML-based messaging layer protocol, typically SOAP [9]
- A service description layer protocol, typically WSDL [10]
- A service discovery layer protocol, typically UDDI [11]

In this document, the assumed web services communication model is SOAP over HTTP. Basic SOAP interactions are asynchronous and unidirectional, but can be combined to implement request/response processes, or even more sophisticated interactions.

SOAP messages are XML based messages for exchanging structured and typed information. SOAP can be used to implement RPC, but the focus shifts to document based information flow in recent web service development.

Next to the originating and receiving node of a web service, intermediate nodes can be defined, as shown in Figure 1. Those intermediate nodes can process the SOAP message, and add extra information to the message (such as a signature on a part of the message).

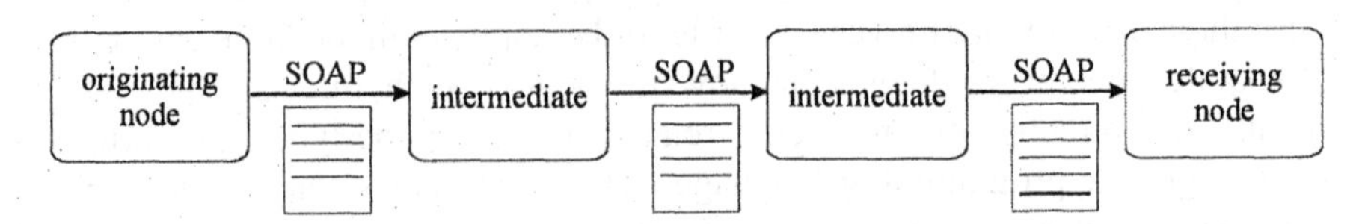

Figure 1. Process flow of a SOAP message.

This document also makes the assumption that WSDL is used to specify the public interface to a web service. A WSDL-based description of a web service can include information on available functions, typing information and address information. WSDL is usually generated by tools, not by hand.

The use of dynamic discovery of web services in web applications is not yet widely used. Hence this document does not consider the service discovery layer.

2.2 Web services in web applications

A generic architecture for web applications is presented in [1]. Within this architecture for web applications, the technology of web services can be used for a variety of purposes. Some examples include:

1. *Wrapping legacy applications:* Incorporating legacy application functionality within a web application is often done by giving the legacy application a web service façade, which can be used by the application server.
2. *Better web server – application server separation:* If the web server communicates with the application server by SOAP/HTTP instead of RPC, the firewall between the DMZ (containing the web server) and the middle tier only needs to open port 80.
3. *Rich Clients:* The browser can download client-side application components (such as Java Applets or .NET assemblies) from the web server. These components can then interact with the web server using web services.
4. *Integration of building block services:* Reusable application services such as authentication or storage can be made available as web services and be used in a variety of web applications.
5. *Multistage processing:* Web services support an asynchronous messaging model. A single request can traverse multiple intermediaries before reaching its final destination. For example, an authentication server as intermediary can authenticate the SOAP message before its arrival at the application server.
6. *Virtual organizations:* Web services can be used for business-to-business integration, creating useful federations of autonomous entities.

Since this paper intends to provide guidelines for Independent Software Vendors building web applications, we assume that the last scenario will be less common. Instead we focus on the most important threats in the other scenarios in the remaining of this paper. These scenarios do not use some of the more advanced features of web services, such as dynamic discovery of services and UDDI. Hence, our threat modelling does not consider these features either. This assumption seems to be in line with the Microsoft Threats and Countermeasures guide [8].

3. OVERVIEW OF ASSETS AND THREAT CATEGORIZATION

This section starts with an overview of the important assets within a web services based web application. Next, a generic classification of threats associated with web services is presented. The section ends with an overview of the attack entry points of web services within a web application.

3.1 Assets

The assets to be protected are subdivided into:

- *Application specific assets*: The data and procedures in the server systems are the main assets, possibly spread over all three tiers. Since we make an abstraction of the application, these cannot be detailed further. For a specific application, further analysis is necessary.
- *Web service specific technology artifacts*. These include elements such as WSDL files, assemblies implementing client and server calls, SOAP messages and so forth. The threats to these assets are the web services technology specific threats. Threats to these assets usually lead indirectly to threats to application specific assets (e.g. leaking of an assembly might give an attacker the necessary information on how to attack a back-end system, a SOAP message will usually include application specific information, tampering with a WSDL file may enable service spoofing, and so forth.)
- *Private information* on the client machine
- *Availability* of the various machines, connections and services in the architectural picture.

3.2 Overview of possible threats

We follow the STRIDE threat categorization [13] for systematically enumerating the threats. In this section, we discuss in a generic way the threats present in a scenario with a single web service consumer and a single web service provider.

1. *Spoofing*: Whenever the communication line between the web service consumer and provider crosses a trust boundary, there is a threat of spoofing. Both the provider and the consumer can be spoofed.
2. *Tampering*: Tampering can be done while data is on the communication channel, while data resides on the consumer

machine, or while it resides on the provider machine. For web services in particular, targets for tampering are the SOAP and WSDL files, the executing code at both consumer's and provider's side, and application specific data on the consumer or provider.

3. *Repudiation*: Repudiation threats are by nature application-specific and are not further detailed here. Web services do provide countermeasure technologies here, such as XML signatures.
4. *Information disclosure*: Information can leak during communication, or while being stored on consumer or provider machine. Similar to the tampering threats, targets for information disclosure are the SOAP and WSDL files, the executing code at both the consumer's and provider's side, and application specific data on the consumer or provider.
5. *Denial of service*: Denial-of-service attacks try to disturb the services by overloading the communication line, or by enforcing a crash or ungraceful degradation of the consumer or provider.
6. *Elevation of privilege*: An elevation of privilege can occur on both the consumer's and producer's machine.

3.3 Attack entry points

On the architectural overview in Figure 2, the possible places where there can be a web service consumer and provider combination are indicated. For each of these web-service instances, each of the generic threats discussed in the previous section is potentially relevant, thus leading to a very high number of potential threats.

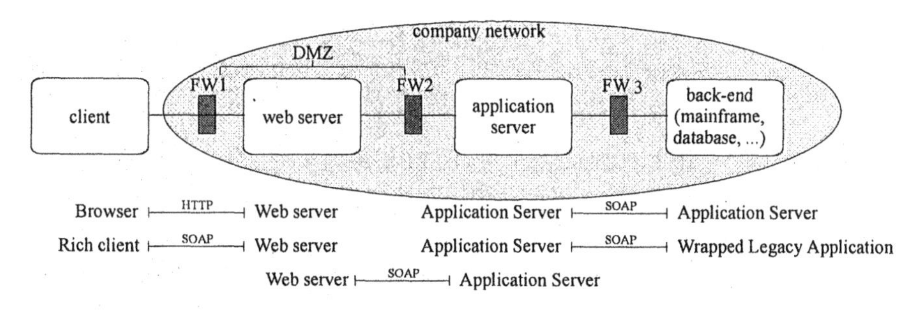

Figure 2. Attack entry points.

4. LIST OF THREATS

In order to keep the list of identified threats reasonable in size, we present only the most relevant threats in this section. For those threats, only a short overview is given here. More details can be found in [14].

To be able to identify the most relevant threats, we make two assumptions. Firstly, we assume that the company network and the servers are secured according to best practices. We do take into account that an internal attacker might get company network access, but with no privileges on any of the server systems. As a consequence, we consider it unlikely that an attacker can get direct access to state kept on any of the server machines. (Of course, indirect access is still possible, e.g. an application exception can leak information to clients.)

Secondly, we assume that attacks will be directed to the server. We do not consider attacks to the client. The rationale for this is that the web application designer/architect typically is concerned with protecting server assets, and does not have much control over the client software anyway.

The threat analysis is done on web applications, running on a Microsoft platform, as introduced in Section 4 of [1].

4.1 Spoofing

Given the possible instances of web services within the web application, the scenario where the client is spoofed in its communication with the web server is considered the most relevant. Weak or no authentication of the client can lead to unauthorized access to the web service.

Two other relevant spoofing threats can occur if the web service crosses a trust boundary. If the DMZ cannot be trusted, there could be a spoofing threat between the web server and the application server. If the application server communicates with a remote application server, there is a considerable spoofing threat in both directions (see [12] for further information).

4.2 Tampering

The highest risk for tampering exists at the client side. An attacker can tamper with all assets residing on the client machine or traveling over the HTTP channel. This leads to the following threats that are considered most relevant in this category.

- A SOAP message is replayed, leading to the unintended duplication of a server action or to inconsistencies on the server.

- A SOAP message is tampered with or maliciously constructed, leading to a whole variety of problems on the server side, such as information disclosure due to thrown exceptions or violations due to malicious input (e.g. SQL injection attacks to the database).
- The WSDL-file sent to the client, containing essential contact information (such as URLs) is tampered with. Changing this information can mislead the client.
- The rich client is reverse engineered and modified. In a rich client scenario, an attacker can gain valuable information by analyzing the browser extension sent to the client. Modifying this extension can enable an attacker to bypass input validation checks, or to construct malicious SOAP calls.

Depending on the context of a particular application, the threat of modifying state information on the servers could be important, but is not further detailed in this document. In particular in the scenario where the web application allows remote upload (or modification) of the content or functionality of the web application, modification of the state information on the server could be an important threat.

4.3 Repudiation

Repudiation threats are by nature application-specific and are not further detailed here. Web services do provide countermeasure technologies here, such as XML signatures.

4.4 Information disclosure

The highest risk for information disclosure exists again at the client side. An attacker can read all assets residing on the client machine or traveling over the HTTP channel. This leads to the following threats that are considered most relevant in this category:

- SOAP messages are disclosed, possibly leaking application specific information such as credit card numbers to an attacker.
- WSDL files are unnecessarily disclosed, giving the attacker information about the application structure.
- Web service implementation leaks information about application internals, for instance by sending stack trace information on errors.

Depending on the context, additional threats that are not detailed in this document could be relevant. In particular, weak host or network security could lead to disclosure of web services specific information such as the files containing the web service code (the .asmx files).

4.5 Denial of service

We consider server denial of service the most relevant threat in this section, causing the server to crash or to degrade ungracefully because of a malicious SOAP call.

In addition, sending a client a malicious assembly in a rich client scenario could do denial of service on that client. Also communication overload could be a threat.

4.6 Elevation of privilege

Again, our focus is on elevation of privilege on any of the servers. We consider the most relevant threat to be the scenario where a web service wraps a legacy application. This can possibly expose legacy software vulnerabilities: the wrapping web service essentially provides a communication path from the Internet to an application written without this connectivity in mind.

5. DESIGN GUIDELINES FOR COUNTERMEASURE SELECTION

A multitude of security technologies is available to counter the threats identified. One of the key challenges for a designer is to make a sensible selection of such countermeasure technologies. In this section, we give an overview of countermeasure technologies, and we provide guidance on how to select appropriate technologies.

The guidance is structured as follows: for each kind of countermeasure we summarize the issues and questions a designer should keep in mind while selecting a technology for implementing that countermeasure, and we give a short overview of the available technologies with their properties.

5.1 Authentication

Authentication counters spoofing threats.

Questions/issues:

- Do you want to authenticate a user or a machine?

- Do you want entity authentication or message authentication? Entity authentication provides evidence that a given entity is actively participating in this communication session, while message authentication provides guarantees about the originator of a message.
- Do you need to propagate the authentication through delegation? If your service relies on other services, you may need to authenticate the client to the other services. Not all authentication technologies support this kind of delegation.
- What assumptions can you make about the authenticated party (e.g. can you install software on the authenticated party's machine)?
- What is the number of users? Some authentication technologies scale better than others.
- Does your application need access to authenticated identities? Some authentication technologies do not provide an API to retrieve authenticated identities at the application level.
- Do you need to integrate in an existing infrastructure? If an authentication infrastructure is already in place, it is probably a good idea to reuse it.
- Security versus ease-of-use? Security mechanisms that are not easy to use can cause the end users to either make mistakes or ignore them altogether.
- Related to data protection and authorization needs: authentication is often done as a precursor to authorization. So make sure authentication and authorization technologies work seamlessly together. Similarly, data protection is often combined with authentication.

Available technologies:

- At the network level, use IPsec. IPsec authenticates machines, but does not provide an API for passing identities to applications. IPsec requires OS support (available from Windows 2000 and up).
- At the transport level, use any of the HTTP authentication mechanisms (basic, digest, forms, passport, integrated windows, or SSL client certificate). For a discussion of the advantages and disadvantages of each of these authentication mechanisms, see [6].
- At the application level, use WS-Security, or XML digital signatures on SOAP messages. XML digital signatures can provide message authentication, but require an infrastructure to manage client certificates.
- Single-sign-on infrastructures such as Microsoft Passport can support the web application in authenticating the client.

- An intermediate authentication and/or authorization server can be used within the web service flow to check the user identity and to approve credentials.

Example designs:

- Basic HTTP authentication over an SSL protected channel is often used for client to web server authentication.
- IPsec is a good choice for mutual authentication between web server and application server.

5.2 Data protection

Data protection counters tampering and information disclosure threats for data in transit.

Questions/issues:

- Do you need selective encryption? Is it feasible to protect all content in the same way, or do some parts have different protection requirements than other parts?
- End-to-end or hop-by-hop? Are all intermediates that process the messages trusted, or do you need protection from potentially untrustworthy intermediates?
- Do you cross a Network Address Translation (NAT) device? Some data protection technologies cannot cross NAT boundaries.
- Related to authentication mechanism: often session keys for data protection are negotiated as part of the authentication process. Make sure you keep in mind these dependencies.

Available technologies:

- At the network level use IPsec/ESP. This is hop-by-hop, non-selective data protection. IPsec does not mix well with NAT.
- At the transport level use SSL or RPC Packet Privacy. Again hop-by-hop, non-selective data protection. SSL can cross NAT boundaries.
- At the message level, use XML encryption of (parts of) SOAP messages. This is the only technology providing selective protection and end-to-end protection.

Example designs:

- SSL is the typical choice for data protection between client and web server.
- Message level protection is needed in some multistage processing scenarios.

5.3 Authorization

Authorization counters tampering and information disclosure on data residing on servers. Authorization can also counter elevation of privilege or denial of service.

5.3.1 Questions/issues:

- What information do you need to make authorization decisions? Do you base access control decisions only on authentication information, or also on application state information?
- What is the granularity of the assets you are protecting access to? Do you need to control access to the application, or to specific functionalities within the application, or to specific objects in the application?
- Do these objects that need protection map naturally on operating system, web server or database resources?
- Do you need to integrate in an existing infrastructure?
- How will the access control policy be managed?
- Authorization technology is related to the authentication mechanism (and identity flow), as discussed in section 5.1.

5.3.2 Available technologies:

- At the machine level, by restricting access to a set of IP addresses (using IPsec, IIS or a firewall). This is a very coarse-grained access control. Keep also in mind that IP addresses can be spoofed to fool IIS access control.
- At the URL level, by configuring IIS. IIS can leverage the Windows access control mechanisms for restricting access to web server files.
- At the application server level, by using .NET or COM+ mechanisms for role-based access control.
- In the application code itself: application code performs the necessary authorization checks, possibly calling a centrally managed authorization engine. See [7] for a detailed discussion of application managed authorization.

- An intermediate authorization server can do access control or prove the client's authority.

5.3.3 Example designs:

- Each of the server machines could use IP-based access control to make sure the server machines are only accessible from expected machines.
- Role-based access control for protecting web application functionality from clients.

5.4 Input validation

Input validation potentially counters any of the STRIDE threats.

Questions/issues:

- As data flows from client to back-end or from client to other client, who will sanitize the data? Consider all data flows originating from an untrustworthy source and make sure they are validated somewhere.
- Is there a strict XML schema describing allowable input? If so, this can be used as a basis for validation. If not, provide a description of allowable input using other means such as regular expressions.
- Where does untrustworthy data go? If it goes to the database, SQL injection is a possible threat. If it is echoed to clients, cross-site scripting could be an issue. If it goes to a wrapped legacy application, there is a threat of buffer overflows.

Available technologies:

- Validating XML parser.
- Regular expression API's.

5.5 Other countermeasure technologies

We briefly summarize other countermeasure technologies. For more detail, we refer to [14].

- *Non-repudiation*: Non-repudiation counters the repudiation threat. This can only be done meaningfully at the application level. Possible technologies include XML signatures and application-level auditing.

- *Sandboxing*: Sandboxing counters elevation of privilege threats, and can be provided by the operating system (process separation) or by .NET Code Access Security.
- *Secure coding*: Secure coding counters all kinds of threats. It is not further discussed here, since it is not a design time countermeasure. See [13] for more information.
- *Intrusion/fraud detection*: Intrusion or fraud detection counters all kinds of threats. As a designer, the process of detecting intrusions or fraud can be made easier by providing good, application-level audit data.
- *Availability related countermeasures*: These countermeasures counter denial-of-service related threats. Available technologies include filtering (rejecting unacceptable requests as quickly as possible, e.g. by using firewall rules) and throttling (limiting the number of unauthenticated requests to your application).

6. CONCLUSION

Threat modelling and countermeasure selection are important steps in an engineering process for building secure software. Documenting the threats inherent in the use of specific technologies and guiding designers in the selection of countermeasures to these threats can make these steps significantly easier. This paper reports on the results of an analysis of the use of web service technologies for web applications from this perspective. The most relevant threats are identified, and rough guidelines on how to mitigate the associated risks are provided. Threats, vulnerabilities and risks are described informally. A potential direction for future work is a more formal description, for instance in a UML profile for risk analysis, such as CORAS [15,16].

7. ACKNOWLEDGEMENTS

This work reported in this paper was developed as part of the *Designing Secure Applications* (DeSecA) project, funded by Microsoft. Partners within this project are the Universita' degli Studi di Milano, the Technical University of Ilmenau, the University of Salford, and the COSIC and DistriNet research groups of the Katholieke Universiteit Leuven.

8. REFERENCES

[1] L. Desmet, B. Jacobs, F. Piessens, and W. Joosen. A generic architecture for web applications to support threat analysis of infrastructural components, Eighth IFIP TC-6 TC-11 Conference on Communications and Multimedia Security (CMS 2004), September 2004, UK, pp155-160

[2] D. De Cock, K. Wouters, D. Schellekens, D. Singelee, and B. Preneel. Threat modelling for security tokens in web applications, Eighth IFIP TC-6 TC-11 Conference on Communications and Multimedia Security (CMS 2004), September 2004, UK, pp 213-223

[3] R. Grimm and H. Eichstädt. Threat Modelling for ASP.NET – Designing Secure Applications, Eighth IFIP TC-6 TC-11 Conference on Communications and Multimedia Security (CMS 2004), September 2004, UK, pp175-187

[4] E. Bertino, D. Bruschi, S. Franzoni, I. Nai-Fovino, and S. Valtolina. Threat modelling for SQL Server, Eighth IFIP TC-6 TC-11 Conference on Communications and Multimedia Security (CMS 2004), September 2004, UK , pp189-201

[5] D. W. Chadwick. Threat Modelling for Active Directory. Eighth IFIP TC-6 TC-11 Conference on Communications and Multimedia Security (CMS 2004), September 2004, UK, pp203-212

[6] Microsoft Patterns and Practices: Building Secure ASP.NET Applications, Microsoft Press, January 2003.

[7] Microsoft Patterns and Practices: Designing Application Managed Authorization, http://msdn.microsoft.com/library/default.asp?url=/library/en-us/dnbda/html/DAMAZ.asp

[8] Microsoft Patterns and Practices: Improving Web application security: Threats and Countermeasures, Microsoft Press, June 2003.

[9] W3C Note, SOAP: Simple Object Access Protocol 1.1, May 2000, http://www.w3.org/TR/2000/NOTE-SOAP-20000508/

[10] W3C Note, Web Services Description Language (WSDL) 1.1, 15 March 2001, http://www.w3.org/TR/2001/NOTE-wsdl-20010315/

[11] UDDI.org white paper, UDDI Technical White Paper, 6 September 2000, http://www.uddi.org/pubs/Iru_UDDI_Technical_White_Paper.pdf

[12] Hartman, Flinn, Beznosov, Kawamoto. Mastering Web Services Security. Wiley Publishing 2003.

[13] Howard, LeBlanc. Writing Secure Code 2nd edition, Microsoft Press, 2003.

[14] Designing Secure Application project (DeSecA), final report, May 2004.

[15] M. Lund, I. Hogganvik, F. Seehusen, and K. Stolen. UML profile for security assessment, Technical report STF40 A03066, SINTEF Telecom and Informatics, December 2003.

[16] M. Lund, F. den Braber, K. Stolen, and F. Vraalsen. A UML profile for the identification and analysis of security risks during structured brainstorming, Technical report STF40 A03067, SINTEF ICT, May 2004.

THREAT MODELLING FOR ASP.NET

Designing Secure Applications

Rüdiger Grimm and Henrik Eichstädt
University of Technology, Ilmenau, Am Eichicht 1, D-98 693 Ilmenau

Abstract: This paper gives a security analysis of Microsoft's ASP.NET technology. The main part of the paper is a list of threats which is structured according to an architecture of Web services and attack points. We also give a reverse table of threats against security requirements as well as a summary of security guidelines for IT developers. This paper has been worked out in collaboration with five University teams each of which is focussing on a different security problem area. We use the same architecture for Web services and attack points.

Key words: web services; asp.net; client-server; security; threats; web application; data storage; threat countermeasures.

1. INTRODUCTION

A Web service is a network of coordinated applications in the backend behind an http-governed Web server. The Web server is addressed by http-clients across the Internet. ASP.NET is one example for the coordination technology. However, the security analysis holds for Web services in general, not only for ASP.NET.

ASP.NET provides a set of components for developers to implement complex functionality in DLL. It is scalable, in that it provides state services to manage session variables (cookies, session ids, temporary URLs) across multiple Web servers in a server farm. It is stable, in that it can detect application failures and recover from them. It addresses both "managed code" (conformant to ASP.NET), as well as "unmanaged code" ("native code") to include "legacy" applications. It is performant, because ASP.NET pages are compiled whereas ASP pages are interpreted. When an ASP.NET page is first requested, it is compiled and cached, or saved in memory, by the

.NET Common Language Runtime (CLR). This cached copy can then be reused for each subsequent request for the page. After the first request, the code can run from a much faster, compiled version, see Butler, Caudill [1] for details.

In this paper we will use an abstract Web services model which allows us to identify different sources and targets of attacks. On the basis of our attack analysis we will provide a structured view on security guidelines which help developers to avoid the most obvious security holes. The security holes derive mainly from the fact that any kind of Web service resides within the open world of Web usage. They are not specific to ASP.NET. However, ASP.NET is an obvious example of a Web services framework.

2. ARCHITECTURE PREREQUISITES

We will base our security analysis on a rather abstract structure of ASP.NET technology which we will refer to as our Web services model. It consists of these four building blocks, which could reside either on the same or different hardware components:

1. a 'pure' ASP.NET component (which serves as a 'gate' between the web server and source code; external components can only be connected from this ASP.NET-component);
2. an 'external' component built with C#, VB or any other language using the Common Language Runtime (CLR); this is so-called 'managed code';
3. an 'old', external component being integrated into the Web service – possibly not integrated into the Common Language Runtime (CLR); this is so-called 'unmanaged code';
4. database(s).

Our Web service structure is a refined version of the architecture model in [2]. We have explicated the application server part by adding application details and communication relations between the components. The structure is shown in Fig. 1 below.

We will not analyse the internal functional structure of the four components any deeper. In this sense we will consider the Web services on the ASP.NET technology as a 'black box': it reacts on input data (both stored and communicated), and it creates some output data (both stored and communicated). Therefore it is inserting, updating, checking and/or deleting data of any kind.

In this Web services model, several assumptions are made which are to be respected by application security policies in the first place. First, our focus is on ASP.NET technology, therefore we address only the Web service. Other services such as FTP, Sendmail, or Telnet are also security relevant, but out of scope of this paper. Furthermore, we assume that the Web Server is organised as follows.

1. A firewall protects the Web Server from the Internet which contains a positive list of ports and protocols to be accepted.
2. The Web Server accepts and responds to 'valid' http(s)-requests only;
   a) 'valid' are requests with correct http syntax, and the URLs of which are within an explicitly accepted name space;
   b) 'validity', however, does not refer to parameter content; on this level, parameter content is not checked and will therefore be addressed by our attack analysis below.
3. On an operating system level the Web service is configured according to these minimal security requirements:
   a) only a minimal set of components and applications is installed: e.g., if not explicitly needed, no ssh / sendmail / telnet / ftp etc. service is addressable through this Web Server; no client browser is available within the Web service;
   b) rights management within the Web service follows the least privileges principle for the relationship 'userid → application';
   c) a minimal set of users (potential attackers) has access to the internal network: with respect to the relationship 'persons → userid'.

3. ATTACK ENTRY POINTS

3.1 SOURCES AND TARGETS

In order to identify attack points, two aspects are to be addressed: sources ("who attacks"), and targets ("what is attacked?"). Attackers may reside inside or outside the server ("sources"). They may aim at assets of the server or of the client ("targets"). Servers do not only organise their own assets, but also assets of clients, for example account levels, private information, or an achieved status of a purchase. An attack on the server can, therefore, also be an attack on a resource inside the server which represents a client's asset. It is in the interest of the server to protect both its own assets (e.g. received payment), as well as the assets of its client as far as it is responsible for them. Otherwise, a server will lose reputation, or even be liable for losses of its clients.

3.2 ATTACK POINT SOURCES

Attacks can be pushed from outside as well as from inside the Web service-network. In a refined view of the Web services model, presented below in Fig. 1, the following six attack sources can be identified:

1. attack from an external aggressor via the standard http(s)-gate
2. Web service attacking the client (delivering malicious code, misuse of personal data)
3. attack from an external aggressor circumventing the ASP.NET gate (=> firewall and webserver are not secured properly)
4. attack from an internal aggressor via the internal network
5. security risks by connecting unmanaged code (native) applications
6. attack from an aggressor application nested inside the Web service structure. This could be any kind of application as database, (web)server, operating system program or any other application.

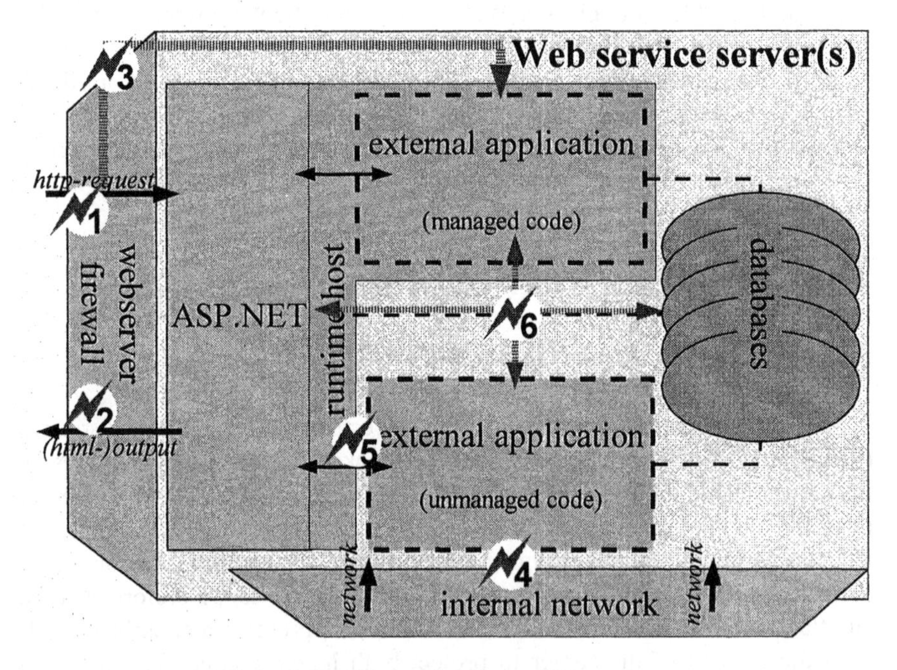

Figure 1. Possible attack points on Web services

There are two general directions of attacks:

- *Server is being attacked*: The target of attacks of a client against the server may be **(a)** the assets of the server, e.g., the client retrieves an electronic good without paying for it. Or the target may be **(b)** the assets of another client through a manipulated server, i.e. by retrieving an electronic good which another client has paid for and who is then prevented from receiving it (impersonation, or stealing of privilege). Case (b) is an attack against the client via an attack against the server, i.e. the attacked client will observe an attack of the server, while the server itself was attacked in order to attack the other client.

- *Client is being attacked*: The target of attacks against the client that will be considered here are always the assets of the client, e.g. his privacy, his money, his knowledge, his privileges, etc.

The following kinds of attack are out of scope of this paper: Servers which attack clients in order to attack other servers through the manipulated client. This can be done either by using the clients' credentials, or by using client resources. The aim would be to enforce attacks (DDoS), or to blame the service provider for an insecure service.

Why is it important to analyse attacks on the client by the server? At first glance, the server is simply regarded as decent, and so there is no point in considering this case. However, there are two reasons why a server (and even more a decent server) is interested in protecting its clients against attacks through the server:

1. Servers want to protect their reputation against suspicion. For example, shops provide read-access to purchase status points, they provide read- and write-access to personal data of their clients (each client only accesses his data), they reveal their privacy policy, they offer privacy mechanisms like P3P, they sign their parts of obligations (like payment receipts), etc. Servers will also have to make clear to their clients that insider attacks are minimized, e.g. by 4-eyes-principle access rules, or other security-certified mechanisms.
2. Servers must be aware that unauthorised intruders (outside attackers) compromise the system in order to attack other clients. From the point of view of a server, this is an outside attack against the server, covered by analysis in case 1 above. From the point of view of the client, however, this is an attack of the server on his assets. Servers must make clear how they minimize this danger.

4. ASSETS VS. ATTACK TARGETS

For a general security analysis of the ASP.NET technology, no concrete assets can be identified, because the technology is not restricted to a specific type of application. Instead, we consider general, abstract assets being in the focus of attackers. In supplement to the Microsoft STRIDE-categories (see [3]) of attack targets, we suggest to introduce the common IT security requirements (see [4][5]) as abstract assets of all ASP.NET services:

- Availability
- Confidentiality
- Integrity
- Authenticity
- Accountability (non repudiation)

These requirements can be understood as abstract assets. The assets can be mapped one-to-one on threats, in that threats are understood as negative requirements.

4.1 IT SECURITY REQUIREMENTS VS. STRIDE ATTACK TARGETS

The same requirements (assets) can be broken (enacted on) by multiple attacks [7]. The abstract assets (i.e. the IT security requirements) can be mapped on the STRIDE categories of attack targets via this matrix:

Table 1. common IT security criteria vs. Microsoft's STRIDE concept

	Availability	Confidentiality	Integrity	Authenticity	Accountability
Spoofing	X	X		X	X
Tampering			X	X	X
Repudiation					X
Information disclosure		X			
Denial of service	X				
Elevation of privileges	X	X	X	X	X

5. LIST OF THREATS / ATTACKS

There are three ways to structure attacks:

1. Attack points oriented (as in Fig. 1 above)
2. Assets/Threats oriented (IT security requirements as abstract assets)
3. Attacks oriented (Microsoft's STRIDE)

We have introduced attack points in Fig. 1 above in the section on attack entry points. Assets/Threats were introduced by abstract IT security requirements in the previous section on assets vs. attack targets. Attacks are introduced by the STRIDE model. In Table 1 of that section we have mapped assets (IT security criteria) on attacks of STRIDE type.

As the same threats can be enacted by multiple attacks, we have decided to follow the attack points orientation, because there is least redundancy - the following list of threats is thus ordered by attack points. In order to keep up with the STRIDE structure, we offer a reverse table of attacks vs. our attack numbers at the end of the attack list in this section.

The threats in this list are numbered according to the following scheme: AST represents 'ASP.NET Threat', the first digit refers to the attack point, the last two digits represent the numbering of the threats inside the attack point. Appended to the threat title is the STRIDE-classification displayed by the initial letter(s) of the applicable STRIDE-category(ies) in parenthesis.

There is one type of threat which can be realized at any point of the Web service. This threat may be a side effect of the other threats listed below or may be applied as preparation of any other threat.

AST001: Provoke errors to reveal system information (I)

Description: The attacker 'misuses' the Web services to provoke the generation of error messages. These messages can be used to gather detailed system information for further attacks.

Countermeasures: Only general/generic error messages should be visible to the client and should not disclose any specific information about the internal system and the nature of the error. Detailed error messages are to be written into a logfile.

5.1 Attack point 1: External Attacker

The most likely way to attack a Web service is to construct input data contrary to the intention of form(field)s.

5.1.1 AST101: any input data is sent to the application (RI)

Description: The attacker fills in data into html-forms that is not intended by the application. False information and executable code could be used to manipulate the application.

Countermeasures: A server-side validation of input data is necessary. Use .NET validation server controls for this task. Additionally, storage of 'false data' can be avoided by checking the data against a 'valid' database. As a minimum, SQL-Syntax should be denied.

5.1.2 AST102: Manipulating form parameters (TRID)

Description: False input data is carefully crafted and sent to the server by manipulating the http-request (either by building a URI with parameters [GET-method] or manipulating the http-body [POST-method]).

Countermeasures: In addition to the AST101 countermeasures, the form data could be checked to be sent by the POST-method (if action is set to be POST). The session-identifier should be authenticated with additional data (e.g. IP-address) and/or the application should re-ask for authentication credentials in case of critical actions.

5.1.3 AST103: Uploading malicious program code (STRIDE)

Description: Some code file containing malicious code is uploaded using an upload form. Subsequently the attacker gets to know the save folder on the server and tries to execute his code or the uploaded file is processed by the server and thus executed.

Countermeasures: The execution of uploaded files has to be denied (either stand-alone execution on the server or HTML-inline execution). Uploaded files should be validated not to be code, the target folder for upload files should be secured - no (direct) access via http. Uploads could be filtered by denying file types with possibly included code/allowing file types from a positive list.

5.2 Attack point 2: Web service attacking client

Though no direct threat to the server, this threat is mentioned because it represents a threat to the servers trustworthiness.

5.2.1 AST201: non-transparent data gathering (I)

Description: The Web service collects data from clients (required form input) that is not or barely necessary for the applications purpose.

Countermeasures: Forms should be constructed in a way that only minimal, necessary data is required. In addition, transparency tools can be used (P3P: publish privacy policies, privacy audit label).

5.2.2 AST202: Web service delivers malicious code (STIE)

Description: The Web service creates and sends code that forces the client to crash. As this could (but needs not) be code created by an attacker, AST103 is a possible origin of this threat.

Countermeasures: Carefully create Web service (HTML-/script-) output and avoid additional/plugin media/technology where possible. Before delivering any code, check if the client supports the needed technology and offer alternative technology.

5.3 Attack point 3: ASP.NET-gate circumvented

As ASP.NET serves as 'gateway' to the web applications, threats could be possible by contacting applications without ASP.NET intervening.

5.3.1 AST301: Reveal location of subordinate application (I)

Description: An attacker causes the server application to generate output that exposes the location of subordinate applications, databases etc.

Countermeasures: Force the applications to receive input data through a central, filtering application that is redirecting the data on the server-side.

5.3.2 AST302: Execute subordinate application directly (STRIDE)

Description: An attacker executes a subordinate application that is intended not to be executed from outside.

Countermeasures: This should not be possible due to the prerequisites. Subordinate applications should be configured not to be executed from outside the Web service. Establish trust management on the server by defining a 'need-to-know' access rules matrix for internal applications (read/write).

5.4 Attack point 4: Internal aggressor

The Web service files could be accessed by an internal attacker being connected to the company network. As a consequence, the www-interface is avoided by accessing the Web service structure from the internal network.

5.4.1 AST401: Accessing applications with internal authentication data (STRIDE)

Description: An attacker from inside the network accesses/executes components with 'insider' privileges. Manipulation of data/communication could be possible with those access rights.

Countermeasures: Web service components should only be executed with restricted privileges. Additionally, a sophisticated rights management prevents execution by real users (run as special, 'virtual' user only). Using 4-

eyes principle access rules for very sensitive actions and data secures those areas.

5.4.2 AST402: Accessing stored data (TRIDE)

Description: An attacker from inside the network accesses data stores (file system, data base) to get information. The data stored is accessed directly through OS means, not via ASP.NET.

Countermeasures: Access to data stores should only be permitted to Web service components.

5.4.3 AST403: Manipulating source code (TIE)

Description: An attacker from inside the network accesses the file system and manipulates the source code files.

Countermeasures: Limit write access, Sign/create hash values for component files and deny execution if authentication of component fails. Additionally, the changes of source code can be logged (logfile, notification mail etc.).

5.5 Attack point 5: Unmanaged Code

As ASP.NET allows the integration of a broad variety of applications, also 'old' code can be used in ASP.NET-based Web services. It is then necessary to exchange data between these (un)managed code components.

5.5.1 AST501: Inconsistent data (ID)

Description: When components running outside the CLR are used, data-types have to be converted but can't always be mapped 'perfectly' between these components. An attacker could use this to cause components to malfunction (by generating a complex piece of data).

Countermeasures: Native code should be ported to .NET code ('partial port' approach according to [6]) and/or the critical native code should be rewritten. Exception handling to catch wrong data types should be implemented.

5.6 Attack point 6: Aggressor application inside Web service

If some application inside the Web service structure is used to attack the Web service, this set of threats is conceivable.

5.6.1 AST601: Revelation of data from inside (I)

Description: Web service data-store components / store controls can easily be contacted by a 'hi-jacked' component to retrieve stored data.

Countermeasures: Implement system integrity checks (viruses, Trojan horses), establish a 'need-to-know' access rules matrix for internal applications (read/write) and define a strong access control. Additionally check if request originally comes from 'outside' and is generated by a http-request through the official, allowed routes. Sign components to prevent manipulation of the hi-jacked components' source code.

5.6.2 AST602: Manipulation of data from inside (STRIDE)

Description: Web service data-store components / store controls can be contacted by a 'hi-jacked' component to manipulate stored data.

Countermeasures: see AST601

5.6.3 AST603: Contacting Applications from inside (STRIDE)

Description: Web service applications can be contacted by a 'hi-jacked' component (Trojan horse or stolen privileges). The component can request the service of other applications without any outside-triggered need.

Countermeasures: see AST601. The 'need-to-know'-rules matrix has to be expanded to cover the execution of components.

5.6.4 AST604: Revelation of configuration information: (I)

Description: If client software (e.g. Browser, .NET Interface) is run on the server, it is possible for an attacker to gather configuration information (OS version, .NET runtime version etc.).

Countermeasures: Deny client software to be run on server.

5.6.5 AST605: Buffer overflow (STRIDE)

Description: Buffer overflows are used to attack the server. Especially Web service components are permanently cached in the CLR using one memory area. This can be used to cause Buffer Overflows and get access to the Web service.

Countermeasures: Cause caching to refresh periodically and implement Buffer Overflow checks. Avoid using unmanaged code.

6. REVERSE TABLE OF ATTACKS

Table 2. ASP.NET-Threats / STRIDE matrix

	S	T	R	I	D	E
AST001				X		
AST101		X	X	X	X	
AST102		X	X	X	X	
AST103	X	X	X	X	X	X
AST201				X		
AST202	X	X		X		
AST301				X		
AST302	X	X	X	X	X	X
AST401	X	X	X	X	X	X
AST402		X	X	X	X	X
AST403		X		X		X
AST501				X	X	
AST601				X		
AST602	X	X	X	X	X	X
AST603	X	X	X	X	X	X
AST604				X		
AST605	X	X	X	X	X	X

7. DESIGN GUIDELINES

1. Validate input data on the server side
   - Validating on the client side is nice for the user, but insecure for your application because it can be bypassed
   - Server-sided validation can't be by-passed, check input data to be of the correct range, expected length and uploaded files to be of the correct data type or among correct/allowed file types. For this validation, use the .Net validation controls.
2. Do not insert data again that was input and validated before, without new validation (only insert and check deltas to previous state)
3. Establish a 'need-to-know' access rules matrix
   - Which application may connect to another application/to a data storage
   - Which application may request what kind of data
   - Which application may modify data
4. Sign components and check correct signature (checksum, hash) within the Web service structure
5. Make sure data can only be accessed via a Web service component
   - Especially do not allow direct request of uploaded files
   - Deny execution of uploaded files
6. Re-ask for credentials if a critical action (modification of user data) is requested

7. Use managed code wherever possible
   - Convert 'old' applications
8. Minimize forms
   - Collect only data that is needed by the application – the user will begin to trust your application
9. Do not reveal internal (configuration / system) data to user
   - Error codes delivered to the user have to be generic ('an error occurred', if it is that bad)
   - Log error codes in detail to a logfile on the server in a secure folder
10. Have a 'pure' server (see prerequisites section)
    - No client applications installed
    - Only needed services installed / active

8. ACKNOWLEDGEMENTS

The work reported in this paper was developed as part of the *Designing Secure Applications* (DeSecA) project, funded by Microsoft. Partners within this project were the Universita' degli Studi di Milano, the Technical University of Ilmenau, the University of Salford, and the COSIC and DistriNet research groups of the Katholieke Universiteit Leuven.

9. REFERENCES

[1] J.Butler, T. Caudill - ASP.NET Database Programming - Weekend Crash Course (John Wiley & Sons Inc, 2002)

[2] L. Desmet, B. Jacobs, F. Piessens, and W. Joosen. A generic architecture for web applications to support threat analysis of infrastructural components, Eighth IFIP TC-6 TC-11 Conference on Communications and Multimedia Security (CMS 2004), September 2004, UK, pp155-160

[3] MSDN Library - Improving web application security: Threats and Countermeasures http://msdn.microsoft.com/library/default.asp?url=/library/en-us/dnnetsec/html/ThreatCounter.asp, 2003

[4] Information Technology Security Evaluation Criteria (ITSEC):/ Provisional Harmonised Criteria. Luxembourg: Office for Official Publications of the European Communities, 1991. Bundesanzeiger Verlagsges., Köln 1992

[5] The Common Criteria for Information Technology Security Evaluation (CC) version 2.1, Sep 2000. Part 1 - Intro & General Model; Part 2 - Functional Requirements; Part 3 - Assurance Requirements. Standardised as ISO/IEC 15408 1999 (E), available from http://csrc.nist.gov/cc/

[6] Don Box - Migrating Native Code to the .NET CLR http://msdn.microsoft.com/library/default.asp?url=/msdnmag/issues/01/05/com/toc.asp, 2001

[7] L. Desmet, B. Jacobs, F. Piessens, and W. Joosen. Threat modelling for web services based web applications. Eighth IFIP TC-6 TC-11 Conference on Communications and Multimedia Security (CMS 2004), September 2004, UK. pp 161-174

THREAT MODELLING FOR SQL SERVERS

Designing a Secure Database in a Web Application

E.Bertino [1], D.Bruschi [2], S.Franzoni [2], I.Nai-Fovino [2], S.Valtolina [2]

[1] *CERIAS, Purdue University, West Lafayette, IN, USA*
[2] *DICO, Universita' degli Studi di Milano, Via Comelico 39, 20135 Milan, Italy*

Abstract: In this paper we present the results from an analysis focusing on security threats that can arise against an SQL server when included in Web application environments. The approach used is based on the STRIDE classification methodology. The results presented provide also some general guidelines and countermeasures against the different attacks that can exploit the identified vulnerabilities.

Key words: Database Systems, Web Services, Security, Threat Model

1. INTRODUCTION

In the last few years the use of the Internet has experienced an exponential growth and the World Wide Web has become the main instrument for information sharing. Such trends have pushed the development of a new kind of service architecture, specifically tailored at supporting data sharing among remotely connected clients, which is based on the concept of *Web Applications*. A web application can be essentially seen as a collection of different entities that collaborate in order to provide services to remote clients. In such an architecture, a client typically communicates with external entities using the HTTP protocol.

Various web application architectures have been devised and can be found in the literature. In this paper we will consider one of the most adopted, i.e. the architecture includes a database, positioned into a backend zone, storing all the information needed to provide the service. Since this data must be accessible from both the internal network and Internet, the database is exposed on the web and can thus become a target of possible attacks [1]. Many of these attacks can be prevented following some guidelines in the design and development of the web applications. In this paper, by using the STRIDE approach [2], we analyze the most frequent threats concerning the database in a generic model of web applications, and we describe the countermeasures to prevent those threats or mitigate the damages subsequent to a successful attack.

2. SQL SERVER

SQL Server [3] is a relational database management system which is part of the Microsoft family of servers. SQL Server was designed for client/server use and is accessed by applications using SQL. It runs on Windows NT version 4.0 or higher and is compliant with the ANSI SQL-92 standard. SQL Server supports symmetric multiprocessing hardware, ODBC, OLE DB, and major open standard communications protocols. It has Internet integration, data replication, transaction management and data warehousing features.

The main role of an SQL Server in a web-based architecture is to store and manage the data required by the authorized web applications. To be able to access data from a database, a user must pass through two authentication phases. The first phase is performed by the SQL Server and the other by the database management system. These two steps are carried out using logins names and user accounts respectively.

2.1 Authentication

A valid login name is required to connect to an SQL Server instance. A login could be a Windows NT/2000 login that has been granted access to SQL Server or an SQL Server login that is maintained within the SQL Server. These login names are stored in the master database. All permissions and ownership of objects in the database are controlled by the user account. SQL Server logins are associated with these user accounts. During a new connection request, SQL Server verifies the login name supplied to make sure that the login corresponds to a subject authorized to access SQL Server. SQL Server supports two authentication modes:

- Windows authentication mode: under this mode there is no need to specify a login name and password to connect to SQL Server. Instead the access to SQL Server is controlled by the user's Windows NT/2000 account (or the group to which the user's account belongs). Database administrators can grant access to the database to the user or the user group specified in the Access Control List provided by the operating system. Under this security mode, SQL Server tracks users by their individual SIDs (Security Identifiers) stored by the operating system itself.

- Mixed mode: users can establish a connection to an SQL server either using Windows authentication or SQL Server authentication. Under this authentication mode, the user must supply the SQL Server login and password when he connects to SQL Server. If the user does not specify an SQL Server login name and password, or request Windows Authentication, he/she is authenticated using Windows Authentication.

2.2 Access Control

Accesses to objects in the database are managed by granting the proper permissions to individual users or by defining user roles. A role is a group to which individual logins/users can be added, so that the permissions can be assigned to the group, instead of assigning them to all individual logins/users. There are three types of roles in SQL Server:

- Fixed server roles: these are server-wide roles. Logins can be added to these roles to gain the associated administrative permissions of the role. Fixed server roles cannot be altered and new server roles cannot be created. An example of a fixed server role is sysadmin, which is authorized to perform any activity in SQL Server.
- Fixed database roles: each database has a set of fixed database roles to which database users can be added. These fixed database roles are unique within the database. While the permissions of fixed database roles cannot be altered, new database roles can be created. An example of a fixed database role is db_owner, which has all permissions in the database.
- Application roles: after creating and assigning the required permissions to an application role, the client application needs to activate this role at run-time to get the permissions associated with that application role. By using application roles, the database administrator does not have to manage permissions at the individual user level; he/she simply needs to create an application role and assign permissions to it. The application that is connecting to the database activates the application role and inherits the permissions associated with that role.

2.3 System Prerequisites

The guidelines discussed in this paper are effective only if the SQL Server is properly installed, configured and patched. In this section we provide a list of actions that we assume have been already taken on the database.

2.3.1 Installation recommendations

We assume that the SQL Server has been installed with a least privilege account. In order to protect the domain hosting the database, the SQL server must not be installed on a primary or secondary domain controller. Instead, we recommend dedicating a machine to the database, without additional services (i.e. Upgrade tools, Replication support Script, Development tools Headers and library files used by C developers and Microsoft Data Access (MDAC), etc.) if they are not required. We assume that after the installation all available patches are applied.

2.3.2 Unused Services

During the installation phase three major services are set up, the SQLSERVERAGENT, the MSSQLServerADHelper and the Microsoft Search. These three services are optional and they must be disabled if they are not necessary. It is also important to notice that the presence of other services not related with SQL Server on the same machine can jeopardize the database security. The installation of such services is discouraged if they are not strictly required.

2.3.3 Unused Protocols

It is a good practice to configure SQL Server to support only clients that connect using the TCP/IP protocol. All the other unused protocols must be disabled. A TCP/IP stack hardening can be also taken into consideration.

2.3.4 Accounts

We assume that for all the accounts configured after the installation, the principle of least privilege has been adopted. The execution of the following actions should be considered:

- Secure the SQL Server service account
- Delete or disable unused accounts
- Disable the Windows guest account
- Rename the administrator account
- Enforce strong password policy (length and complexity, expiration time)
- Restrict remote logins
- Disable null sessions (anonymous logons)

2.3.5 File system and directory

An important prerequisite for a proper SQL Server installation is a strongly secure directory and file-system permission management. We take for granted the execution of the follow steps:

- Verification of permissions on SQL Server install directories.
- Verification that the Everyone group does not have permissions to SQL Server files.
- Secure setting up of log files.
- Securing or removing tools, utilities, and SDKs.

3. ASSETS

The first step that must be taken into account in a threat modelling process is the identification of the assets that need to be protected. In fact, they represent the value the attacker is looking for. In our particular case, the principal asset that we want to protect is the data stored in the database. It must be pointed out that not all the data stored have the same relevance. For example, a company can decide to publish on the Web only a partial database, while the whole enterprise data are kept offline. In such a case, the loss of the data accessible from the Web is much less serious than damages to the data stored in the backend database, as we discuss in Section 4. Data protection involves satisfying two main requirements: the integrity of stored data and their confidentiality. These two properties have both been taken into account in our threat modelling phase, as explained in Section 6.

In addition to data, the second fundamental asset that needs to be protected is the data management service, for which availability is crucial; a database should always be able to provide the data required to authorized users.

The data and the data management system can thus be considered the "crucial" assets of an SQL server, but there are some other assets not strictly connected with data stored in the database that can be valuable for an attacker. Some examples are the data accounts of authorized users, the database system, since it can be exploited for more sophisticated attacks, and the integrity of the host machines. Weaknesses in a host machine can be exploited to perform attacks against other machines in the enterprise network.

4. ARCHITECTURAL SCENARIOS

We consider two possible scenarios. In the first one, as described in the architecture overview, the SQL Server is located in the backend subnet. This is the most straightforward method for providing web access to the database. The web application server forwards the client requests to the database across the internal network.

The second scenario is characterized by a general architecture which is similar to the architecture of the first scenario. The main difference is that the backend database is not accessible from the web application. The client can only access a partial mirror database located in another subnet. The mirror database contains only the data to be accessed from the Internet. In this way, an attack exploiting the web application or the web server would compromise only the data stored in the database located in this partial database and not all the enterprise data. When adopting this configuration, this database must be synchronized with the backend SQL server, and these update operations need to be performed in a secure way.

When considering these scenarios, we must take into account that there is a non-negligible risk: we protect the database from an outside attacker, but we cannot say anything about an attacker that has already the control of other servers inside the backend subnet and that can use these servers in order to start an attack to the SQL Server. This issue can be addressed assuming that the backend subnet is trusted, or that the database is located in a dedicated subnet.

The threats concerning the two scenarios are in general the same; what changes is the difficulty with which these threats can be realized and the dimension of the final damage. For example, if an attacker can disrupt the data stored in the SQL server in the first scenario, the enterprise will lose all its data, with an enormous damage. If the same threat succeeds in the second scenario, the company will lose only the data published on the public mirror database, but not the sensitive data stored in the main SQL database.

5. ATTACK ENTRY POINTS

One of the most important issues in threat modelling activity is to identify the attack entry points of the system being analyzed. Based on the vulnerabilities of a SQL Server and the above architectural scenarios, we have identified three attack points:

- The client side of the web application: an attacker can use the normal web interface of a client in order to insert some malicious code or perform unauthorized or dangerous operations. It is very difficult to control this entry point. The main problem is that it is not possible to make any assumption about the client identity. Moreover we generally do not have control over the configuration and security of the client machine. Thus the client machine can be trojanized and controlled by a third malicious party. For all these reasons we assume that the client is not trusted. A general good practice is thus to perform strong input validation, to inhibit dynamic SQL, and to use an effective password management policy.

- Network: an attacker with a direct access to the network can intercept information or data flow between the client and web application or between the web application and SQL Server. It is important to note that this entry point is not only located on the external network, but it also involves the internal enterprise network. The attacker can also mount some complex attack like a man-in-the-middle attack. In order to protect this entry point a good practice is the use of a secure channel (IPsec, SSL etc.) between the different actors involved in the web application (client, web server, SQL server etc.)
- SQL Server port: an attacker can try to directly send requests and malicious code (Slammer worm for example acted in this way) to the SQL Server bypassing the web application. A strong access control policy and ad-hoc firewall rules can mitigate the vulnerability of this entry point.

6. SQL SERVER THREATS

As explained above, in order to identify the different threats on SQL Server, we have adopted the STRIDE classification that groups the different types of attack into six main classes (Spoofing identity, Tampering with data, Repudiation, Information disclosure, Denial of service and Elevation of privilege). Table 1 provides a mapping between the STRIDE classes and the common attacks we have identified.

In the remainder of this section, we describe in more detail the different types of attack and their respective countermeasures.

Table 1 Mapping between the STRIDE classes and the common attacks

	S	T	R	I	D	E
SQL injection		X		X		X
Unauthorized access	X	X		X		X
Network eavesdropping	X			X		X
Denial of service					X	
Timing analysis				X		
Error analysis				X		
Malicious Data Mining				X		

6.1 SQL Injection

This is a technique which exploits vulnerabilities in input validation to run arbitrary commands in the database [1]. It can occur when the application uses input to construct dynamic SQL statements to access the database. It can also occur if the code uses stored procedures that are passed strings containing unfiltered user input. The issue is magnified if the application uses an over-privileged account to connect to the database. In this instance it is also possible to use the database server to run operating system commands and potentially compromise other servers, in addition to being able to retrieve, manipulate, and destroy data.

Usually this attack affects applications that incorporate non-validated user input into database queries. Particularly susceptible is code that constructs dynamic SQL statements with unfiltered user input.

6.1.1 Countermeasures

In order to prevent this kind of attack the application should validate its input prior to sending a request to the database. Other preventive countermeasures are the use of type safe SQL parameters for data access, the execution of checks against parameter types and length, the use of injected code as literal data instead of executable code for the database. The use of restricted accounts can be useful too.

To discover if this type of attack has been performed, the only possible countermeasure that can be adopted is logging all requests sent to the database and then executing an off-line analysis. Because the logging and analysis activities can be very expensive, when designing the database and the database application it is important to identify which kind of data flow must be logged and analyzed in order to avoid overloading the logging system.

6.2 Network Eavesdropping

This threat is related to the unauthorized interception of information sent across a network [1]. This attack is usually carried out by means of a packet sniffer program which can monitor the traffic on the network. An attacker may exploit poorly configured network devices. Common vulnerabilities include weak default installation settings of the communication channels between client and web server and between web server and database server.

6.2.1 Countermeasure

There are different types of countermeasure that can be taken in order to protect against this type of threat. For example the use of Windows authentication to avoid sending credentials over the network can be useful to protect the system from the discovery of authorized user accounts. In this respect, the installation of a server certificate on the database server and the use of an encrypted channel like SSL or IPsec is a good practice to protect the integrity and confidentiality of the data exchanged on the network.

This type of attack assumes that a malicious user is able to capture the traffic between the different actors of the web application. Usually, as explained above such type of attacks is made possible by Sniffer tools. To detect the use of these tools on the enterprise network, the use of some "discovery sniffer" tools is suggested [4,5,6].

6.3 Error Analysis

This threat arises because of a general good practice concerning well designed code [1]. Indeed in a well designed software system, when an error occurs, a detailed error message is returned as feedback in order to understand where the problem is. Exception conditions can arise because of configuration errors, bugs in the code, or malicious input. Unfortunately, a malicious client can use these error messages in order to guess sensitive information about the location and nature of the data source in addition to valuable connection details.

Targets of this type of attack can be applications that incorporate non-validated user input into database queries and that do not use exception handling or implement it poorly. Particularly susceptible is code that constructs dynamic SQL statements with unfiltered user input or code that does not check input parameters.

6.3.1 Countermeasures

In order to avoid a malicious use of message errors, an approach is to filter them. Effective filtering can be achieved by ensuring that the database accepts connections only from the application (the application thus acts as a filter), by using exception handling throughout the application's code base and by returning a generic, harmless error messages to the client.

Log and traffic analysis is the only way for detecting this threat.

6.4 Denial of Service

Denial of service denies [1] legitimate users access to a server or services. It can focus on two targets: the former type of DoS arises because of the structure of the Internet. Therefore there are no effective countermeasures at the database server level. The latter type of DoS is performed to make the server unable to provide its services, by means like application crashing or resource consumption. Stored procedures executing non-optimized code, stored procedures executing code with weak controls over variable size and type, or stored procedures executing code with a bad resource allocation and management policy are examples of the possible target of this attack class.

6.4.1 Countermeasures

To avoid the execution of this type of attack the following operations should be considered. Strong input validation should be performed on the client side with the aim of avoiding the insertion of malicious or unusual requests.

Because most of the security holes with respect to the second class of DoS attacks are usually located in the stored procedures, a good practice is to allow the execution of only secure stored procedures. By secure stored procedures we mean stored procedure whose implementation is well known. Other suggested countermeasures include the adoption of a resource allocation policy combined with a service monitor tool and the profiling of the stored procedures also under stress conditions [7].

6.5 Unauthorized accesses

This threat is common to all systems in which there is no strong password management policy. Attackers typically try to guess the passwords of authorized users. This type of threat can also arise in all systems that are affected by buffer overflow vulnerability [8,9]. In this case once the attacker has obtained a remote root shell, he/she has gained access to the database.

6.5.1 Countermeasures

The best strategies for protecting against unauthorized accesses are the use of Windows authentication, the adoption of a strong password policy and a strong input validation to avoid the insertion of buffer overflow code. The only way to detect this type of threat is a log analysis.

6.6 Sensitive Information Disclosure

This threat can be posed even by users having limited access rights to the database. By manipulating the results of regular queries by means of data mining techniques an attacker can extract sensitive information.

6.6.1 Countermeasures

The only countermeasure to this threat can be database sanitization [10] or the publication of a partial database containing only non-sensitive information.

7. DESIGN GUIDELINES

We now summarize the major design guidelines that we have devised.

A first important protection measure is to adopt an architecture for protecting the SQL Server from exploit attempts and at the same time protecting the enterprise subnets from attacks performed using an eventually exploited SQL Server. A logical separation between the network hosting the SQL Server and the other networks is strongly recommended and also the presence of a mirror SQL Server is a good practice in order to guarantee the survivability of the system.

A second protection measure is the use of the Windows authentication whenever possible. With Windows authentication, it is possible to make use of the system account and password management policies, so there is no need to store database connection strings with embedded credentials and to have to transmit these credentials across the network. Windows and SQL Server must both recognize the account from which the application runs. The account must be granted a login to SQL Server and the login needs to have associated permissions to access a database.

If SQL authentication must be adopted, it is necessary to take additional precautions in order to secure the database connection string, since it contains the user login and password. The connection string must not be sent over the network in clear text, but it must be encrypted.

The application login to the database must be properly authorized and restricted. The application should use a least privileged account that has limited permissions in the database; this can limit the potential damage if the account is compromised or malicious code is injected.

A third relevant protection measure is to never connect to an SQL Server using the **sa** account or any account that is a member of the SQL Server **sysadmin** or **db_owner** roles. If the connection is established using an over-privileged account, for example an account provided with the SQL Server **sysadmin** role, the attacker can perform any operation in any database on the server.

Other important protection measures are based on the use of parameterized stored procedures that should be used for data access where possible. Stored procedures can enhance data access security in several ways. Database users can be given permissions to execute a stored procedure without being granted permissions to directly access the database objects on which the stored procedure operates. Besides, stored procedures can validate user input, and their parameters cannot be treated as executable code. All this helps mitigate the risk posed by SQL injection attacks. However, only stored procedures whose origin and behavior is well known should be used.

If parameterized stored procedures cannot be used for some reason and the application needs to construct SQL statements dynamically, it is crucial to use typed parameters and parameter placeholders to ensure that input data are checked with respect to their length and type.

Another protection technique is related to error management by the application software. It is important to trap all the exceptions the application may raise and return only generic error messages which do not reveal details about the inner database structure.

Finally sensitive data should be encrypted when stored in the database and protected, when being transmitted across the network, by using an SSL connection between the Web server and database server and/or an IPSec encrypted channel.

8. ACKNOWLEDGEMENTS

This work reported in this paper was developed as part of the *Designing Secure Applications* (DeSecA) project, funded by Microsoft. Partners within this project are the Universita' degli Studi di Milano, the Technical

University of Ilmenau, the University of Salford, and the COSIC and DistriNet research groups of the Katholieke Universiteit Leuven.

9. REFERENCES

[1] J.D. Meier and others, Improving Web Application Security. Threats and countermeasures, Microsoft press, 2003
[2] M. Howard and D. LeBlanc, Writing secure code 2nd edition , Microsoft press, 2003
[3] SQL Server 2000, Resource kit, Microsoft press, 2001
[4] http://sniffdet.sourceforge.net/download.html
[5] http://www.atstake.com/antisniff/
[6] http://www.packetfactory.net/Projects/sentinel/
[7] E. Whalen, M. Garcia and others, SQL Server 2000 Performance tuning, Microsoft press, 2001
[8] A. One, Smashing The Stack For Fun And Profit, .oO Phrack 49 Oo. Volume Seven, Issue Forty-Nine File 14
[9]] M. Howard, Reviewing Code for Integer Manipulation Vulnerabilities, Secure Windows Initiative, 2003
[10] V. S. Verykios, E. Bertino, I. Nai Fovino, L. Parasiliti Provenza, Y. Saygin, Y. Theodoridis, State-of-the-art in privacy preserving data mining, ACM SIGMOD Record, Volume 33 Issue 1, 2004

THREAT MODELLING FOR ACTIVE DIRECTORY

David Chadwick
ISI, University of Salford, Salford, M5 4WT, England.

Abstract: This paper analyses the security threats that can arise against an Active Directory server when it is included in a Web application. The approach is based on the STRIDE classification methodology. The paper also provides outline descriptions of countermeasures that can be deployed to protect against the different threats and vulnerabilities identified here.

Key words: security, LDAP, active directory, threats, vulnerabilities

1. INTRODUCTION

Active Directory (AD) is Microsoft's LDAP product offering, first introduced with Windows 2000 servers. Whilst being reasonably conformant to many of the LDAP set of standards e.g. [1,2,3], nevertheless it is non-conformant in some aspects. For example, it does not support some standardized features, such as multi-valued relative distinguished names (RDNs) or country based naming, but it does support many proprietary features, such as a tight coupling with the operating system and Microsoft's DNS server. It has also replaced several standardized features with its own proprietary ones. For these reasons customers using Microsoft's operating systems are well advised not to try to replace Active Directory with an alternative more standards' conformant LDAP product such as OpenLDAP.

Active Directory is a core service holding user and server account details and security information. For example, Windows authentication uses credentials stored in the Active Directory. Active Directory is therefore fundamental to the correct operation of a Microsoft domain. For this reason most Microsoft based Web applications will need to access Active Directory either directly or indirectly at some point during their business processing, often during the authentication and/or authorization phases, but also at different stages of the business process.

Access to Active Directory therefore needs to be well controlled and protected, otherwise an attacker could severely impair the correct functioning of both the Web application and the back office by successfully launching an attack on Active Directory. Web application builders need to understand the vulnerabilities of Active Directory and the threats that can potentially exploit these vulnerabilities. In common with the other papers in this series [4, 5, 6, 7] we use the STRIDE approach [8] to categorize the most frequent or damaging threats that can arise against Active Directory when deployed as part of the generic model for Web applications described in [9]. Finally we describe the countermeasures that can be used to prevent these threats or to mitigate against the damages subsequent to a successful attack.

2. ASSUMPTIONS

The guidelines discussed in this paper will be effective only if the Active Directory is properly installed, configured and patched with the latest updates and service packs as released by Microsoft.

Correct configuration requires that that the Access Control Lists (ACLs), that are used to control access to objects in the Active Directory, are set up to give minimum privileges to the users (and to the Application Server acting as a user or a proxy for the users).

The assumption is that the Application Server will communicate with the Active Directory server by RPC messages generated by the Active Directory Service Interfaces (ADSI), using one of the various scripting or programming languages that it supports e.g. C++, Visual Basic or Java.

It is assumed that there is only a limited amount of trust between the Active Directory Server and the Application Server, and between the Application Server and the Web Server. By this, we mean that the Active Directory Server will not let the Application Server have unrestricted access to its resources, but will impose some controls on what the Application Server can do. For example, the AD server may have an administrative limit on the number of LDAP entries that can be returned to any ADSI request; the AD server may have controls on the complexity and number of filter items that can be included in a Search filter; and the AD server will have properly configured access controls that limit which directory entries and which operations the Application Server (and its users) are allowed to access. Likewise, the Application Server will have some controls on the messages originating from the Web Server and will validate and restrict their contents. From a security perspective, the less trust that there is between the AD server and the Application Server, and between the latter and the Web Server, the better, as more controls will be imposed by the AD server on what the Application Server is allowed to do, and by the Application Server on what the Web Server can do. For example, at one extreme the AD server may forbid any modification operations to originate from the Application Server. The more trust that there is, the more careful the application developer will need to be to ensure that this trust is not abused by an application server that may become compromised, or that is just badly programmed.

The final assumption is that there is no (or very little) trust between the Web Server and the client, or between the Web Server and the network over which the client's http messages are transported. Thus eavesdropping of messages on the network is possible, and in extreme cases, message modifications. Furthermore, the Web Server must expect the client to try to circumvent whatever client controls are placed on the messages that it sends. Consequently the Web Server and all subsequent servers that receive client messages, for example SOAP messages that are relayed through the Web Server, must be designed to protect against threats emanating from modified or badly formed client messages, by rigorously validating their contents.

3. SECURITY REQUIREMENTS

We can look at security requirements from two perspectives: the security requirements placed on the design of the web application because it has little or no trust in the client and the external network, and the security requirements placed on the Active Directory because it only has limited trust in the web application.

The security requirements placed on the web application i.e. the web server and the Application Server, partially depend upon the type of application that is being built. At one extreme, we may have an application that is only retrieving public information from the AD server. At the other extreme we may have an application that is accessing highly confidential directory information and writing to the AD server by adding, modifying and deleting objects in the Directory Information Tree (DIT).

In the former case the web application may have very few security requirements placed on it, and may allow unauthenticated user access over unsecured http links. Example applications might be: one that accesses the contact information of people in the marketing and sales department, or one that retrieves certificate revocation lists (CRLs) for a PKI application. The main security function of the web application will be to validate the contents of the client requests (see below) and ensure that only a predefined limited set of Search requests, and no modification requests, are sent to the Active Directory.

In the latter case the web application will have very strict security requirements placed on it. An example application might be one that supports single sign on (SSO) and user authorisation by checking user credentials in and retrieving their privileges from the AD server, whilst simultaneously supporting dynamic provisioning and management of user rights. In such cases, the web application will demand strong authentication of the user to prevent masquerade, and will require all messages to be carried across encrypted links to protect against eavesdropping and message modification. The web application should never request nor accept user passwords passed in the clear from the client. This will facilitate password capture over an insecure network. The application should always require passwords to be sent over an encrypted link e.g. using SSL or IPsec, or use HMAC hashing which creates one-time passwords. When using SSL, the web server should check that the SSL cipher suite that has been negotiated with the client is a minimum of 128 bit encryption, and that it has not been negotiated down to plain text (no encryption) or weak encryption. The same holds true for the Application Server if it is using an insecure link to communicate with the Web Server. In addition rigorous checking and validation of all client provided fields and requests should take place as described next.

Preferably, and whenever possible, limit the choices that are available to the client by having picking lists of predefined values so that the client cannot create its own values (this is very important for attribute type names, matching rules, the distinguished names of subtree roots, the name of the AD server and its connection details, although the latter of these will usually be pre-configured into the Application Server and the client will not have any control over them). For fields where the client must usually have complete freedom of choice over the input values, for example, attribute values for Search filters, then the Application Server should perform rigorous validation of these values. Firstly determine the maximum length of each field and check that it has not been exceeded by the client. Reject client operations in which fields are too long. Secondly, treat each field as a literal and make sure that it is encoded as such, for example by enclosing the user's input in quotation marks. Consider the following: say that the client interface had separate input fields for attribute types and values when creating a Search filter. The code might put them together to create a filter such as (<user type>=<user value>). An attacker might place the following in the Attribute Type field

&(objectCategory=person)(!salary>=10000)(commonName

and the code would then create the following valid complex filter

(&(objectCategory=person)(!salary>=10000)(commonName=<user value>)

thereby allowing the attacker to create whatever Search filters they want to. Input field validation and checking is thus extremely important.

Because the Active Directory only has limited trust in the web application, the security requirements placed on the Active Directory and on the design of the web application are common, regardless of the type of application that is being built. Firstly the Active Directory should be configured so that the Application Server has no (or very limited) access privileges to data in the Active Directory. This will help to protect against elevation of privileges, whereby a user gains the access privileges of the application rather than his/her own. Secondly the Active Directory should limit the types of request from and the volume of data returned to the Application Server. Finally, the Application Server should Bind to the Active Directory using the client's user context rather than its own.

When an application Binds to an object in the Active Directory, the access privileges that the application has to that object are based on the user context specified during the Bind operation. For the ADSI binding functions and methods (IADsOpenDSObject::OpenDSObject, ADsOpenObject, ADsGetObject, GetObject) an application can implicitly use the credentials of the caller, or explicitly specify the credentials of a user account, or use an unauthenticated user context (Guest). The Application Server should never Bind to the AD server using a stronger form of authentication than that used by the client, nor should it use a user account that has higher privileges than the client's (for example, the LocalSystem account on a domain controller has complete access to Active Directory whereas a typical user has only limited access to some of the objects in the directory). Ideally, the Application Server should either use the credentials provided by the user, and validate them by passing them to the AD server either implicitly or explicitly, or should discard the user credentials altogether and use the Guest context. In the former case the Application Server is acting as a proxy for the client and will thus only have the same access rights to the directory data as if the client were binding directly. In the latter case, the Application Server will only gain minimum/public access rights to the directory data. For example, an application policy might say that local users who access the Active Directory when they are at a remote site should only have Guest access to public data in the directory, in which case their credentials would be discarded by the Application Server when they contact it from a remote location.

4. ACTIVE DIRECTORY THREATS AND COUNTERMEASURES

4.1 Spoofing

Spoofing can take one of two forms. Either an attacker attempts to spoof a user or an attacker attempts to spoof the Active Directory. In the former case the attacker captures or guesses a user's credentials and then masquerades as the user when accessing the Active Directory. In the latter case the attacker tricks a client into believing that information came from the Active Directory when it did not, or tricks the client into sending confidential data to it that should have been sent to the Active Directory. Spoofing results from vulnerabilities in the client or in the network. Spoofing the directory could be achieved by social engineering (e.g. sending a wrong URL to users), misdirecting operations or modifying data in transit. The use of SSL links will counteract the latter two, and user education will help to protect against social engineering, although this is notoriously difficult to fully protect against.

Spoofing a user can be aided by vulnerabilities in the network, vulnerabilities in the Active Directory Information Base and vulnerabilities in the Application Server. An attacker can sniff the network to obtain user account names and passwords, or access the Active Directory to retrieve valid user account names and then find the password by either a dictionary attack or modifying the password attribute in the directory. Since the Active Directory is often designed to return user account names, it may be difficult to stop attackers from gaining this information, but if clients generally don't need to know user account names, then these should not be returned to the client interface. The use of encrypted connections such as SSL or IPsec will stop network sniffing, as will the use of HMAC [10] or Kerberos authentication. Dictionary attacks can be prevented by having the Application Server count the number of failed login attempts per user account name, writing them to audit trails, and then disabling the account when a threshold number is exceeded. Modification of password attributes can be prevented by the Application Server not providing a modification capability to the client, but if this is essential, then the server should carefully validate all modification operations and trap ones that try to modify the password attribute.

4.2 Tampering

With this threat, an attacker tries to modify directory data either in transit to the client, or whilst it is stored in the AD server. This can be due to vulnerabilities in the network, vulnerabilities in the Active Directory Information Base or vulnerabilities in the Application Server. Threats to the AD server can arise from masquerade, poorly configured access controls and the injection of modification operations via the Application Server. Countermeasures include protecting data in transit by using either SSL or IPsec. Masquerade has been dealt with in Section 4.1. The Application Server should be configured to reject all Modification operations, or if this is not possible, to very carefully validate all user input fields and to reject operations with "invalid" arguments. The Application Server should Bind to the AD server using the user provided credentials so that the user does not inherit the possibly higher privileges of the Application Server process.

4.3 Repudiation

Repudiation is when users deny that they have performed specific actions or transactions. Keeping adequate audit trails will provide evidence of who did what and will help to counteract this type of threat. Auditing should be performed by both the AD server and the Application Server, and in this way insider attacks directed straight to the AD server will be more easy to identify. Requiring relatively strong client authentication will minimize the chances that an attacker can perform actions on behalf of a client which will subsequently be repudiated.

4.4 Information Disclosure

Information disclosure occurs when a user gains read access to information that (s)he is not supposed to have access to. This can be due to vulnerabilities in the network, vulnerabilities in the Active Directory or vulnerabilities in the Application Server. Vulnerabilities in the AD software, other than those caused by badly configured access controls, are outside the scope of this document. An attacker may sniff the network, masquerade as another user, or generate valid or invalid search or modify requests. Network sniffing and masquerade have already been dealt with in section 4.1. Generating invalid search or modify requests may return useful error diagnostic messages, which can provide the attacker with valuable information. The countermeasure to this is for the Application Server to scrub useful information from error messages and to return bland generic error messages to the client, whilst writing the full error message to its audit trail.

The Application Server should exert control over the Search requests that clients can perform. In general only specific limited Searches should be allowed by clients, otherwise attackers may generate very broad searches that trawl the entire directory. All user input should be validated, and only a fixed subset of ADSI arguments should to be allowed. Searches with "invalid" arguments should be rejected. However, a determined attacker may even circumvent this by generating multiple valid Search requests that only return snippets of information each time. If this is done a sufficient number of times, the sum total of information gained by the attacker may be more than the application designers ever intended to be revealed. For example, retrieving details of individual users in each Search request, may enable an attacker to retrieve details of the entire organizational workforce. Such attacks are very difficult to stop. Even building an audit trial and refusing access after a set number of searches might not stop the problem if the attacker has access to multiple user accounts.

Similarly, the Application Server should exert tight control over Modification operations. Ideally, it should refuse to allow any Modification operation through the interface, or if this is not possible, it should ensure that only authenticated users can perform modification operations, whilst simultaneously very carefully validating all user input fields and rejecting those with "invalid" arguments. For example, an attacker may try to modify the heuristic status of attributes, by setting bit 1 (which will make the attribute visible to unauthenticated users) or unsetting bit 3 (which removes operational attribute status).

4.5 Denial of Service

In a denial of service attack, the attacker denies access to the AD server for normal users. This can be aided by vulnerabilities in the Active Directory server and vulnerabilities in the Application Server. Denial of Service attacks are typically very hard to protect against.

The attacker may try to crash the AD server, or more likely, consume excessive resources. The easiest way to consume excessive resources is to launch CPU or network intensive Search operations. The former can be started by creating Searches with inefficient and/or complex filters, or ones containing multiple ambiguous name resolution elements (i.e. those where the attribute type is set to anr) [11]. Network intensive Searchers are designed to return lots of entries – the entire AD contents if possible.

Countermeasures to the above are as follows. The Application Server should validate all filters input by the user and only allow a predefined subset of filters to get through. In addition, the AD server should be configured to reject complex filters, and to only return a pre-defined maximum number of entries for any Search request.

An attacker may try to open up multiple connections to the Application

Server and/or AD server, preferably using SSL which consumes more resources. Countermeasures include timing out inactive sessions, keeping a record of the usernames of each active session and only allowing a fixed number of sessions per user at any one time.

More sophisticated attacks, which would normally require administrator level privileges, include: switching off indexing which kills the performance of most search operations; starting replication between AD servers which again kills performance; or updating the schema which might actually crash the AD server. Careful validation of the allowed modification operations by the Application Server should trap operations such as these.

4.6 Elevation of Privileges

Elevation of privileges can occur when an attacker either masquerades as a user with higher privileges than his own, or modifies data in the directory, for example, by adding a user to a group, or modifying ACLs in directory objects. Masquerade has already been described in Section 4.1. Illegal modification of directory data can be prohibited by disallowing any Modification operation to originate from the Application Server, or if this is not possible, by very carefully validating all user input fields and rejecting operations with "invalid" arguments. Correctly configured Access Control Lists in the AD server, and Binding with minimum privileges are also essential.

5. CONCLUSIONS

Whilst many different vulnerabilities and threats exist, they can nearly all be protected against by a few common countermeasures:

- Encrypt and authenticate messages that pass over insecure networks by using either SSL or IPsec
- Always have the Application Server Bind to the Active Directory using the same or lower privileges than those possessed by the client
- Ensure that the Access Control Lists in the AD server are correctly configured to give minimum privileges to clients.
- Severely limit the number and scope of directory operations that the Application Server sends to the AD server on behalf of the client. Always try to restrict the range of parameters that can be set or chosen by the client, and validate all user input fields for their content. If possible, ensure that no Modification operations are ever sent.
- Restrict the error diagnostic messages that are returned to the client.

With these countermeasures in place, it will significantly reduce the risk that an attacker will be able to launch a successful STRIDE attack against an Active Directory server.

6. ACKNOWLEDGEMENTS

The work reported in this paper was developed as part of the *Designing Secure Applications* (DeSecA) project, funded by Microsoft. Partners within this project were the Universita' degli Studi di Milano, the Technical University of Ilmenau, the University of Salford, and the COSIC and DistriNet research groups of the Katholieke Universiteit Leuven.

7. REFERENCES

[1] M. Wahl, T. Howes, and S. Kille. Lightweight Directory Access Protocol (v3), RFC 2251, December 1997

[2] Wahl, M., Coulbeck, A., Howes, T., Kille, S. "Lightweight Directory Access Protocol (v3): Attribute Syntax Definitions". RFC 2252. December 1997.

[3] Kille, S et.al. "Using Domains in LDAP/X.500 Distinguished Names", RFC 2247, Jan 1998

[4] E. Bertino, D. Bruschi, S. Franzoni, I. Nai-Fovino, and S. Valtolina. Threat modelling for SQL Servers. Eighth IFIP TC-6 TC-11 Conference on Communications and Multimedia Security (CMS 2004), September 2004, UK, pp189-201

[5] R. Grimm and H. Eichstädt. Threat modelling for ASP.NET – Designing Secure Applications. Eighth IFIP TC-6 TC-11 Conference on Communications and Multimedia Security (CMS 2004), September 2004, UK, pp175-187

[6] D. De Cock, K. Wouters, D. Schellekens, D. Singelee, and B. Preneel. Threat modelling for security tokens in web applications. Eighth IFIP TC-6 TC-11 Conference on Communications and Multimedia Security (CMS 2004), September 2004, UK, pp 213-223

[7] L. Desmet, B. Jacobs, F. Piessens, and W. Joosen. Threat modelling for web services based web applications. Eighth IFIP TC-6 TC-11 Conference on Communications and Multimedia Security (CMS 2004), September 2004, UK, pp161-174

[8] MSDN Library - Improving web application security: Threats and Countermeasures http://msdn.microsoft.com/library/default.asp?url=/library/en-us/dnnetsec/html/ThreatCounter.asp, 2003

[9] L. Desmet, B. Jacobs, F. Piessens, and W. Joosen. A generic architecture for web applications to support threat analysis of infrastructural components, Eighth IFIP TC-6 TC-11 Conference on Communications and Multimedia Security (CMS 2004), September 2004, UK, pp155-160

[10] Wahl, M., Alverstrand, H., Hodges, J., Morgan, R. "Authentication Methods for LDAP", RFC 2829, May 2000

[11] MSDN Library - Creating More Efficient Microsoft Active Directory-Enabled Applications. http://msdn.microsoft.com/library/en-us/dnactdir/html/efficientadapps.asp?frame=true

THREAT MODELLING FOR SECURITY TOKENS IN WEB APPLICATIONS

Danny De Cock, Karel Wouters, Dries Schellekens, Dave Singelee and Bart Preneel
COSIC Research Group, Dept. Electrical Engineering-ESAT, Katholieke Universiteit Leuven, Kasteelpark Arenberg 10, B-3001 Leuven, Belgium

Abstract: In the last couple of years, several European countries have started projects which intend to provide their citizens with electronic identity cards, driven by the European Directive on Electronic Signatures. One can expect that within a few years, these smart cards will be used in a wide variety of applications. In this paper, we describe the common threats that can be identified when using security tokens such as smart cards in web applications. We illustrate each of these threats with a few attack scenarios. This paper is part of a series of papers, written by several academic teams. Each paper focuses on one particular technological building block for web applications.

Key words: Smart card applications, security, threat modeling

1. INTRODUCTION

This paper analyzes threats that occur when smart cards are used in web applications. This analysis is part of the *Designing Secure Applications* (DeSecA) project [5], funded by Microsoft. The aim of this project is to provide an application developer with a tool that allows him to prevent the exploitation of a broad range of threats. Several academic teams investigated common threats in five areas, each focusing on one particular technological building block for web applications [1,2,3,4]. One of these is the smart card, and in particular the electronic identity card (eID card). Many European countries have started to develop such smart card projects, driven by the European Directive on Electronic Signatures [11]. We expect that these projects will be very successful in several European countries in the short term and in most European countries within a couple of years from now. This means that it is important to identify common threats before large scale software applications are developed and used. These threats involve the use of smart cards where the application developer's decisions can make the difference: well known attacks on smart cards (e.g. timing attacks, power analysis and fault attacks [8,9,10]), are not included in the scope of this study. In the following sections, we give an overview of the targeted security tokens, a list of attack entry points and the most relevant mitigation techniques. We conclude with an enumeration of threats with potential countermeasures.

2. SECURITY TOKENS

Our threat modeling for security tokens mainly focuses on electronic identity (eID) cards and smart cards used for digital signatures.

An eID card is mainly used to

- Obtain strong authentication of the cardholder, e.g. through client authentication when using a website secured with SSL. This client authentication is accomplished by having the client sign data, which is specified by the challenge-response protocol of SSL. The digital signature is computed by the cardholder's security token, e.g. a smart card, securID token or a software key store. The token only produces the digital signature after some form of cardholder verification, e.g. using a personal identification number (PIN) or a password. Once the client has successfully been authenticated, specific services may be available to the client (cf. authorization).
- Generate advanced electronic signatures. These signatures, in combination with a qualified certificate, are equivalent to hand-written signatures (cf. [11]). The production of an advanced electronic signature also relies on the cardholder verification through PIN or password validation. Note that the generation and verification of advanced electronic signatures is a very complicated matter (more legally than technically).
- Obtain information on the cardholder (e.g. address, social security number, date of birth, gender). It is common to acquire this type of information without any cardholder verification.
- Decrypt confidential data which is intended for the cardholder only.

Figure 1 gives an overview of the different entities which are active in a web application scenario that uses strong client authentication. The smart card may contain user data (e.g., e-business card, home address, birth information, picture), secret information (private keys to sign or decrypt information) and reference data (e.g. a genuine copy of the root certificate of the cardholder's certification authority). The smart card is inserted into a smart card reader which is connected to the user's PC. The smart card communicates with an application on the user's PC through the smart card reader, and the user authenticates himself to his smart card using a PIN or password, depending on the web server's requirements. This PIN or password can be entered on the smart card reader, on the keyboard of the user's PC, or it may have been cached on the user's PC for convenience reasons.

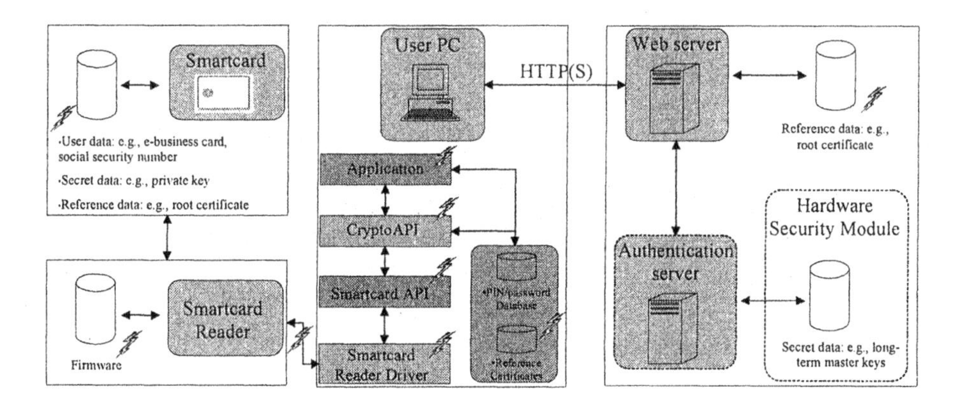

Figure 1. Overview of the entities in a web-based application using smart cards.

3. DESCRIPTION OF THE ATTACK ENTRY POINTS

The overview of the entities involved when using smart cards in a web application, shown in Fig. 1, points out the different attack entry points: every entity and every connection between the entities can be hijacked. It is therefore very important to use and carefully configure every entity to prevent these attacks.

In the following, we list the different attack entry points. Note that we do not mention the Crypto API, as such an API is typically available on any user machine.

3.1 The smart card itself

An obvious point of attack is the smart card itself, as it contains private or secret cryptographic keys. Different keys may be stored in the smart card, depending on the required security level of the application:

1. A smart card used for data authentication usually contains secret long-term master keys (which are commonly used to compute session keys) or private signing keys. The signing key used to produce advanced electronic signatures should ideally be generated in the smart card; it should not be possible for the signing key to leave the smart card. Before performing a private key operation, the presence of the cardholder must be verified by means of a PIN or password.
2. A smart card used for user authentication usually contains one or more signing keys or one or more secret long-term master keys.
3. A smart card used to protect the confidentiality of data contains decryption keys. As with signing keys, all usage of these keys must be protected by a cardholder verification using a PIN presentation. It is clear that a backup copy of these keys should be available to restore encrypted data if the smart card should be lost or damaged.

3.2 The smart card reader

This device should behave as expected and should forward the information exchanged between the PC and the smart card. If it is possible to upgrade the firmware of the smart card reader, this upgrade should not compromise the correct behavior of the reader.

3.3 The smart card driver software

The smart card API, which is used to address the smart card, is essential for the system to operate as specified. The introduction of a Trojan horse or a modified version of this driver software may enable an attacker to gain unauthorized access to the computer system and the smart card.

3.4 The application

The application using the Crypto API or the smart card API performs PIN management. This may be a vulnerable point. The PIN and/or passwords database should never hold PINs or passwords that may compromise the trustworthiness of advanced electronic signatures.

3.5 The user

It is clear that the cardholder also may be an attack entry point: the security of a system in which smart cards are used depends on (a) the possession of the smart card, (b) the knowledge of the appropriate PIN or password to activate some of the card's functions, and (c) the cardholder's approval of the secret or private key operation, which gives us three attack entry points. Also, the visualization of the signature/decryption request can be a point of attack.

3.6 Web servers

A web server usually delegates the validation of the authentication information of a client to an authentication server. This authentication server typically relies on a hardware security module to validate this information. Strong client authentication can only be achieved by consulting up-to-date certificate status information. A possible attack would be to prevent and/or to spoof the gathering of these data.

4. MITIGATION TECHNIQUES AND RECOMMENDATIONS

The mitigation techniques to alleviate security threats can be divided into two sub categories: technical and procedural solutions. Technical solutions can be implemented on all the different components of the system: the smart card, the smart card reader, software components on the user's PC and the web server.

4.1 Technical solutions for the security token

- An adequate access control mechanism should protect the token (smart card, hardware security module, key store...). The software designer should, if possible,
  - Limit the number of password/PIN trials.
  - Specify a fixed number of operations which can be performed without requiring a new or additional user authentication.
- Security tokens which allow the recovery of (secret) data should be avoided: it should not be possible to recover data which the user has invalidated.
- The user of a security token should have the possibility to specify for each security-critical service offered by his security token an individual

PIN or password: if a single PIN or password is used to activate the generation of an advanced electronic or authentication signature, the decryption of encrypted data, the retrieval of privacy-sensitive information, updating privacy-sensitive information, etc, then the user has no control on the actual operations that are launched to the security token.

- The data stored in a security token should be time stamped to avoid replay or substitution.
- The integrity of the data stored in a security token should be protected so that unauthorized modifications can easily be detected.
- Confidential data should not be stored in the clear.
- One should only use security tokens which support and implement state of the art cryptographic algorithms.

4.2 Technical solutions for the smart card reader

- A smart card reader with a secure PIN pad and a secure display should be used to guarantee that the information showed to the user is genuine. The secure PIN pad reader should ideally only display information which comes from the smart card, i.e., which is sent through a secure channel between the smart card and the smart card reader.
- The firmware of the smart card reader should require some kind of user authentication so that a malicious firmware update cannot take place without being noticed.

4.3 Technical solutions for the user's PC

- PINs and passwords which give access to the security token's functionality should never be stored persistently (e.g., cache, swap file, post-it), and should always be obfuscated when used in volatile memory.
- The software designer should inform the user of the reason why a PIN is requested (e.g., user authentication), which type of operation requires this PIN or password (sign, decrypt, read or write sensitive data…), and in which type of session this occurs (e.g., decryption session, authentication session …).
- The most recent accesses and usages of the token should be logged, and the integrity of this log should be protected.
- The PC application or web server should set up a secure communications channel with the security token to avoid attacks which involve a malicious smart card reader.

- The access conditions to services of the security token should be specified as restrictive as reasonable, e.g., so that only the functionality which is strictly necessary can be used.
- The integrity of all the relevant software (e.g., client applications, driver software...) should be protected, e.g., using code signing techniques which can easily be validated.
- One should not rely on garbage collector techniques to erase or clear sensitive information (cryptographic keys, user data, PINs, passwords...). This data should explicitly be reset by the software designer and developer.

4.4 Technical solutions for the web server

- All security-critical information of a web server should be stored in trustworthy hardware such as a hardware security module.

4.5 Procedural techniques

- The targeted audience should be trained to become (more) security-aware. Users who deal with security tokens must be informed such that they know how to correctly use their security tokens and how to spot potential attacks or preparations for such attacks. The users should be informed: of how to protect their security tokens both logically and physically to avoid them from being stolen, lost or damaged; and that their PINs and passwords must be kept secret and only used in the correct context.
- All procedural mitigation techniques should be clearly described and documented in easy to understand terms.
- The procedures which specify how the user should effectively protect his machine (including operating system and applications) should also specify guidelines to avoid malicious software, e.g., using a virus scanner and a personal firewall.

Note that legitimate users can also be potential attackers. It is therefore very important not to forget the impact of the threats triggered by insiders as they can easily study the (in)security of a given system, even without raising any suspicion, use the system legitimately and subsequently mount an attack on its vulnerabilities.

5. LIST OF THREATS

In this section, we give an overview of threats that are relevant to the use of smart cards in (web) applications. For each threat, we describe some scenarios that lead to the successful exploitation of the threat. We also propose some countermeasures, specific to the use of smart cards. General countermeasures, such as the installation of virus scanners, are mentioned in the previous section and are not repeated here. A much more detailed description of the threats can be found in [5].

5.1 List of threats

5.1.1 Token is no longer in the possession of the genuine holder.

If a token is no longer in the possession of the genuine holder, it is not easy to determine whether an attacker has obtained the token, or whether the token will remain inactive forever. This type of threat can be seen as a denial of service attack as the legitimate user can no longer use the token's services. An attacker may also prevent the user from using the services of the token, in order to make the token available to him/herself.

In order to avoid potential abuse of a token which is lost or damaged, the security services of that token should be revoked as soon as the legitimate user discovers the unavailability of the security token.

5.1.2 Token is damaged or unusable

If a security token is damaged, it may no longer operate correctly. This may render the key material and other sensitive data in the token unusable, both for the genuine token holder and a potential attacker, e.g., due to a hardware fault or an attacker's intervention. This type of threat is a denial of service attack as the legitimate user can no longer rely on the token's services.

Any physical damage of a security token can be detected easily. If this event occurs, the token must be revoked to avoid potential abuse of this hardware failure.

5.1.3 Secret data extraction from the token

The attacker obtains the secret data stored in a token. This leads to the existence of cloned tokens. The attacker can use this new token to impersonate the genuine user of that token. This attack is very hard to counter if the token user has not been properly trained to discover abnormal behaviour while (s)he is using his/her token.

The application designer should pay special attention to the handling of sensitive (user) data, and should never manipulate them in unobfuscated form to avoid the extraction of secret information on this data, even if the memory is dumped to disk.

5.1.4 Bypassing the access control mechanisms of the security token

The attacker may obtain a copy of the (software) security token, or obtain the PIN or password which gives access to the services of the security token, e.g., by observation of the PIN while the genuine user uses the token, or by social engineering. Once the attacker has access to the functionality of the token, (s)he can impersonate its legitimate user whenever the user uses the token in an environment controlled by the attacker.

This attack is very hard to counter as the attacker may be very well prepared, and the user may discover the abuse of his token much later than the moment of the attack.

5.1.5 Remote private/secret key operations

An attacker may set up a scenario in which he can perform operations which use the cryptographic keys of the legitimate user's security token, e.g., to generate authentication or advanced electronic signatures, or to decrypt encrypted data, without the consent of the legitimate token owner. The attacker may gain this access through social engineering or after a successful Trojan Horse attack which can either reveal the legitimate user's PIN or password, or which immediately executes additional operations which were not authorized by the legitimate token user.

This type of attack is very hard to counter and requires careful training of the token users. An additional countermeasure consists of the limitation of the number of operations that a security token can execute before a new user authentication is necessary.

5.1.6 Tampering with data in the token

An attacker may be able to alter the data stored in a security token, e.g., through the update, insertion, invalidation or removal of data without the user's explicit approval. E.g., if the token contains a root certificate of a certification authority that the token holder blindly trusts, the attacker can add an additional root certificate of a malicious party during the same session which was authorized by the user. By doing this, the malicious party abuses the authorization by the legitimate token user.

6. CONCLUSION

This article focuses on the countermeasures and recommendations, which a software developer of web applications in which security tokens are used for client and/or server authentication should keep in mind in order to counter common threats. We have described the most important threats, proposed reasonably possible attack scenarios to exploit them, and recommended countermeasures. We conclude that the awareness of the user is the most vulnerable link in the security chain which builds secure (web) applications which rely on user tokens. It is clear that the need for proper user education and training cannot be over-emphasized enough. This should not come as a surprise, as the entire purpose of using security tokens such as smart cards is actually moving the trust (and hence the target of an attack) to the user. The application developer can play a crucial role in the user awareness process. Another important element is the user's computer system: if this gets compromised in one way or another, the entire system's security guarantees are at risk.

7. ACKNOWLEDGEMENTS

This work reported in this paper was developed as part of the *Designing Secure Applications* (DeSecA) project, funded by Microsoft. Partners within this project were the Universita' degli Studi di Milano, the Technical University of Ilmenau, the University of Salford, and the COSIC and DistriNet research groups of the Katholieke Universiteit Leuven.

8. REFERENCES

[1] D. W. Chadwick. Threat Modelling for Active Directory. Eighth IFIP TC-6 TC-11 Conference on Communications and Multimedia Security (CMS 2004), September 2004, UK, pp 203-212

[2] R. Grimm and H. Eichstädt. Threat Modelling for ASP.NET – Designing Secure Applications. In *Eighth IFIP TC-6 TC-11 Conference on Communications and Multimedia Security (CMS 2004)*, September 2004, UK, pp 175-187.

[3] E. Bertino, D. Bruschi, S. Franzoni, I. Nai-Fovino, and S. Valtolina. Threat modelling for SQL Server. In *Eighth IFIP TC-6 TC-11 Conference on Communications and Multimedia Security (CMS 2004)*, September 2004, UK, pp 189-201

[4] L. Desmet, B. Jacobs, F. Piessens, and W. Joosen. Threat Modelling for Web Services Based Web Applications. In *Eighth IFIP TC-6 TC-11 Conference on Communications and Multimedia Security (CMS 2004)*, September 2004, UK, pp 161-174.

[5] *Designing Secure Application project (DeSecA).* final report, May 2004.

[6] M. Howard and D. LeBlanc. *Writing Secure Code 2nd edition.* Microsoft Press, 2003

[7] Microsoft Patterns and Practices, *Improving Web application security: Threats and Countermeasures.* Microsoft Press, June 2003.

[8] P. Kocher. Timing attacks on implementations of Diffie-Hellman, RSA, DSS, and other systems. In *Advances in Cryptology – CRYPTO '96,* pages 104-113, Lecture Notes in Computer Science 1109, N. Koblitz, Ed., Springer-Verlag, 1996.

[9] P. Kocher, J. Jaffe, and B. Jun. Differential power analysis. In *Advances in Cryptology Conference – CRYPTO '99*, pages 388-397, Lecture Notes in Computer Science 1666, M. Wiener, Ed., Springer-Verlag, 1999.

[10] D. Boneh, R.A. DeMillo and R.J. Lipton. On the importance of eliminating errors in cryptographic computations, *J. Cryptology*, 14(2):101-119, 2001.

[11] European Parliament. *Directive 1999/93/EC of the European Parliament and of the Council of 13 December 1999 on a Community Framework for Electronic Signatures.* Official Journal L 013, p.0012-0020, January 2000.

ANALYSIS OF THE DVB COMMON SCRAMBLING ALGORITHM

Ralf-Philipp Weinmann and Kai Wirt
Technical University of Darmstadt
Department of Computer Science
Darmstadt, Germany
{weinmann,kwirt}@cdc.informatik.tu-darmstadt.de

Abstract The Common Scrambling Algorithm (CSA) is used to encrypt streams of video data in the Digital Video Broadcasting (DVB) system. The algorithm cascades a stream and a block cipher, apparently for a larger security margin. In this paper we set out to analyze the block cipher and the stream cipher separately and give an overview of how they interact with each other. We present a practical attack on the stream cipher. Research on the block cipher so far indicates it to be resistant against linear and algebraic cryptanalysis as well as simple slide attacks.

Keywords: Block cipher, stream cipher, cryptanalysis, DVB, pay-tv

1. Introduction

The DVB Common Scrambling Algorithm is an ETSI-specified algorithm for securing MPEG-2 transport streams such as those used for digitally transmitted Pay-TV. It was adopted by the DVB consortium in May 1994, the exact origin and date of the design is unclear. Until 2002, the algorithm was only available under a Non-Disclosure Agreement from an ETSI custodian. This NDA disallowed and still disallows licensees to implement the algorithm in software for "security reasons". The little information that was then available to the public is contained in an ETSI Technical Report [European Telecommunications Standards Institute, 1996] and patent applications [Bewick, 1998], [Watts et al., 1998]. This changed in the Fall of 2002, when a Windows program called FreeDec appeared which implemented the CSA in software. It was quickly reverse–engineered and details were disseminated on a web site [Pseudonymous authors, 2003].

For keying the CSA, so called *control words* are used. These control words are provided by a conditional access mechanism, which generates them from encrypted control messages embedded in the transport stream. Conditional access mechanisms vary between broadcasters and can be more easily changed than the actual scrambling algorithm. Examples for commonly used conditional access mechanisms are Irdeto, Betacrypt, Nagravision, CryptoWorks etc. A new common key is usually issued every 10–120 seconds. The great relevance of CSA lies in the fact that every encrypted digital Pay-TV transmission in Europe is secured using this algorithm. A practical break of CSA would thus affect all broadcasters and could not be remedied by changing the conditional access mechanism.

The scrambling algorithm can be seen as the layering of two cryptographic primitives: a 64-bit block cipher and a stream cipher. Both ciphers employ a common key; the stream cipher uses an additional 64-bit nonce, the origin of which we will discuss later.

In this paper we investigate the two ciphers independently and show weaknesses. Although we do not present a break of the scrambling algorithm we present a known-plaintext attack on the stream cipher and show preliminary results on the block cipher.

The rest of this paper is organized as follows: Section 2 defines the notation used. In Section 3 we describe the two ciphers and how they are combined in the CSA. Our attack on the stream cipher as well as a presentation of properties of the block cipher follow in Sections 4 respectively 5. Section 6 concludes.

2. Definitions

In the rest of this paper we use the following notation:

K	the common key. A 64 bit key used for both the stream and the block cipher
k_i	denotes the i-th bit of K
K^E	denotes the expanded key which is derived through the key schedule of the block cipher
SB_i	is the i-th 8-byte block of the scrambled data stream SB_0 is used as nonce in the stream cipher
CB_i	is the i-th 8-byte block of stream cipher output
IB_i	intermediate blocks. See Figure 3.1 for details.
DB_i	is the i-th 8-byte block of descrambled data
R	denotes the residue and
SR	is used for the scrambled residue
IV	an initialization vector. Always equals the zero block.
rol	bitwise rotation to the left by one bit
$\|\|$	denotes concatenation
t_i	state of the stream cipher after i clocks t_{-31} is the starting state, t_0 the state after the initialization
I^A	is an additional input for the stream cipher generated from the nonce
l_w	denotes the cycle length, i.e. the smallest number $j - i$ for which $t_j = t_i$
l_s	is the length of a small cycle, i.e. the smallest number $j - i$ for which the feedback shift register 1 has the same value in t_j and t_i

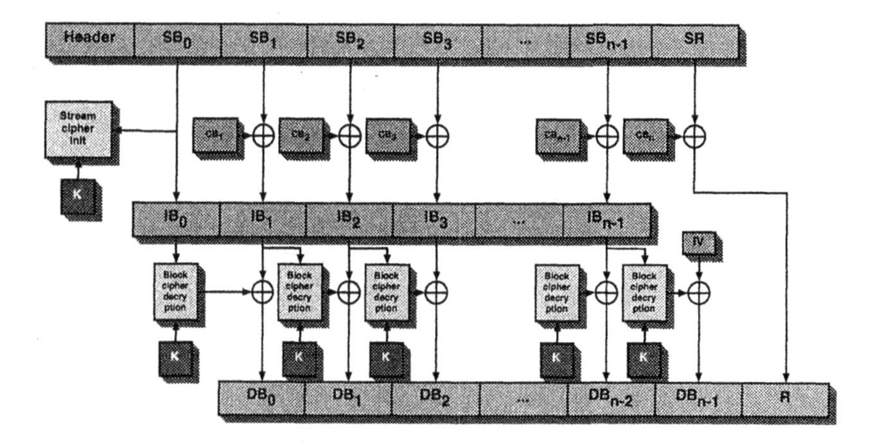

Figure 1. Combination of block- and stream cipher.

3. Description

3.1 Cascading the Block and the Stream Cipher

The scrambling algorithm can be seen as a cascade of a block cipher and a stream cipher. Both ciphers use the same 64-bit key K, which is called the *common key*. We will now describe how the block and the stream cipher are combined. Figure 3.1 depicts the descrambling process.

For scrambling the payload of an m-byte packet, it is divided into blocks (DB_i) of 8 bytes each. If an adaption field was used, it is possible that the length of the packet is not a multiple of 8 bytes. Thus the last block is $n < 8$ bytes long and shall be called *residue*.

The sequence of 8-byte blocks is encrypted in reverse order with the block cipher in CBC mode, whereas the residue is left untouched. The last output of the chain IB_0 is then used as a nonce for the stream cipher. The first m bytes of keystream generated by the stream cipher are XORed to the encrypted blocks $(IB_i)_{i \geq 1}$ followed by the residue.

3.2 The Stream Cipher

3.2.1 Overview. The stream cipher is built of two feedback-shift-registers and a combiner with memory. The overall layout is shown in Figure 3.2.1. The registers p, q and c are bit registers. All other registers are 4 bit wide.

The stream cipher operates in one of two modes. The first one is the initialization mode in which the starting state of the cipher is set up. The second one is the generating mode in which the cipher produces two pseudo-random bits per clock cycle.

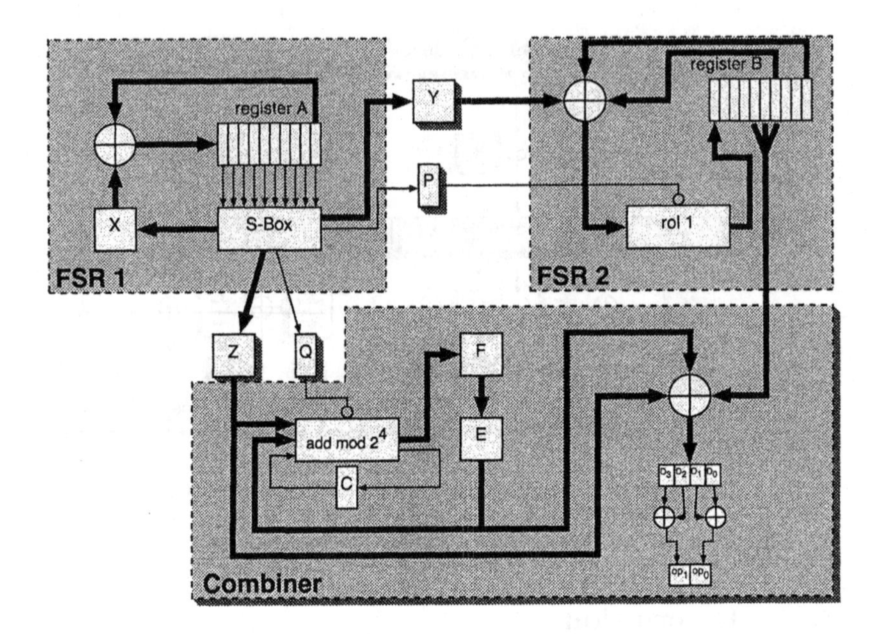

Figure 2. The stream cipher.

3.2.2 Key Schedule. The cipher uses the common key K and the first scrambled block of the transport stream SB_0 as a nonce to set up the initial state. At first all registers of the cipher are set to 0. Then the common key $K = k_0, \dots, k_{63}$ is loaded into the shift registers $A := a_{0,j}, \dots, a_{9,j}$ and $B := b_{0,j}, \dots, b_{9,j}$ with $0 \le j \le 3$ according to the following rule:

$$a_{i,j} = \begin{cases} k_{4 \cdot i+j} & i \le 7 \\ 0 & \text{else} \end{cases}$$

$$b_{i,j} = \begin{cases} k_{32+4 \cdot i+j} & i \le 7 \\ 0 & \text{else} \end{cases}$$

In the following a_i and b_i denote the 20 4-bit registers $a_{i,0}, \dots, a_{i,3}$ and $b_{i,0}, \dots, b_{i,3}$ respectively.

Hereafter the cipher is in initialization mode. It uses SB_0 and the feedback register D as input and performs 32 clock cycles to calculate the starting state. The inputs for feedback shift registers 1 and 2 are derived from SB_0:

$$(I^A, I^B) := \begin{cases} (SB_0 \text{ div } 2^4, SB_0 \text{ mod } 2^4) & \text{in state } t_i, i \in \{-31, -29, \dots\} \\ (SB_0 \text{ mod } 2^4, SB_0 \text{ div } 2^4) & \text{else} \end{cases}$$

Thus in every odd cycle number I^A is the high nibble of SB_0 whereas I^B is the low nibble. In even cycles the nibbles are used the other way round. See below for the equations which update the internal cipher state.

3.2.3 Generation Mode.

Feedback shift register 1. The feedback a'_0 of shift register A is calculated as

$$a'_0 := \begin{cases} a_9 \oplus X & \text{if not in init mode} \\ a_9 \oplus X \oplus D \oplus I^A & \text{else} \end{cases}$$

The next value A' for register A is then given by

$$A' := (a'_0, a_0, \ldots, a_8)$$

Feedback shift register 2. The feedback b'_0 of shift register B is given by

$$b'_0 := \begin{cases} b_6 \oplus b_9 \oplus Y & \text{if not in init mode} \\ b_6 \oplus b_9 \oplus Y \oplus I^B & \text{else} \end{cases}$$

and the new value B' for B is

$$B' := \begin{cases} (b'_0, b_0, \ldots, b_8) & p = 0 \\ (rol(b'_0), b_0, \ldots, b_8) & \text{else} \end{cases}$$

Other registers. New values for the other registers, namely X, Y, Z, p and q are derived from seven 5×2 S-Boxes. Table 1 shows which bits from shift-register A are used as input for the S-Boxes and how the new register values are constructed. The S-Boxes itself are shown in Table 4. Table 6 gives an algebraic description of the S-Boxes, with a being the most significant input bit and e the least significant.

Combiner. The stream cipher uses a combiner with memory to calculate two bits of output per clock. The memory of the combiner consists of registers E, F and c. In each cycle a new state for these registers is determined according to

$$(E, F)' := \begin{cases} (F, E) & q = 0 \\ (F, E + Z + c \bmod 2^4) & \text{else} \end{cases}$$

c is unchanged if $q = 0$. Otherwise it is 1 if $E + Z + c \geq 2^4$ and 0 else.

The output of the generator is calculated by $D_2 \oplus D_3 || D_0 \oplus D_1$ where $D := E \oplus Z \oplus B^{out}$ with B^{out} given by

$$\begin{aligned} B_3^{out} &:= b_{2,0} \oplus b_{5,1} \oplus b_{6,2} \oplus b_{8,3} \\ B_2^{out} &:= b_{5,0} \oplus b_{7,1} \oplus b_{2,3} \oplus b_{3,2} \\ B_1^{out} &:= b_{4,3} \oplus b_{7,2} \oplus b_{3,0} \oplus b_{4,1} \\ B_0^{out} &:= b_{8,2} \oplus b_{5,3} \oplus b_{2,1} \oplus b_{7,0} \end{aligned}$$

3.3 The Block Cipher

CSA employs an iterated block cipher that operates bytewise on 64-bit blocks of data and uses a 64-bit key, the common key K. Each round of the cipher employs the same round transformation ϕ, which takes an 8-byte vector along with a single byte of the expanded key as input and outputs an 8-byte vector. This round transformation is applied 56 times. One could also lump together 8 successive rounds of the cipher into a round function ϕ' and describe a 7-round cipher which uses 64-bit subkeys; however we feel that the description we give below is more natural and easier to comprehend.

3.3.1 The Key Schedule. Let ρ be the bit permutation on 64-bit strings which is defined in Table 2. The expanded key $K^E = (k_0^E, \ldots, k_{447}^E)$ consists of a total of 448 bits which are recursively computed as follows:

$$k^E_{0,\ldots,63} = k_{0,\ldots,63}$$

$$k^E_{64i,\ldots,64i+63} = \rho(k^E_{64(i-1),\ldots,64i-1}) \oplus \mathtt{0x0}i\mathtt{0}i\mathtt{0}i\mathtt{0}i\mathtt{0}i\mathtt{0}i\mathtt{0}i\mathtt{0}i \quad 1 \leq i \leq 6$$

where the expression $\mathtt{0x0}i\mathtt{0}i\mathtt{0}i\mathtt{0}i\mathtt{0}i\mathtt{0}i\mathtt{0}i\mathtt{0}i$ is to be interpreted as a hexadecimal constant. We note that the key schedule is entirely $GF(2)$-linear.

3.3.2 The Round Function. At the core of the round transformation ϕ are the nonlinear functions f and f'. These are distinct

Table 1. S-Box input and generation of new register values.

S_1	$a_{3,0}$	$a_{0,2}$	$a_{5,1}$	$a_{6,3}$	$a_{8,0}$
S_2	$a_{1,1}$	$a_{2,2}$	$a_{5,3}$	$a_{6,0}$	$a_{8,1}$
S_3	$a_{0,3}$	$a_{1,0}$	$a_{4,1}$	$a_{4,3}$	$a_{5,2}$
S_4	$a_{2,3}$	$a_{0,1}$	$a_{1,3}$	$a_{3,2}$	$a_{7,0}$
S_5	$a_{4,2}$	$a_{3,2}$	$a_{5,0}$	$a_{7,1}$	$a_{8,2}$
S_6	$a_{2,1}$	$a_{3,1}$	$a_{4,0}$	$a_{6,2}$	$a_{8,3}$
S_7	$a_{1,2}$	$a_{2,0}$	$a_{6,1}$	$a_{7,2}$	$a_{7,3}$

X	$S_{4,0}$	$S_{3,0}$	$S_{2,1}$	$S_{1,1}$
Y	$S_{6,0}$	$S_{5,0}$	$S_{4,1}$	$S_{3,1}$
Z	$S_{2,0}$	$S_{1,0}$	$S_{6,1}$	$S_{5,1}$
p	$S_{7,1}$			
q	$S_{7,0}$			

Table 2. Key bit permutation.

i	0	1	2	3	4	5	6	7	8	9	10	11	12	13	14	15
$\rho(i)$	17	35	8	6	41	48	28	20	27	53	61	49	18	32	58	63
i	16	17	18	19	20	21	22	23	24	25	26	27	28	29	30	31
$\rho(i)$	23	19	36	38	1	52	26	0	33	3	12	13	56	39	25	40
i	32	33	34	35	36	37	38	39	40	41	42	43	44	45	46	47
$\rho(i)$	50	34	51	11	21	47	29	57	44	30	7	24	22	46	60	16
i	48	49	50	51	52	53	54	55	56	57	58	59	60	61	62	63
$\rho(i)$	59	4	55	42	10	5	9	43	31	62	45	14	2	37	15	54

permutations on the set of all byte values and can be seen as the S-Boxes of the cipher. Both permutations have maximum cycle length and are related to each other by a bit permutation σ, i.e. $f' = \sigma \circ f$. This bit permutation maps bit 0 to 1, bit 1 to 7, bit 2 to 5, bit 3 to 4, bit 4 to 2, bit 5 to 6, bit 6 to 0 and bit 7 to 3. See Table 5 for the actual values described by f.

Let $S = (s_0, \ldots, s_7)$ be the vector of bytes representing the internal state of the block cipher in an arbitrary round. The function ϕ taking the internal state S from round i to round $i+1$ can then be defined as

$$\begin{aligned}\phi(s_0, \ldots, s_7, k) &= (s_1, s_2 \oplus s_0, s_3 \oplus s_0, s_4 \oplus s_0, \\ &\quad s_5, s_6 \oplus f'(k \oplus s_7), s_7, s_0 \oplus f(k \oplus s_7))\end{aligned}$$

whereas for decrypting a block of ciphertext we need the inverse function:

$$\begin{aligned}\phi^{-1}(s_0, \ldots, s_7, k) &= (s_7 \oplus f(s_6 \oplus k), s_0, \\ &\quad s_7 \oplus s_1 \oplus f(s_6 \oplus k), s_7 \oplus s_2 \oplus f(s_6 \oplus k), \\ &\quad s_7 \oplus s_3 \oplus f(s_6 \oplus k), s_4, s_5 \oplus f'(s_6 \oplus k), s_6)\end{aligned}$$

3.3.3 Encryption/Decryption. Encrypting a plaintext $P = (p_0, \ldots, p_7)$ is accomplished by

$$\begin{aligned}S^0 &= P \\ S^r &= \phi(S^{r-1}, (k^E_{8r}, \ldots, k^E_{8r+7})) \qquad 1 \le r \le 56 \\ C &= S^{56}\end{aligned}$$

which yields the ciphertext $C = (c_0, \ldots, c_7)$. For decrypting this ciphertext the following sequence of operations needs to be carried out:

$$\begin{aligned}S^0 &= C \\ S^r &= \phi(S^{r-1}, (k^E_{448-8r}, \ldots, k^E_{455-8r})) \qquad 1 \le r \le 56 \\ P &= S^{56}\end{aligned}$$

4. Analysis of the Stream Cipher

In the following we denote with t_0 the stream cipher's state after the initialization. That means t_{-31} is the initial state, in which the common key is loaded in the registers A and B respectively. Given this notation we define a full cycle to be the smallest number $l_w := j - i$ for which the values of all registers in state t_i are equal to the values in t_j. Also we define a small cycle to be the smallest number $l_s := j - i$ when the values of X and A in state t_i are equal to the values in t_j.

4.1 Observation

The CSA stream cipher's state consists of 103 bits. This means that the maximum period length is 2^{103}. For cryptographic purposes, one would expect the cycle to go through a minimum of 2^{80} states. Using Floyd's cycle-finding algorithm however, we observed that after a relatively short preperiod there exist only a few different cycle lengths for different key/nonce combinations; all of these have a length of $l_w < 10^9$, which of course is much smaller than 2^{80}. When comparing the set of states in several cycles with the same length which where generated by different key/nonce pairs, one notices that these are disjunct; many different cycles with length l_w exist.

On the other hand, taking only A and X in account shows that if two cycles have the same length l_w then l_s is equal too. Moreover the sequence of states in feedback-shift-register 1 is equal. This means that if l_w is equal for two cycles then the registers A and X for these cycles are going through the same values.

We conducted a total of 10^5 experiments with random key/nonce pairs to determine the most probable period lengths for the state transition function operating on register A. Table 3 shows some small cycle lengths l_s together with the number of times $n(l_s)$ we observed a cycle of this length in our test and $a(l_s)$ the average length of the pre-period for a given cycle length.

Table 3. Probability distribution for small cycles.

$n(l_s)$	l_s	$a(l_s)$
36106	22778	152854.6
24196	97494	83098.3
18054	121992	27726.2
15171	42604	65556.8
3244	25802	17643.8
1495	108	21051.6
131	2391	3138.5

In 1.6% of all cases we observed cycle lengths not listed in the above table. For each of these the probability of occurrence must be lower than 0.2%. This observation leads to the following attack:

1: Calculate a table T with the states of the small cycles
2: **for** every state in T **do**
3: Test if the state is correct
4: Reconstruct the remaining registers
5: **end for**

It remains to show how one can determine if the state is correct and how the remaining registers can be reconstructed.

4.2 Finding the Correct Value for FSR1

The trivial method of finding the correct value for FSR1 is to simply try all possible values. That means that one searches through all states which belong to one of the small cycles. Summing up the number of states in Table 3 shows that in 98.4% of all cases testing 313 169 possibilities is sufficient; this is far less than the 2^{44} possible values for A and X.

4.3 Reconstructing the Remaining Registers

The stream cipher's output is calculated by XORing Z, E and B^{out}. Since we can now consider A to be known, Z is fully determined. For all possible 2^9 values of E, F and c do the following:
Consider all bits of B at clock cycle t as variables with values in $GF(2)$. Generate a system of equations describing the two output bits at clock cycle $t + k$ as linear equations of bits of these variables. This system is linear since the additional inputs for the feedback shift register are fully determined by A and hence are known. In other words: for every state of A a system of linear equations that fully describes B with respect to B^{out} exists. Therefore this system can be efficiently solved using Gaussian elimination. If the system is inconsistent then the guess for E, F and c was wrong and has to be altered.

The last step of the attack is to determine which of the possible solutions for the linear equations system is the correct one. This has to be done because different values for E, F and c may lead to a solution of the system. The correct value can be determined simply by running the keystream generator with the calculated state and checking if the output corresponds to the actual output of the generator.

4.4 Results

Some of the generated equations are linearly dependent. Experimentally we derived that for finding a unique solution to the system described above, 60 equations are sufficient.

For carrying out the attack one thus needs to solve approximately $2^{19} \cdot 2^9 = 2^{28}$ systems of linear equations, each of which contains 60 equations in 40 unknowns. Experiments showed that this can be done in less than an hour on a 1.25 GHz PowerPC G4. We stress that our attack leaves much room for improvement. It might be possible to increase our chances at guessing the correct value for A from statistical deviation in the output of the stream cipher. But already our unoptimized version shows that the stream cipher can be broken in a very short time. Also, this attack is well suited to parallelization.

5. Analysis of the Block Cipher

We note that the round function ϕ is a weak permutation. Given the inputs x_1, x_2 and outputs $y_1 = \phi(x_1, k)$ and $y_2 = \phi(x_2, k)$ of a single round it is trivial to determine the round subkey k. The key schedule however seems to make the cipher resistant against slide attacks [Biryukov and Wagner, 1999].

5.1 Linear Approximation of the S-Boxes

The maximum bias of both S-Boxes is $\frac{17}{128}$. Trying to find a linear path through several rounds of the cipher we see that the number of active S-Boxes in the path increases exponentially in the number of rounds. Because of this fact and the high number of rounds, the authors believe that classical linear cryptanalysis poses not threat to the cipher.

5.2 Polynomial Interpolation of the S-Boxes

We have interpolated the S-Boxes as polynomials over fields $GF(2^8) = GF(2)[X]/m(X)$ for all $m \in GF(2)[X]$ with $\deg(m) = 8$ and m irreducible. The resulting polynomials are all dense and of maximum degree. Interpolating bit traces of the S-Boxes results in polynomials consisting of 117–137 terms. Two of them are of degree 8, the other 6 of degree 7.

Thus we conclude that both representations are not useful for algebraic cryptanalysis of the cipher.

6. Conclusion

In this paper we described the Common Scrambling Algorithm and presented an analysis of the underlying stream and block cipher parts. We showed that the stream cipher is weak and can be efficiently broken. We also pointed out some properties of the block cipher which eventually could be used in an successful attack. However, since the block cipher uses 56 rounds we believe that such an attack would have to use sophisticated techniques.

Cryptanalyzing both stream and block cipher at the same time seems to be a task too daunting to attempt. Finding special cases where plaintext and corresponding ciphertext can be obtained that is encrypted with only one of the ciphers facilitates easier cryptanalysis. For the stream cipher these are packets with a residue. A sufficiently long adaption field on the other hand can lead to packets which are only protected by the block cipher.

We believe that extending the attack on the stream cipher to a key recovery is not a trivial task. Since the state update function of the stream cipher is irreversible and nonlinear, the only option we see at this point for recovering the key is to solve a large system of polynomial equations for different nonces and key streams. The nonlinear equations in this system are of the form seen in Table 6.

There are various directions for future research on these topics. First of all the attack presented offers room for further improvements like the reduction of the necessary register guesses. Investigating how to recover the Common Key K from a known state of the stream cipher is another logical step. Finally, the block cipher needs more scrutiny.

7. Appendix

Table 4. S-Boxes of the stream cipher.

Input	S_1	S_2	S_3	S_4	S_5	S_6	S_7
00000	10	11	10	11	10	00	00
00001	00	01	00	01	00	01	11
00010	01	00	01	10	00	10	10
00011	01	10	10	11	01	11	10
00100	10	10	10	00	11	01	11
00101	11	11	11	10	10	10	00
00110	11	11	11	01	11	10	00
00111	00	00	01	10	10	00	01
01000	11	01	01	01	00	00	11
01001	10	11	01	10	01	01	00
01010	10	10	00	00	11	11	01
01011	00	01	11	01	11	00	11
01100	01	00	11	11	01	10	01
01101	01	00	00	00	00	11	10
01110	00	01	10	00	10	01	10
01111	11	10	00	11	01	11	01

Input	S_1	S_2	S_3	S_4	S_5	S_6	S_7
10000	00	11	01	01	10	10	01
10001	11	01	11	00	11	11	00
10010	11	00	00	11	10	00	11
10011	00	11	01	01	00	10	11
10100	10	11	11	10	00	11	00
10101	10	10	00	11	11	00	01
10110	01	00	10	00	01	01	01
10111	01	10	10	11	01	01	10
11000	10	00	10	00	01	10	10
11001	10	00	00	11	00	01	11
11010	00	01	01	10	11	01	01
11011	11	10	10	00	10	10	00
11100	01	10	00	01	11	00	10
11101	01	01	11	10	01	11	11
11110	11	11	11	10	00	11	00
11111	00	01	01	01	10	00	10

Table 5. S-Box of the block cipher. Output arranged row-wise; lower nibble on horizonal, upper on vertical.

	0x00	0x01	0x02	0x03	0x04	0x05	0x06	0x07	0x08	0x09	0x0A	0x0B	0x0C	0x0D	0x0E	0x0F
0x00	0x3A	0xEA	0x68	0xFE	0x33	0xE9	0x88	0x1A	0x83	0xCF	0xE1	0x7F	0xBA	0xE2	0x38	0x12
0x01	0xE8	0x27	0x61	0x95	0x0C	0x36	0xE5	0x70	0xA2	0x06	0x82	0x7C	0x17	0xA3	0x26	0x49
0x02	0xBE	0x7A	0x6D	0x47	0xC1	0x51	0x8F	0xF3	0xCC	0x5B	0x67	0xBD	0xCD	0x18	0x08	0xC9
0x03	0xFF	0x69	0xEF	0x03	0x4E	0x48	0x4A	0x84	0x3F	0xB4	0x10	0x04	0xDC	0xF5	0x5C	0xC6
0x04	0x16	0xAB	0xAC	0x4C	0xF1	0x6A	0x2F	0x3C	0x3B	0xD4	0xD5	0x94	0xD0	0xC4	0x63	0x62
0x05	0x71	0xA1	0xF9	0x4F	0x2E	0xAA	0xC5	0x56	0xE3	0x39	0x93	0xCE	0x65	0x64	0xE4	0x58
0x06	0x6C	0x19	0x42	0x79	0xDD	0xEE	0x96	0xF6	0x8A	0xEC	0x1E	0x85	0x53	0x45	0xDE	0xBB
0x07	0x7E	0x0A	0x9A	0x13	0x2A	0x9D	0xC2	0x5E	0x5A	0x1F	0x32	0x35	0x9C	0xA8	0x73	0x30
0x08	0x29	0x3D	0xE7	0x92	0x87	0x1B	0x2B	0x4B	0xA5	0x57	0x97	0x40	0x15	0xE6	0xBC	0x0E
0x09	0xEB	0xC3	0x34	0x2D	0xB8	0x44	0x25	0xA4	0x1C	0xC7	0x23	0xED	0x90	0x6E	0x50	0x00
0x0A	0x99	0x9E	0x4D	0xD9	0xDA	0x8D	0x6F	0x5F	0x3E	0xD7	0x21	0x74	0x86	0xDF	0x6B	0x05
0x0B	0x8E	0x5D	0x37	0x11	0xD2	0x28	0x75	0xD6	0xA7	0x77	0x24	0xBF	0xF0	0xB0	0x02	0xB7
0x0C	0xF8	0xFC	0x81	0x09	0xB1	0x01	0x76	0x91	0x7D	0x0F	0xC8	0xA0	0xF2	0xCB	0x78	0x60
0x0D	0xD1	0xF7	0xE0	0xB5	0x98	0x22	0xB3	0x20	0x1D	0xA6	0xDB	0x7B	0x59	0x9F	0xAE	0x31
0x0E	0xFB	0xD3	0xB6	0xCA	0x43	0x72	0x07	0xF4	0xD8	0x41	0x14	0x55	0x0D	0x54	0x8B	0xB9
0x0F	0xAD	0x46	0x0B	0xAF	0x80	0x52	0x2C	0xFA	0x8C	0x89	0x66	0xFD	0xB2	0xA9	0x9B	0xC0

Table 6. Algebraic description of the S-Boxes used in the stream cipher.

$$
\begin{aligned}
S_{1,0} &= abce + abc + abd + bde + ab + ae + be + ce + b + d \\
S_{1,1} &= abcd + abde + abc + abd + acd + ade + bcd + bce + \\
&\quad ab + ac + bc + bd + be + cd + ce + de + a + d + e + 1 \\
S_{2,0} &= abce + abde + ade + bce + bde + ab + ac + ce + c + d + 1 \\
S_{2,1} &= abde + abc + abd + abe + acd + cde + cd + ce + b + d + e + 1 \\
S_{3,0} &= ce + de + a + b + d \\
S_{3,1} &= abcd + acde + abe + ac + abc + acd + ace + ade + bcd + bde + \\
&\quad cde + ad + bc + bd + be + cd + ce + a + b + d + e + 1 \\
S_{4,0} &= abcd + abde + acde + abc + abe + bde + ab + ad + ae + bc + \\
&\quad be + de + c + d + 1 \\
S_{4,1} &= abcd + abde + acde + abc + abe + bcd + cde + ad + ab + ae + \\
&\quad de + a + b + c + e + 1 \\
S_{5,0} &= abde + acde + acd + abe + abd + ace + bce + cde + ab + ac + \\
&\quad ae + bd + be + ce + de + c \\
S_{5,1} &= abcd + abce + acde + abd + abe + acd + bcd + bce + \\
&\quad bde + cde + ac + ad + ae + be + cd + ce + de + b + d + e + 1 \\
S_{6,0} &= abcd + abde + acde + acd + ade + bcd + cde + bc + bd + cd + \\
&\quad c + e \\
S_{6,1} &= abe + ade + bce + bde + bc + ce + a + d \\
S_{7,0} &= abde + abd + cde + bc + cd + de + a + b + c + e \\
S_{7,1} &= abcd + abdebc + acde + acd + ade + bde + ac + ae + de + \\
&\quad b + c + d + e
\end{aligned}
$$

References

[Bewick, 1998] Bewick, Simon (1998). Descrambling DVB data according to ETSI common scrambling specification. UK Patent Applications GB2322994A / GB2322995A.

[Biryukov and Wagner, 1999] Biryukov, Alex and Wagner, David (1999). Slide attacks. In Knudsen, Lars, editor, *Fast Software Encryption: 6th International Workshop, FSE'99, Rome, Italy, March 1999. Proceedings*, volume 1663 of *Lecture Notes in Computer Science*, pages 245–. Springer-Verlag Heidelberg.

[European Telecommunications Standards Institute, 1996] European Telecommunications Standards Institute (1996). ETSI Technical Report 289: Support for use of scrambling and Conditional Access (CA) within digital broadcasting systems.

[Golomb, 1967] Golomb, Solomon W. (1967). *Shift Register Sequences.* Holden-Day San Francisco.

[Pseudonymous authors, 2003] Pseudonymous authors (2003). CSA – known facts and speculations. `http://csa.irde.to`.

[Rueppel, 1986] Rueppel, Rainer A. (1986). *Analysis and design of stream ciphers.* Springer-Verlag New York, Inc.

[Watts et al., 1998] Watts, Davies Donald, Ashley, Rix Simon Paul, and Jacobus, Kuehn Gideon (1998). System and apparatus for blockwise encryption and decryption of data. US Patent Application US5799089.

References

AN EXTENSION OF TYPED MSR FOR SPECIFYING ESOTERIC PROTOCOLS AND THEIR DOLEV-YAO INTRUDER

Theodoros Balopoulos, Stephanos Gritzalis, and Sokratis K. Katsikas
Laboratory of Information and Communication Systems Security
Department of Information and Communication Systems Engineering
University of the Aegean
Karlovassi, Samos, GR-83200, Greece
{tbalopoulos,sgritz,ska}@aegean.gr

Abstract Esoteric protocols, such as electronic cash, electronic voting and selective disclosure protocols, use special message constructors that are not widely used in other types of protocols (for example, in authentication protocols). These message constructors include blind signatures, commitments and zero-knowledge proofs. Furthermore, a standard formalization of the Dolev-Yao intruder [6] does not take into account these message constructors, nor does it consider some types of attacks (such as privacy attacks, brute-force dictionary attacks and known-plaintext attacks) that esoteric as well as other types of protocols are designed to protect against. This paper aims to present an extension of typed MSR [3, 4] in order to formally specify the needed message constructors, as well as the capabilities of a Dolev-Yao intruder designed to attack esoteric protocols.

Keywords: Specification of security protocols, Dolev-Yao intruder, esoteric protocols, privacy, typed MSR

1. Introduction

This paper builds on the typed MSR specification language [3, 4] and aims to make it suitable for the specification of esoteric protocols, as well as for the specification of a version of the Dolev-Yao intruder that is designed to attack such protocols. Some aspects of these extensions are useful in other types of protocols as well. The term "esoteric protocols" is taken from Chapter 6 of [9], and refers to a family of protocols such as electronic cash, electronic voting and selective disclosure protocols.

The paper is organized as follows. In Section 2, we give an overview of the standard version of typed MSR, as well as our extensions of the language's message constructors. In Section 3, we demonstrate how our extensions can be used to make abstraction of two simple esoteric protocols. In Section 4, we give an overview of typing in typed MSR, present our typing extensions and apply them to our newly introduced message constructors. In Section 5, we use our syntactical and typing infrastructure to formally specify the capabilities of a Dolev-Yao intruder targeted for esoteric protocols. We conclude the paper with Section 6.

2. Typed MSR

Typed MSR is a strongly typed specification language for security protocols, aiming to discover errors in their design. It is particularly suitable for esoteric protocols because it features memory predicates, which enable it to faithfully encode systems consisting of a collection of coordinated subprotocols — a common characteristic of esoteric protocols (consider for example the electronic cash protocol, which consists of a issuing and a showing/spending subprotocol). However, the standard language does not support the message constructors needed for esoteric protocols. In Section 2.1 we give an overview of messages in the standard version of typed MSR, and in Section 2.2 we introduce the needed message constructors.

2.1 Overview of Messages in Typed MSR

In typed MSR, messages are obtained by applying message constructors to a variety of atomic messages. Typically, the atomic messages include principals, keys, nonces and raw data. This is formalized by the following grammatical production:

$$
\begin{array}{llcll}
\textit{Atomic messages:} & a & ::= & \mathsf{A} & (\textit{Principal}) \\
 & & | & \mathsf{k} & (\textit{Key}) \\
 & & | & \mathsf{n} & (\textit{Nonce}) \\
 & & | & \mathsf{m} & (\textit{Raw data})
\end{array}
$$

In typed MSR A, k, n and m range over principal names, keys, nonces and raw data respectively. Raw data denotes pieces of data whose sole function in a protocol is that they are transmitted.

The message constructors typically present in typed MSR are those formalized by the following grammatical production:

$$
\begin{array}{llcll}
\textit{Messages:} & t & ::= & a & (\textit{Atomic messages}) \\
 & & | & x & (\textit{Variables}) \\
 & & | & t_1\, t_2 & (\textit{Concatenation}) \\
 & & | & \{t\}_k & (\textit{Symmetric-key encryption}) \\
 & & | & \{\!\{t\}\!\}_k & (\textit{Asymmetric-key encryption}) \\
 & & | & [t]_k & (\textit{Digital Signature})
\end{array}
$$

We will use the letter t (possibly sub-scripted) to range over messages. We will write A, k, n and m (possibly sub-scripted) for atomic constants or variables that are principals, keys, nonces and raw data respectively. We will also use the letter B for principals and the letter S for servers (which are also principals). Note that in typed MSR, the seriffed letters are used whenever the object we want to refer to cannot be but a constant.

In this paper we choose a different meaning for the digital signature constructor than the meaning chosen in standard MSR. Instead of $[\,t\,]_k$ denoting both the message t *and* its digital signature using key k, here it will denote only the latter. This will become evident in Section 3, where we present a high level view of some esoteric protocols.

2.2 Adding Message Constructors for Esoteric Protocols

To cope with esoteric protocols we add message constructors for blinding, commitment and zero-knowledge proofs:

Messages:	t	$::=$	$\ldots$	*(see above)*
		$\mid$	$\langle\, t\,\rangle_n^k$	*(Blinding)*
		$\mid$	$\|t\|_n$	*(Commitment)*
		$\mid$	$\mathcal{Z}(t, n_s, k, n_f)$	*(Zero-knowledge proof)*

The abstraction of blinding is based on Chaum's blinding [8, 2, 5], according to which the construction of a blinded message depends on a blinding factor (which we can abstract as a nonce) and on a public key. The fundamental property is that if message $\langle\, t\,\rangle_n^k$ is signed using k' (the private key corresponding to public key k), the resulting message can be unblinded by those who know nonce n to produce the digital signature of message t signed using k'.

The abstraction of commitment is based on the non-interactive bit commitment using one-way hash functions [9, 2]. According to this method, the commitment of a message is the hash of the concatenation of the message with a salt value (which we can abstract as a nonce). The fundamental property is that someone who sees $\|t\|_n$, t and n will be convinced that t and n were the values used in the computation of $\|t\|_n$, and that no other values could have been used.

The abstraction of a zero-knowledge proof is based on the non-interactive cut-and-choose protocol introduced in the selective disclosure protocol of Holt and Seamons. The interested reader can refer to Section 3.2.2 of [7]. The fundamental property is that someone who observes $\mathcal{Z}(t, n_s, k, n_f)$ will deduce the values of t and $\langle\, \|t\|_{n_s}\,\rangle_{n_f}^k$ and he will gain no knowledge about the values of n_s, k and n_f. To make the protocol descriptions more readable, we will sometimes annotate a zero-knowledge proof message constructor with the information one gets by observing it as follows:

$$\mathcal{Z}(t, n_s, k, n_f) \rightsquigarrow t,\ \langle\, \|t\|_{n_s}\,\rangle_{n_f}^k$$

Notice that we have chosen to make all our new message constructors non-interactive, so that they share this property with the standard message constructors of Section 2.1.

3. Esoteric Protocols Overview

At this point, we will demonstrate how the message constructors described above may be used to make abstractions of two simple esoteric protocols: an electronic cash protocol and an electronic voting protocol. The aim is not to make abstractions of real-world esoteric protocols, but only to justify the introduction of our new message constructors.

3.1 Electronic Cash Protocol

Issuing. Alice wants to have some e-cash issued by her bank. To do this, Alice authenticates herself to the bank server (so that the server can know which account to debit) and sends a zero-knowledge proof. The server verifies the proof, checks that message m has the format of an e-coin (e.g. it is equal to the message $\texttt{value} = \$10$), debits Alice's account, signs the blinded e-coin's commitment and sends the signature to Alice.

$$\begin{array}{lllll} A & \rightarrow & S & : & \mathcal{Z}(m, s, k_S, f) \rightsquigarrow m,\ \langle\, \|m\|_s \,\rangle_f^{k_S} \\ S & \rightarrow & A & : & [\,\langle\, \|m\|_s \,\rangle_f^{k_S}\,]_{k'_S} \end{array}$$

Showing. Alice unblinds the signature of the blinded commitment, which gives her the signature of the commitment. To spend the money at Bob's shop, she uses an anonymous channel to send to Bob the signature of the commitment and the data used in the computation of the commitment. Bob verifies the bank server's signature and checks that the commitment is indeed computed using the data sent. He then authenticates himself to the bank server and forwards to it all the e-coin data. The server verifies its signature, checks again the commitment's computation, checks further that the e-coin has not been spent before (double spending) and credits Bob's account.

$$\begin{array}{lllll} A & \rightarrow & B & : & m, s, [\,\|m\|_s\,]_{k'_S} \\ B & \rightarrow & S & : & B, m, s, [\,\|m\|_s\,]_{k'_S} \end{array}$$

Notice that the server does not know s, so even if Bob and the server cooperate in an effort to disclose Alice's identity, they will fail.

3.2 Electronic Voting Protocol

Issuing. Alice wants to participate in an electronic election held by a trusted voting server. To do this, Alice authenticates herself to the server (so that the server knows she is eligible for voting) and sends a zero-knowledge proof for each of the possible votes of this election. The server verifies the proofs, checks that messages $m_1, m_2, \ldots$ represent the possible votes, signs the blind commitment of each vote and sends the signatures back to Alice.

$$\begin{array}{lllll} A & \rightarrow & S & : & \mathcal{Z}(m_1, s_1, k_S, f_1),\ \mathcal{Z}(m_2, s_2, k_S, f_2),\ \ldots \\ S & \rightarrow & A & : & [\langle \| m_1 \|_{s_1} \rangle_{f_1}^{k_S}]_{k'_S},\ [\langle \| m_2 \|_{s_2} \rangle_{f_2}^{k_S}]_{k'_S},\ \ldots \end{array}$$

Showing. Alice unblinds the signatures of the blinded commitments, which gives her the signatures of the commitments. She can now choose the commitment of the vote she wishes to cast, and send the corresponding signature to the server via an anonymous channel, together with the data used in the computation of the commitment (one of which is the vote's representation). The server verifies its own signature and after checking that the commitment is indeed computed using the data send, it accepts Alice's vote.

$$A \rightarrow S : m_a, s_a, [\| m_a \|_{s_a}]_{k'_S}$$

Notice that the server has no way of linking s_a to Alice.

4. Types

Typed MSR employs types to enforce basic well-formedness conditions (e.g. that only keys can be used to encrypt a message), as well as to provide a statically checkable way to ascertain desired properties (e.g. that no principal can grab a key he is not entitled to access).

4.1 Overview of Types in Typed MSR

The typing of typed MSR is based on the notion of *dependent product types with subsorting* [1] and the basic types used are summarized in the following grammar:

$$\begin{array}{llll} \textit{Types:} & \tau ::= & \mathsf{principal} & (\textit{Principals}) \\ & \mid & \mathsf{nonce} & (\textit{Nonces}) \\ & \mid & \mathsf{shK}\ A\ B & (\textit{Shared keys}) \\ & \mid & \mathsf{pubK}\ A & (\textit{Public keys}) \\ & \mid & \mathsf{privK}\ k & (\textit{Private keys}) \\ & \mid & \mathsf{msg} & (\textit{Messages}) \end{array}$$

We will use the letter τ (variously decorated) to range over types. The types principal and nonce are used to classify principals and nonces respectively. The type shK A B is used to classify the keys shared between A and B. The type pubK A is used to classify the public keys of A. The type privK k is used to classify the private key that corresponds to the public key k. Finally, the type msg is used to classify generic messages, which include raw data, but also all the other stated types.

The notion of dependent product types with subsorting we mentioned above accommodates our need of having multiple classifications within a hierarchy. For example, everything that is of type nonce, is also of type msg — but the inverse is not true. Therefore, we say that nonce is a *subsort* of msg. We will use the notation $\tau :: \tau'$ to state that τ is a subsort of τ'. The following rules can now be presented:

$$\frac{}{\mathsf{principal} :: \mathsf{msg}} \qquad \frac{}{\mathsf{nonce} :: \mathsf{msg}} \qquad \frac{}{\mathsf{shK}\ A\ B :: \mathsf{msg}}$$

$$\frac{}{\mathsf{pubK}\ A :: \mathsf{msg}} \qquad \frac{}{\mathsf{privK}\ k :: \mathsf{msg}}$$

4.2 Adding Types for Esoteric Protocols

To better cope with esoteric protocols, we add types for tractable, semi-tractable and intractable messages:

Types:	τ	::=	...	(*see above*)
		|	tract	(*Tractable messages*)
		|	semitract	(*Semitractable messages*)
		|	intract	(*Intractable messages*)

These three types are used to classify messages according to their commonness. In other words, they qualitatively classify the number of possible values a message can have.

The type tract is used to classify messages that are very common. Because of the tractable number of their possible values, we consider that an intruder (regardless of whether these messages are publicly known or not) is able to to find them out by successfully employing a brute-force dictionary attack on them. On the other hand, if a principal reveals the same (tractable) message in more than one protocol or subprotocol execution, the intruder will not be able to link these executions together (at least not because of this particular message). Therefore, this classification isolates pieces of information on the *secrecy* of which it is erroneous to base the correctness of a protocol, but on the *anonymity* of which it is safe to do so.

The type intract is used to classify messages that are extremely uncommon. These are pieces of information on the secrecy of which it is safe to base the correctness of a protocol, but on the anonymity of which it is certainly erroneous to do so.

The type semitract is used to classify messages that are common enough to be considered realistic candidates for brute-force dictionary attacks, but not common enough to be considered anonymous. It is not safe to base the correctness of a protocol either on the secrecy of such pieces of information, nor on their anonymity.

We will now classify each of the standard types according to their tractability. Private keys, shared keys and nonces should be regarded as intractable. Principals should be regarded as semitractable: we should not base the correctness of protocols on the number of available principals. Public keys should also be regarded as semitractable for the same reason. Notice that this classification conveniently enforces that everyone has access to public keys. The following rules can now be presented:

$$\frac{}{\mathsf{principal} :: \mathsf{semitract}} \qquad \frac{}{\mathsf{nonce} :: \mathsf{intract}} \qquad \frac{}{\mathsf{shK}\ A\ B :: \mathsf{intract}}$$

$$\frac{}{\mathsf{pubK}\ A :: \mathsf{semitract}} \qquad \frac{}{\mathsf{privK}\ k :: \mathsf{intract}}$$

The classification of messages that are not keys, nor nonces, nor principals will be dealt with by *signatures*, which are described in Section 4.3. To complete our subsorting rules, we add rules that classify tractable, semitractable and intractable messages as messages:

$$\frac{}{\mathsf{tract} :: \mathsf{msg}} \qquad \frac{}{\mathsf{semitract} :: \mathsf{msg}} \qquad \frac{}{\mathsf{intract} :: \mathsf{msg}}$$

4.3 Signatures

Typed MSR has typing rules that check whether an expression built according to the syntax of messages can be considered a ground message. These rules systematically reduce the the validity of a composite message to the validity of its sub-messages. In this way, it all comes down to what the types of atomic messages are. Typed MSR uses signatures to achieve independence of rules from atomic messages. A signature is a finite sequence of declarations that map atomic messages to their type. The grammar of a signature is given below:

Signatures:	Σ	$::=$	$\cdot$	(*Empty signature*)
		$\mid$	$\Sigma,\ a : \tau$	(*Atomic message declaration*)

For our extended type system, we will need two signatures. Signature Σ will map atomic messages to one of the standard types, and signature Γ will map them to one of the extended types, i.e. classify them into tractable, semitractable or intractable. We will write $t :_{\Sigma} \tau$ to say that message t has type τ

in signature Σ, and we will write $t :_\Gamma \tau'$ to say that message t has type τ' in signature Γ. Hence the following two rules:

$$\frac{}{(\Sigma, \alpha : \tau, \Sigma') \vdash \alpha :_\Sigma \tau} \qquad \frac{}{(\Gamma, \alpha : \tau, \Gamma') \vdash \alpha :_\Gamma \tau}$$

4.4 Type Rules for Message Constructors

We will now introduce type rules for all the message constructors presented in Sections 2.1 and 2.2 that use the new types introduced in Section 4.2 in order to further check the groundness of messages.

Concatenation. The concatenation of two messages of the same type will yield a message of that type.

$$\frac{\Gamma \vdash t_1 : \tau \quad \Gamma \vdash t_2 : \tau}{\Gamma \vdash t_1\, t_2 : \tau}$$

The concatenation of two messages of different types will yield a message of the least tractable type among the types of the original messages.

$$\frac{\Gamma \vdash t_1 : \mathsf{tract} \quad \Gamma \vdash t_2 : \mathsf{semitract}}{\Gamma \vdash t_1\, t_2 : \mathsf{semitract} \quad \Gamma \vdash t_2\, t_1 : \mathsf{semitract}}$$

$$\frac{\Gamma \vdash t_1 : \mathsf{tract} \quad \Gamma \vdash t_2 : \mathsf{intract}}{\Gamma \vdash t_1\, t_2 : \mathsf{intract} \quad \Gamma \vdash t_2\, t_1 : \mathsf{intract}}$$

$$\frac{\Gamma \vdash t_1 : \mathsf{semitract} \quad \Gamma \vdash t_2 : \mathsf{intract}}{\Gamma \vdash t_1\, t_2 : \mathsf{intract} \quad \Gamma \vdash t_2\, t_1 : \mathsf{intract}}$$

Note that in typed MSR concatenated messages can be taken apart.

Symmetric-key and asymmetric-key encryption. The tractability of the resulting ciphertext is defined to be the same as the tractability of the plaintext.

$$\frac{\Gamma \vdash t : \tau \quad \Sigma \vdash k : \mathsf{shK}\; A\; B}{\Gamma \vdash \{t\}_k : \tau} \qquad \frac{\Gamma \vdash t : \tau \quad \Sigma \vdash k : \mathsf{pubK}\; A}{\Gamma \vdash \{\!\{t\}\!\}_k : \tau}$$

The implication is that the ciphertext of a tractable or semitractable message can now be cryptanalyzed by an intruder and the original plaintext will instantly be made available. The aim is to enforce that only intractable messages are enciphered, so that known-plaintext attacks are not possible. One way to make a tractable or semitractable message into an intractable one is to concatenate it with a nonce (see rules for concatenation).

We believe that these type rules are fully in line with the black-box view on cryptography that the Dolev-Yao abstraction adopts. The type rules only enforce a safer use of cryptography; they do not poison the abstraction with low-level details.

Digital signature. Similar considerations apply to digital signatures.

$$\frac{\Gamma \vdash t : \tau \quad \Sigma \vdash k' : \mathsf{privK}\ k}{\Gamma \vdash [t]_{k'} : \tau}$$

Commitment. Commitments may be considered to be intractable because of the nonce (salt value) used in the calculation.

$$\frac{\Gamma \vdash t : \tau \quad \Sigma \vdash n_s : \mathsf{nonce}}{\Gamma \vdash \|t\|_{n_s} : \mathsf{intract}}$$

Blind signatures. Blind signatures may be considered to be intractable because of the nonce (blinding factor) used in the calculation.

$$\frac{\Gamma \vdash t : \tau \quad \Sigma \vdash k : \mathsf{pubK}\ A \quad \Sigma \vdash n_f : \mathsf{nonce}}{\Gamma \vdash \langle t \rangle^{k}_{n_f} : \mathsf{intract}}$$

Zero-knowledge proofs. The zero-knowledge proof itself can be considered to be intractable, as two nonces are used in its calculation (a salt value and a blinding factor). However, we require that the underlying message of a zero-knowledge proof is tractable in order to enforce anonymity, and thus protect privacy. Consider for example that, if e-coins were issued at any possible denomination, the bank would be able to identify the spender in most cases.

$$\frac{\Gamma \vdash t : \mathsf{tract} \quad \Sigma \vdash n_s : \mathsf{nonce} \quad \Sigma \vdash k : \mathsf{pubK}\ A \quad \Sigma \vdash n_f : \mathsf{nonce}}{\Gamma \vdash \mathcal{Z}(t, n_s, k, n_f) : \mathsf{intract}}$$

5. The Dolev-Yao Intruder

The Dolev-Yao abstraction [6] assumes that elementary data, such as keys or nonces, are atomic rather than strings of bits, and that the operations needed to assemble messages, such as concatenation or encryption, are pure constructors in an initial algebra. Typed MSR fits very well in this abstraction: elementary data are indeed atomic and messages are constructed solely by message constructors.

In this Section, we present a version of the Dolev-Yao intruder which is useful in discovering more types of attacks in esoteric (as well as other types of) protocols. The rules that formally describe the new capabilities of the intruder are represented in the same way as in [3], i.e. using the format shown in the following diagram:

$$\left(\boxed{\begin{array}{c}\text{Universal}\\\text{quantifiers}\end{array}} \boxed{\begin{array}{c}\text{Left-hand}\\\text{side}\end{array}} \rightarrow \boxed{\begin{array}{c}\text{Existential}\\\text{quantifiers}\end{array}} \boxed{\begin{array}{c}\text{Right-hand}\\\text{side}\end{array}} \right)^{\text{Owner}}$$

It has been proved [10] that there is no point in considering more than one Dolev-Yao intruder in any given system. Therefore, we can select a principal, I say, to represent the Dolev-Yao intruder. Furthermore, we associate I with an MSR memory predicate $\mathsf{M}_\mathsf{I}(\_)$, whose single argument can hold a message, to enable I to store data out of sight from other principals.

5.1 Standard Version of the Dolev-Yao Intruder

The standard version of the Dolev-Yao intruder can do any combination of the following operations:

- Intercept and learn messages
- Transmit known messages
- Decompose known (concatenated) messages
- Concatenate known messages
- Decipher encrypted messages if he knows the keys
- Encrypt known messages with known keys
- Sign messages with known keys
- Access public information
- *Generate fresh data*

The interested reader can refer to [3] for the formal specification of these operations in typed MSR.

5.2 Extended Version of the Dolev-Yao Intruder

The version of the intruder that is presented here is an extended version in two ways.

Firstly, one of the intruder's standard operations will be generalized in line with the new types introduced in Section 4.2. More specifically, we will replace the last operation, i.e. the intruder's ability to generate fresh data, with two new operations: the ability to generate fresh intractable data, and the ability to guess tractable and semitractable data. The intruder will be able either to guess the exact message required for his/her attack if this is possible, or to generate a fresh message of the required type otherwise.

Secondly, the intruder will now be able to handle messages constructed using the message constructors introduced in Section 2.2.

We will now formally specify the new operations in typed MSR.

Generate fresh intractable data. The intruder may generate fresh nonces, fresh private keys, fresh shared keys, as well as other intractable messages.

$$(\cdot \;\rightarrow\; \exists t :_{\Gamma} \mathsf{intract}.\;\; \mathsf{M}_\mathsf{I}\,(t))^{\mathsf{I}}$$

Guess tractable and semitractable data. The intruder may guess or get access to public keys, principals, as well as other tractable or semitractable messages.

$$(\forall t :_{\Gamma} \mathsf{tract}. \ \cdot \ \rightarrow \ \mathsf{M_I}\,(t))^{\mathsf{I}} \qquad (\forall t :_{\Gamma} \mathsf{semitract}. \ \cdot \ \rightarrow \ \mathsf{M_I}\,(t))^{\mathsf{I}}$$

Notice that this rule can be used together with the previous one to allow the intruder to generate a key-pair by first generating a fresh private key, and then by 'guessing' the corresponding public key. However, the intruder is not able to guess the private keys of other principals.

Blind messages. The intruder may blind a message given a public key and a blinding factor (nonce).

$$\left(\begin{array}{lcl} \forall t :_{\Sigma} \mathsf{msg}. & & \\ \forall A :_{\Sigma} \mathsf{principal}. & \begin{array}{l}\mathsf{M_I}\,(t) \\ \mathsf{M_I}\,(k) \\ \mathsf{M_I}\,(n)\end{array} & \rightarrow \ \mathsf{M_I}\left(\langle\, t \,\rangle_n^k\right) \\ \forall k :_{\Sigma} \mathsf{pubK}\ A. & & \\ \forall n :_{\Sigma} \mathsf{nonce}. & & \end{array}\right)^{\mathsf{I}}$$

Unblind messages. The intruder may unblind a (blinded) message given the blinding factor (nonce).

$$\left(\begin{array}{lcl} \forall t :_{\Sigma} \mathsf{msg}. & & \\ \forall A :_{\Sigma} \mathsf{principal}. & \begin{array}{l}\mathsf{M_I}\left(\langle\, t \,\rangle_n^k\right) \\ \mathsf{M_I}\,(n)\end{array} & \rightarrow \ \mathsf{M_I}\,(t) \\ \forall k :_{\Sigma} \mathsf{pubK}\ A. & & \\ \forall n :_{\Sigma} \mathsf{nonce}. & & \end{array}\right)^{\mathsf{I}}$$

Unblind signatures. The intruder may unblind a (blinded) signature given the blinding factor (nonce), if the public key used in the blinding corresponds to the private key used in the signing.

$$\left(\begin{array}{lcl} \forall t :_{\Sigma} \mathsf{msg}. & & \\ \forall A :_{\Sigma} \mathsf{principal}. & & \\ \forall k :_{\Sigma} \mathsf{pubK}\ A. & \begin{array}{l}\mathsf{M_I}\left([\,\langle\, t \,\rangle_n^k\,]_{k'}\right) \\ \mathsf{M_I}\,(n)\end{array} & \rightarrow \ \mathsf{M_I}\,([\,t\,]_{k'}) \\ \forall k' :_{\Sigma} \mathsf{privK}\ k. & & \\ \forall n :_{\Sigma} \mathsf{nonce}. & & \end{array}\right)^{\mathsf{I}}$$

Commit to a message. The intruder may commit to a message given a salt value (nonce).

$$\left(\begin{array}{lcl} \forall t :_{\Sigma} \mathsf{msg}. & \mathsf{M_I}\,(t) & \rightarrow \ \mathsf{M_I}(\|\,t\,\|_n) \\ \forall n :_{\Sigma} \mathsf{nonce}. & \mathsf{M_I}\,(n) & \end{array}\right)^{\mathsf{I}}$$

Generate a zero-knowledge proof. The intruder may generate a zero-knowledge proof given a message, a salt value (nonce), a public key and a blinding factor (nonce).

$$\begin{pmatrix} \forall t :_{\Sigma} \mathsf{msg}. & & \\ \forall n_s :_{\Sigma} \mathsf{nonce}. & \mathsf{M_I}\,(t) & \\ \forall A :_{\Sigma} \mathsf{principal}. & \mathsf{M_I}\,(n_s) & \rightarrow\ \mathsf{M_I}\,(\mathcal{Z}(t, n_s, k, n_f)) \\ \forall k :_{\Sigma} \mathsf{pubK}\ A. & \mathsf{M_I}\,(k) & \\ \forall n_f :_{\Sigma} \mathsf{nonce}. & \mathsf{M_I}\,(n_f) & \end{pmatrix}^{\mathsf{I}}$$

Observe a zero-knowledge proof. The intruder will get the same information as anyone else who observes the zero-knowledge proof (see Section 2.2).

$$\begin{pmatrix} \forall t :_{\Sigma} \mathsf{msg}. & & \\ \forall n_s :_{\Sigma} \mathsf{nonce}. & & \mathsf{M_I}\,(t) \\ \forall A :_{\Sigma} \mathsf{principal}. & \mathsf{M_I}\,(\mathcal{Z}(t, n_s, k, n_f)) \rightarrow & \mathsf{M_I}\left(\langle\, \|t\|_{n_s} \rangle_{n_f}^{k}\right) \\ \forall k :_{\Sigma} \mathsf{pubK}\ A. & & \\ \forall n_f :_{\Sigma} \mathsf{nonce}. & & \end{pmatrix}^{\mathsf{I}}$$

6. Summary and Conclusions

In this paper, we have presented an extension of typed MSR that makes it more suitable for the specification of esoteric protocols. The introduced non-interactive message constructors for blind signatures, commitments and zero-knowledge proofs make the standard language rich enough to specify protocols such as electronic cash, electronic voting and selective disclosure protocols. The introduced type rules make the standard language more capable of statically checking for desired properties in esoteric, as well as other types of protocols. More specifically, the introduced types can be used in the specification of protocols in order to statically check against attacks on privacy, brute-force dictionary attacks and known-plaintext attacks. Finally, the introduced version of the Dolev-Yao intruder creates a formal framework on which attacks on esoteric protocols may be attempted.

Further work will include the development of a stricter and richer type system and the formal specification of real-world esoteric protocols in the extended language.

References

[1] D. Aspinall and A. Compagnoni. Subtyping dependent types. In E. Clarke, editor, *Proceedings of the 11th Annual Symposium on Logic in Computer Science*, pages 86–97. IEEE Computer Society Press, July 1996.

[2] Theodoros Balopoulos and Stephanos Gritzalis. Towards a logic of privacy-preserving selective disclosure credential protocols. In J. Lopez and G. Pernul, editors, *Proceedings of the DEXA 2003 — TRUSTBUS'03 2nd International Workshop on Trust and Privacy in Digital Business*, pages 396–401, Prague, Czech Republic, September 2003. IEEE Computer Society Press.

[3] Iliano Cervesato. Typed Multiset Rewriting Specifications of Security Protocols. In A. Seda, editor, *First Irish Conference on the Mathematical Foundations of Computer Science and Information Technology — MFCSIT'00*, pages 1–43, Cork, Ireland, 19–21 July 2000. Elsevier ENTCS 40.

[4] Iliano Cervesato. Typed MSR: Syntax and Examples. In V.I. Gorodetski, V.A. Skormin, and L.J. Popyack, editors, *First International Workshop on Mathematical Methods, Models and Architectures for Computer Networks Security — MMM'01*, pages 159–177, St. Petersburg, Russia, 21–23 May 2001. Springer-Verlag LNCS 2052.

[5] David Chaum. Security without identification: transaction systems to make big brother obsolete. *Communications of the Association for Computing Machinery*, 28(10):1030–1044, October 1985.

[6] D. Dolev and A. C. Yao. On the security of public key protocols. *IEEE Transactions on Information Theory*, 2(29):198–208, 1983.

[7] Jason E. Holt and Kent E. Seamons. Selective disclosure credential sets. *Accessible as http://citeseer.nj.nec.com/541329.html*, 2002.

[8] Alfred J. Menezes, Paul C. van Oorschot, and Scott A. Vanstone. *Handbook of Applied Cryptography*. CRC Press, 1997.

[9] Bruce Schneier. *Applied Cryptography*. John Wiley & Sons, 1996.

[10] Paul Syverson, Catherine Meadows, and Iliano Cervesato. Dolev-Yao is no better than Machiavelli. In P. Degano, editor, *First Workshop on Issues in the Theory of Security — WITS'00*, pages 87–92, July 2000.

ROBUST VISUAL HASHING USING JPEG 2000

Roland Norcen and Andreas Uhl
Department of Scientific Computing, Salzburg University

Abstract Robust visual hash functions have been designed to ensure the data integrity of digital visual data. Such algorithms rely on an efficient scheme for robust visual feature extraction. We propose to use the wavelet-based JPEG2000 image compression algorithm for feature extraction. We discuss the sensitivity of our proposed method against different malicious data modifications including local image alterations and Stirmark attacks.

Keywords: Image authentication, robust feature extraction, JPEG 2000

1. Introduction

The widespread availability of digital image and video data has opened a wide range of possibilities to manipulate these data. Compression algorithms change image and video data usually without leaving perceptible traces. Beside, different image processing and image manipulation tools offer a variety of possibilities to alter image data without leaving traces which are recognizable to the human visual system.

In order to ensure the integrity and authenticity of digital visual data, algorithms have to be designed which consider the special properties of such data types. On the one hand, such an algorithm should be robust against compression and format conversion, since such operations are a very integral part of handling digital data. On the other hand, such an algorithm should be able to recognize a large amount of different intentional manipulations to such data.

Classical cryptographic tools to check for data integrity like the cryptographic hash functions MD5 or SHA-1 are designed to be strongly dependent on every single bit of the input data. This property is important for a big class of digital data (for instance compressed text, executables,...). Such classical hash functions are not suited for the class of typical multimedia data.

To account for these properties new techniques are required which do not assure the integrity of the digital representation of visual data but its visual appearance or content. In the area of multimedia security two types of approaches have been proposed so far: semi-fragile watermarking and robust multimedia hashes (Fridrich, 2000; Fridrich and Goljan, 2000; Kalker et al., 2001; Radhakrishnan et al., 2003; Skrepth and Uhl, 2003; Venkatesan et al., 2000).

Robust hash functions usually rely on a method for feature extraction to create a robust scheme for ensuring data integrity. Here, different algorithms have been proposed to extract a specific set of feature values from image or video data. The algorithms are designed to extract features which are sensitive to intentional alterations of the original data, but not sensitive to different standard compression algorithms like JPEG or JPEG2000.

The most efficient methods for feature extraction use transformation-based techniques. The DCT or the wavelet transform are two examples which can be employed in this case (Skrepth and Uhl, 2003).

In this work we discuss the possibilities how to use JPEG2000 for robust feature extraction. The basis for our method is a recently proposed algorithm (Norcen and Uhl, 2004) where an authentication scheme for JPEG2000 bitstreams is discussed, and its robustness regarding JPEG2000 and JPEG compression and recompression is shown. Here, we will show detailed results regarding the sensitivity towards local and global image alterations and we will discuss application scenarios how this approach can be used in real applications.

2. JPEG2000

The JPEG2000 (Taubman and Marcellin, 2002) image coding standard uses the wavelet transform as energy compaction method, and operates on independent, non-overlapping blocks whose bit-planes are coded in several passes to create an embedded, scalable bitstream.

The final JPEG2000 bitstream is organized as follows: the main header is followed by packets of data which are all preceded by a packet header. In each packet appear the codewords of the code-blocks that belong to the same image resolution (wavelet decomposition level) and layer (which roughly stand for successive quality levels). Depending on the arrangement of the packets, different progression orders may be specified (e.g., resolution and layer progression order).

2.1 Using the JPEG2000 bitstream for feature extraction

The JPEG2000 bitstream is analyzed for useful robust feature values. Therefore, the bitstream is scanned from the very beginning to the end, and the data of each data packet – as they appear in the bitstream, excluding any header structures – are collected sequentially to be then used as visual feature values.

Testing of the JPEG2000 coding options in Norcen and Uhl, 2004 showed the best set of coding parameters to be used for feature extraction: these options include the JPEG2000 standard parameter setting as well as coding in lossy mode in layer progression order, together with a varying wavelet-transform decomposition level.

3. Experiments: Sensitivity Results

We use classical 8bpp image data in our experiments, including the well known lena image at varying image dimensions (512×512, 1024×1024, and 2048×2048 pixels), the houses (see 2.a), the plane (see 1.a), the graves image (see 3.a), the goldhill image (see 1.c), and frame no. 17 from the surfside video sequence (see 4.a). In the following we present detailed results regarding the sensitivity towards different local image alterations and global Stirmark modifications:

- local: different intentional image modifications:

  plane: plane without call sign (see Figure 1.b)

  graves: one grave removed (see Figure 3.b)

  houses: text removed (see Figure 2.b)

  goldhill: walking man removed (see Figure 1.d)

  surfside frame: twisted head (see Figure 4.b)

- global: different Stirmark attacks (see `www.cl.cam.ac.uk/~mgk25/stirmark/`)

The experiments are conducted as follows: first, the feature values (i.e. packet data) are extracted from the JPEG 2000 codestream. Subsequently, the codestream is decoded and the image alteration is performed. Finally, the image is again JPEG 2000 encoded using the coding settings of the original codestream and the feature values are extracted and compared to the original ones.

The results which are presented in the following show the number of feature values (in bytes) required to detect a global or local image modification. A value of – for instance – 42 means that the first 41 bytes

(a) plane original (b) plane attacked – no call sign

(c) goldhill original (d) goldhill attacked – without walking man

Figure 1. Local attacks.

of feature values are equal when comparing the computed features from the modified image to the feature values of the corresponding original image. The value itself can be easily interpreted: the higher the value, the more robust is the proposed method against the tested attack. In general, we want to see high values against JPEG2000 and JPEG compression, but low values against all other tested attacks. Norcen and Uhl, 2004 showed that the feature extraction method is robust against moderate JPEG and JPEG2000 compression. In most cases, feature values of 50 or more were required for detecting JPEG and JPEG2000 compression ratios up to 1 or 0.8 bits per pixel. Here we want to detect all the described image alterations reliably. Therefore, we want to see significant lower feature values in all tests.

Table 1 lists the obtained results for the different local attacks with respect to a chosen wavelet decomposition level. The wavelet decom-

(a) houses original

(b) houses attacked – without text

Figure 2. Local attacks.

(a) graves original

(b) graves attacked – removed grave

Figure 3. Local attacks.

(a) surfside fr.17 original

(b) surfside fr.17 – twisted head

Figure 4. Local attacks.

Table 1. Local attacks: different wlev used for feature extraction.

	wlev9	wlev8	wlev7	wlev6	wlev5	wlev4	wlev3
goldhill without man	7	7	28	44	29	48	155
houses without text	6	5	3	4	17	60	187
graves attacked	2	4	11	10	28	23	84
plane, no callsign	3	5	34	37	73	27	74
surfside, twisted head	6	17	7	20	2	68	412

position level obviously influences the ability of our algorithm to detect local image modifications. At a higher wlev parameter all local image modifications are detected with a low number of feature values. At wlev 9 for instance, only 7 feature values are needed to detect any of the tested local attacks. The modification of the graves image is detected with 2 feature values, in the plane image case only about 3 values are needed. At lower decomposition levels, more feature values are needed in general to detect the tested local image manipulations. At a wlev of 3, 412 feature values are needed to recognize the twisted head in the surfside frame, at wlev 4, only 68 are needed, and at the highest tested wlev, only about 6 are needed. Since the local changes are kept relatively small, the sensitivity regarding local image manipulations can be considered as high (depending on the wavelet decomposition level) – which of course is desired.

The Stirmark benchmark is used to rate the robustness and efficiency of various watermarking methods. Therefore, numerous image attacks are defined including rotation, scaling, median filtering, luminance modifications, gaussian filtering, sharpening, symmetric and asymmetric shearing, linear geometric transformations, random geometric distortions, and others. More details about the different attacks can be downloaded from the web page `www.cl.cam.ac.uk/~mgk25/stirmark/`, where the Stirmark testsetting is discussed at length. Our robust feature extraction method is tested against the standard Stirmark attacks, and due to the field of application our proposed method should be sensitive regarding all Stirmark attacks. In Table 2 a selection of the obtained results against global modifications is listed. Here we see the sensitivity against Stirmark attacks with parameter i, b, as well as global luminance modifications.

Again the results are delivered with respect to a chosen wlev for feature extraction, and only the results for the lena image at a resolution of 512×512 pixels are given. We can observe a high sensitivity against the presented global image alterations, except for a minimum change of the global luminance by a factor of 1, which shows a worse result.

Table 2. Different attacks/lena512: different wlev used for feature extraction.

	wlev9	wlev8	wlev7	wlev6	wlev5	wlev4	wlev3
stirmark i=1	1	3	6	1	5	1	1
stirmark i=2	1	6	7	2	6	1	1
stirmark b=1	1	6	6	2	3	1	1
stirmark b=2	1	4	5	12	1	1	1
luminance+1	1	4	7	12	36	9	3
luminance+2	1	1	7	2	12	9	3
luminance+3	1	1	6	1	6	5	3

Nevertheless, the sensitivity is high enough – as desired. Interestingly, a lower wlev parameter also shows a higher sensitivity against the Stirmark attacks with parameter i and parameter b. This effect can also be seen in other Stirmark attacked images. For this reason, a lower wlev could be preferred to be used for the feature extraction algorithm, since a lower wlev is also more robust against JPEG2000 and JPEG compression. However, all the local attacks presented in Table 1 could not be detected any longer when using such a low wlev parameter.

In Table 3 and Table 4 the results for the standard Stirmark testsetting are listed. Again, only results for the lena image at a resolution of 512×512 pixels are given with respect to a specific wlev. The first column of both tables clearly identifies the applied Stirmark attack and should be self-contained. Overall we can see that the sensitivity against all tested attacks is very high for a low and a high wlev value. For a wlev of 5 and 6, only the Gaussian filtering shows slightly higher feature values of about 36 and 23. Also a minor rotation and scale is slightly harder detectable. Here we need about 31 and 18 (wlev 5,6) feature values (see Table 4 first data row). The results for the other testimages are similar and therefore not listed here. In general, the sensitivity regarding Gaussian filtering as well as slight rotations and scalings is slightly inferior as compared to the other Stirmark tests. Regarding the graves image, these two test attacks are detected at a lower number of feature values, since the graves image is more sensitive to any image modification than the other tested images.

There is the need for a compromise between the sensitivity against intentional image modifications on the one side, but robustness against JPEG2000 and JPEG compression on the other side. Regarding the robustness results in Norcen and Uhl, 2004, a wlev of about 6 or 5 seems to be best suited to be used for JPEG2000 bitstream feature extraction. In this case, we see a good sensitivity against local and global image attacks, and robustness against JPEG2000 and JPEG compression up to moderate compression ratios.

4. Application Scenarios

Using parts of the JPEG2000 bitstream as robust visual features has important advantages, especially in the context of real world usability:

- Soft- and hardware to perform JPEG2000 compression will be readily available in large quantities in the near future which makes our proposed scheme a very attractive one (and also potentially cheap one).
- JPEG2000 Part 2 allows to use different types of wavelet transforms in addition to the Part 1 pyramidal scheme, in particular anisotropic decompositions and wavelet subband structures may be employed in addition to freedom in filter choice. This facilitates to add key-dependency to the hashing scheme by concealing the exact type of wavelet decomposition in use, which would create a robust message authentication code (MAC) for visual data. This could significantly improve the security against attacks (compare Meixner and Uhl, 2004).
- Most robust feature extraction algorithms require a final conversion stage to transform the computed features into binary representation. This is not necessary since JPEG2000 is of course given in binary representation.

We get two scenarios where our method can be applied in a straightforward manner: first, our method can be applied to any raw digital image data, via computing the JPEG2000 bitstream and then the JPEG2000 feature values. Second, any JPEG2000 bitstream can be used itself as starting point. In this case, the considered bitstream is the original data which should be protected, and the features are extracted directly from the investigated JPEG2000 bitstream. This scenario is useful, where some image capturing device directly produces JPEG2000 coded data instead of raw uncompressed data (i.e. JPEG200 compression implemented in hardware, no raw data saved).

After having extracted the feature values out of the JPEG2000 bitstream, three strategies may be followed:

- The extracted features are fed into the decoder stage of error correcting codes or linear codes to reduce the number of hash bits and to increase robustness. This approach has the advantage that different hash strings can be compared by evaluating the Hamming distance which serves as a measure of similarity in this case.

Table 3. Standard stirmark testsetting, lena512: different wlev used for feature extraction.

	wlev9	wlev8	wlev7	wlev6	wlev5	wlev4	wlev3
17_row_5_col_removed	4	4	3	1	2	1	1
1_row_1_col_removed	5	6	26	7	12	5	7
1_row_5_col_removed	6	4	15	2	12	2	1
3x3_median_filter	3	1	3	7	1	4	13
5_row_17_col_removed	4	4	9	1	5	2	1
5_row_1_col_removed ·	4	4	7	7	5	5	1
5x5_median_filter	3	1	3	4	1	12	13
7x7_median_filter	3	1	3	4	3	4	8
9x9_median_filter	3	1	3	4	3	4	13
Gaussian_filtering_3_3	1	5	7	23	36	5	23
Sharpening_3_3	1	4	7	2	15	9	3
cropping_1	4	4	6	1	5	1	1
cropping_10	1	3	1	1	1	1	1
cropping_15	1	1	1	1	1	1	1
cropping_2	2	4	6	1	5	1	1
cropping_20	2	1	1	1	1	1	1
cropping_25	3	1	1	1	1	1	1
cropping_5	1	4	1	1	1	1	1
cropping_50	1	2	1	1	1	1	1
cropping_75	1	1	1	1	1	1	1
flip	1	1	1	1	1	1	1
linear_1.007_0.010_0.010_1.012	1	2	2	1	1	2	1
linear_1.010_0.013_0.009_1.011	1	2	2	1	1	2	1
linear_1.013_0.008_0.011_1.008	1	2	2	1	1	2	1
ratio_x_0.80_y_1.00	3	1	3	1	1	1	1
ratio_x_0.90_y_1.00	3	1	3	1	1	1	1
ratio_x_1.00_y_0.80	1	1	2	1	1	1	1
ratio_x_1.00_y_0.90	1	4	3	1	2	1	1
ratio_x_1.00_y_1.10	1	1	3	1	2	1	2
ratio_x_1.00_y_1.20	1	1	1	1	2	1	1
ratio_x_1.10_y_1.00	1	2	1	2	1	1	1
ratio_x_1.20_y_1.00	1	2	2	2	1	1	1
rotation_-0.25	4	4	6	2	6	1	1
rotation_-0.50	4	4	6	1	5	1	1
rotation_-0.75	4	4	6	1	4	1	1
rotation_-1.00	4	4	6	1	1	1	1
rotation_-2.00	2	4	4	1	1	1	1
rotation_0.25	4	4	12	2	12	1	1
rotation_0.50	4	4	6	2	12	1	1
rotation_0.75	4	4	6	2	12	1	1
rotation_1.00	2	4	6	2	6	1	1
rotation_10.00	2	3	1	1	1	1	1
rotation_15.00	2	1	1	1	1	1	1
rotation_2.00	2	3	6	1	6	1	1
rotation_30.00	1	1	1	1	1	1	1
rotation_45.00	1	1	1	1	1	1	1
rotation_5.00	2	3	1	1	1	1	1
rotation_90.00	1	1	1	1	1	1	1

Table 4. Standard stirmark testsetting, lena512: different wlev used for feature extraction.

	wlev9	wlev8	wlev7	wlev6	wlev5	wlev4	wlev3
rotation_scale_-0.25	4	4	6	18	31	4	11
rotation_scale_-0.50	4	4	6	16	6	4	5
rotation_scale_-0.75	4	4	6	1	6	4	1
rotation_scale_-1.00	4	4	6	1	1	1	1
rotation_scale_-2.00	1	4	4	1	1	2	2
rotation_scale_0.25	6	4	6	2	3	1	5
rotation_scale_0.50	6	4	6	2	3	1	1
rotation_scale_0.75	6	4	6	2	3	1	1
rotation_scale_1.00	3	4	6	2	3	1	1
rotation_scale_10.00	2	3	1	1	1	1	1
rotation_scale_15.00	2	3	1	1	1	1	1
rotation_scale_2.00	2	4	6	2	1	1	1
rotation_scale_30.00	1	1	1	1	1	1	1
rotation_scale_45.00	1	1	1	1	1	1	1
rotation_scale_5.00	2	3	1	1	1	1	1
rotation_scale_90.00	1	1	1	1	1	1	1
scale_0.50	4	1	1	1	1	1	1
scale_0.75	2	1	1	1	1	1	1
scale_0.90	2	4	3	1	1	1	1
scale_1.10	1	2	1	1	1	1	1
scale_1.50	1	1	1	1	1	1	1
scale_2.00	1	1	1	1	1	1	1
shearing_x_0.00_y_1.00	5	4	11	1	3	5	1
shearing_x_0.00_y_5.00	3	4	3	1	1	1	1
shearing_x_1.00_y_0.00	4	5	7	2	12	1	1
shearing_x_1.00_y_1.00	5	6	7	1	5	1	1
shearing_x_5.00_y_0.00	1	3	2	2	4	1	2
shearing_x_5.00_y_5.00	1	3	2	1	4	1	1

Whereas it is desirable from the point of view of the applications to estimate the amount of difference between images by using those hash functions, this property severely threatens security and facilitates "gradient attacks" by iteratively adjusting hostile attacks to minimize a change in the hash value.

- A classical cryptographic hash function (like MD5 or SHA-1) is applied to the feature data to result in an overall robust but cryptographically secure robust visual hash procedure. The possibility to measure the amount of difference between two hash strings is lost in this case, however, gradient attacks and other security flaws are avoided.

- The extracted feature values are used as hash strings as they are without any further processing. The obvious disadvantages in terms of the higher amount of hash bits and lower security against attacks is compensated by the possibility to localize and approximately reconstruct detected image alterations since the hash string contains data extracted from a low bitrate compressed version of the original image.

In the latter case, with the available feature value data (consisting of JPEG2000 packet body data), and the corresponding packet headers which need to be generated and inserted into the codestream, the original image can be reconstructed up to the point the codeblock data is available in the packet bodies. A packet header indicates, among other information, which codeblocks are included in the following packet body, whereas the body contains the codeblocks of compressed data itself. Without the packet header, a reconstruction of the corresponding packet body is not possible in general. Therefore, these packet headers need to be inserted.

In Figures 5 and 6 we visualize the approximations of the original images using feature value data of the lena and the graves image only. In each case, the first 512, 1024, and 2048 bits of feature values are used.

Since the given number of feature value bits which are used for the visual reconstruction include packet body data only, the overall number of bits used for reconstruction – including the needed packet header data – must be somewhat bigger. Table 5 shows the number of bits which are required for the corresponding images. The first column gives the number of feature bits used, and the entries in the table show the overall number of bits which are needed for the visual reconstruction. We see that a considerable number of "extra" bits are needed. These "extra bits" stem from the corresponding packet headers and are needed to reconstruct the image data up to the point where codeblock packet body data is given in the features.

Table 5. Signature bits (including packet header data).

	lena512	graves512	plane512
512 bits	552	552	552
1024 bits	1144	1136	1136
2048 bits	2224	2208	2224

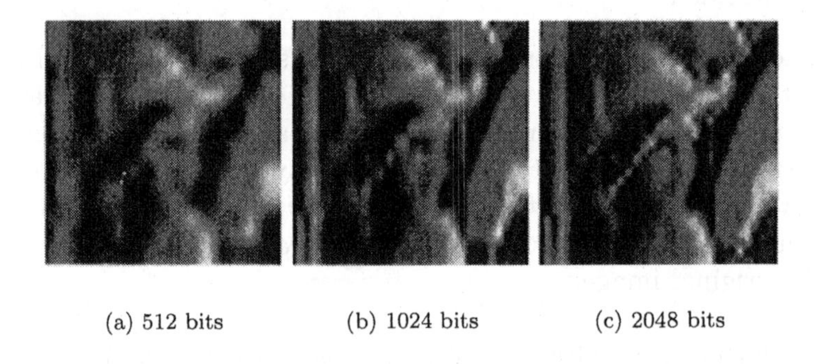

(a) 512 bits (b) 1024 bits (c) 2048 bits

Figure 5. Reconstruction of lena.

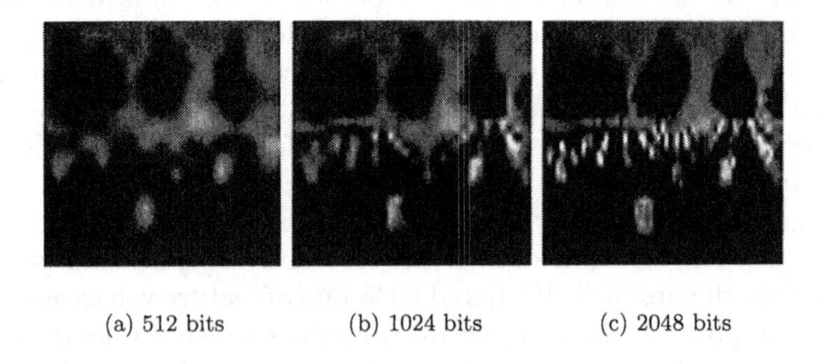

(a) 512 bits (b) 1024 bits (c) 2048 bits

Figure 6. Reconstruction of graves.

The number of feature bits used have been chosen in a way to demonstrate a possible application where the hash string could be signed using a digital signature algorithm like ElGamal or RSA. In this context, using a 512 feature bits signature already could help to localize and approximately reconstruct severely manipulated regions in the image, whereas a

2048 feature bits signature allows to gain information about some details as well.

5. Conclusion

The JPEG2000 algorithm can be employed to extract robust features from an image. The presented method has shown to be robust against moderate JPEG2000 and JPEG compression. In this work we showed that the method is also very sensitive regarding global and local image alterations including Stirmark attacks and different intentional local image modifications. Application scenarios for our approach are discussed and show this method to be of interest for practical employment.

References

Fridrich, Jiri (2000). Visual hash for oblivious watermarking. In Wong, Ping Wah and Delp, Edward J., editors, *Proceedings of IS&T/SPIE's 12th Annual Symposium, Electronic Imaging 2000: Security and Watermarking of Multimedia Content II*, volume 3971, San Jose, CA, USA.

Fridrich, Jiri and Goljan, Miroslav (2000). Robust hash functions for digital watermarking. In *Proceedings of the IEEE International Conference on Information Technology: Coding and Computing*, Las Vegas, NV, USA.

Kalker, T., Oostveen, J. T., and Haitsma, J. (2001). Visual hashing of digital video: applications and techniques. In Tescher, A.G., editor, *Applications of Digital Image Processing XXIV*, volume 4472 of *Proceedings of SPIE*, San Diego, CA, USA.

Meixner, Albert and Uhl, Andreas (2004). Analysis of a wavelet-based robust hash algorithm. In Delp, Edward J. and Wong, Ping W., editors, *Security, Steganography, and Watermarking of Multimedia Contents VI*, volume 5306 of *Proceedings of SPIE*, San Jose, CA, USA. SPIE. To appear.

Norcen, R. and Uhl, A. (2004). Robust authentication of the JPEG2000 bitstream. In *CD-ROM Proceedings of the 6th IEEE Nordic Signal Processing Symposium (NORSIG 2004)*, Espoo, Finland. IEEE Norway Section.

Radhakrishnan, R., Xiong, Z., and Memom, N. D. (2003). Security of visual hash functions. In Wong, Ping Wah and Delp, Edward J., editors, *Proceedings of SPIE, Electronic Imaging, Security and Watermarking of Multimedia Contents V*, volume 5020, Santa Clara, CA, USA. SPIE.

Skrepth, Champskud J. and Uhl, Andreas (2003). Robust hash-functions for visual data: An experimental comparison. In Perales, F. J. et al., editors, *Pattern Recognition and Image Analysis, Proceedings of IbPRIA 2003, the First Iberian Conference on Pattern Recognition and Image Analysis*, volume 2652 of *Lecture Notes on Computer Science*, pages 986–993, Puerto de Andratx, Mallorca, Spain. Springer Verlag, Berlin, Germany.

Taubman, D. and Marcellin, M.W. (2002). *JPEG2000 — Image Compression Fundamentals, Standards and Practice.* Kluwer Academic Publishers.

Venkatesan, Ramarathnam, Koon, S.-M., Jakubowski, Mariusz H., and Moulin, Pierre (2000). Robust image hashing. Vancouver, Canada.

A SYSTEM FOR END-TO-END AUTHENTICATION OF ADAPTIVE MULTIMEDIA CONTENT

Takashi Suzuki,[1] Zulfikar Ramzan,[2] Hiroshi Fujimoto,[1] Craig Gentry,[2] Takehiro Nakayama,[1] and Ravi Jain[2]

[1]*NTT DoCoMo Media Computing Group*
lastname@mml.yrp.nttdocomo.co.jp

[2]*DoCoMo Communications Laboratories, USA*
lastname@docomolabs-usa.com

Abstract We present a multimedia content delivery system that preserves the end-to-end authenticity of original content while allowing content adaptation by intermediaries. Our system utilizes a novel multi-hop signature scheme using Merkle trees that permits selective element removal and insertion. To permit secure element insertion we introduce the notion of a placeholder. We propose a computationally efficient scheme to instantiate placeholders based on the hash-sign-switch paradigm using trapdoor hash functions. We developed a system prototype in which the proposed signature scheme is implemented as an extension of the W3C XML signature standard and is applied to content meta-data written in XML. Evaluation results show that the proposed scheme improves scalability and response time of protected adaptive content delivery systems by reducing computational overhead for intermediaries to commit to the inserted element by 95% compared to schemes that use conventional digital signatures.

Keywords: Digital signatures, content adaptation, multimedia security

1. Introduction

The popularity of mobile internet services, such as NTT DoCoMo's i-mode [1], has dramatically increased the amount of content delivered to mobile devices. The recent proliferation of third-generation (3G) mobile networks has not only accelerated the increase but also made richer (i.e., bandwidth and CPU intensive) multimedia content available to mobile devices. Due to various service contexts or user preferences that mobile devices can signal to service providers, coupled with the usual mobile device constraints (e.g., viewing time, battery life, and display), content adaptation is expected to play an important role in multimedia content delivery for mobile environments [2]. While such adaptation is useful, there is a cost. In particular, existing systems cannot handle dynamic data adaptation while preserving end-to-end security. The IETF

OPES working group pointed out security issues related to services deployed at application-level network intermediaries [7]. The present paper addresses integrity among the issues. Consider digital signatures - once data is signed, subsequent modifications to it invalidate the signature. *Our goal is to concurrently achieve multimedia content adaptation and end-to-end authenticity.*

We assume a multimedia streaming system where meta-data specifying how media components are handled is provided prior to actual content delivery. Adaptation for such a system can be performed at the meta-data level and the media-data level. For media-data adaption, one may apply transcoding techniques such as multi-rate switching or scalable compression. For meta-data adaptation, one may manipulate the composition of audio and video components in the scene according to user preferences or service contexts.

Several works provide related but different features for adaptive content protection. Teranishi et al. propose an information sharing system with management of content derivation [10]. The primary content provider in their system (called the tier-1 provider here) manages content adaptation by binding usage rules to the meta-data. Their system does not, however, protect content from malicious corruption; instead, they assume that all modifications are performed on trusted hosts. *We, on the other hand, lift this assumption by employing, at our cryptographic core, a novel multi-hop message signature scheme that enables end-to-end authenticity of the usage rule and meta-data.*

Our new signature scheme incorporates techniques from [22, 12] which permit selective adaptive content removal. Merkle trees are used to create a message digest, and deletions involve creating a small cover for the subset of removed data items. Our contribution is to enable secure insertion of secondary content by extending the Merkle hash tree based signature scheme to support placeholders where the tier-2 provider can add its content. We propose a computationally efficient scheme to accommodate the placeholder based on the hash-sign-switch paradigm utilizing trapdoor hash functions [18].

In this paper we focus on the meta-data level signature scheme, although media-data level signatures for streaming media has additional challenges such as delay and scalability – see [4] for a discussion of such issues.

The paper is organized as follows. Section 2 discusses related work. Section 3 explains the proposed system architecture. Section 4 describes the multi-hop signature at our cryptographic core. Section 5 details the system prototype we built and gives performance results. Section 6 makes concluding remarks.

2. Background and Related Work

Many content protection systems [5, 21] take an approach where a content author packages multimedia content with meta-data that contains usage rights information regarding how the content should be used. However, these existing systems presume content delivery with end-to-end consistency and thwart malicious entities who wish to tamper with content or meta-data; thus they do not permit tier-2 providers to perform adaptation.

The OPES (open pluggable edge services) working group [8] investigates security threats and risks for services deployed at application-level intermediaries, which are relevant to our adaptive content delivery system. In our signature scheme, we introduce placeholders in the Merkle hash tree to support dynamic content insertion by tier-2 providers. Placeholders can be viewed as indicators for OPES callout servers to identify the place for their content. Amongst security threats, this paper addresses policy enforcement at intermediaries that are innately un-trusted by original content providers, and end-to-end authentication of content. Other threats, such as denial of service attacks, end-to-end encryption, are out of the scope of this paper.

To allow adaptation by intermediaries, an information sharing system that enables tier-1 content providers to manage derivative works is proposed in [10]. They define a language for providers to write content usage rules that express the restrictions imposed on derivative works. Modifications are checked against the rules to detect malicious behavior. Their system does not, however, protect content and usage rules from malicious corruption; instead, they assume all modifications are performed on *trusted* hosts, and the content and usage rules never leave a trusted domain. Although one may argue the assumption can be lifted using a conventional signature scheme, the solution assumes that the tier-1 provider trusts tier-2 providers to sign content and usage rules on its behalf. Another solution is that the tier-1 provider sends a signed content with callout indicators that locate content to be inserted. This requires tier-2 providers to register content pointers which they cannot change after the original content is signed.

We alleviate these assumptions by using a novel multi-hop message signature scheme that enables end-to-end authenticity even with content-adapting tier-2 providers. Such trust alleviation enables various service scenarios where tier-2 providers are not trusted entities. For example, it enables personal users to legitimately use commercial music clips to create personal video clips, and distribute them subject to usage policies of original content.

3. Proposed System Architecture

Figure 1 illustrates the basic architecture of our adaptive multimedia content delivery system. It supports both meta-data and media-data content adaptation. The tier-1 provider (T_1) creates media files which constitute multimedia content and generates meta-data containing information on how to access the media files and how to compose them. Meta-data is delivered to user devices through tier-2 providers (T_2). The actual media files are stored in media servers

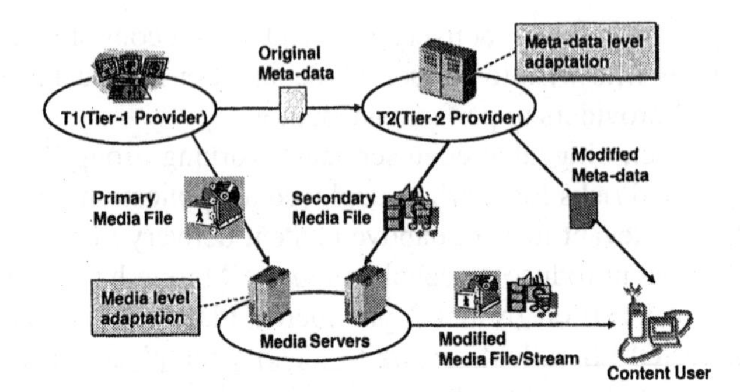

Figure 1. Basic architecture of adaptive content delivery system which supports two-level adaptation: meta-data level and media-data level.

and are delivered to user devices by downloading or streaming. These media servers may be operated by T_1, T_2, or other third-party providers. T_2 may perform adaption on meta-data elements. Each element represents an actual media file; T_2 inserts/deletes a media file to/from a composition by manipulating meta-data without touching the internal content of the files. Examples of such adaptation are dynamic insertion of (targeted) advertisements or removing elements to create a digest.

We assume weak trust between T_1 and T_2. T_2 acquires from T_1 the right to create and re-distribute content derived from the primary content, subject to usage rules specified by T_1. We envision that their relationship is as loose as that between an e-commerce site and consumers. T_1 may have no reason to trust T_2, and presumes it might try to perform illegal modifications on the content and usage rules. Further, T_2 does not trust other tier-2 providers or end-users, and assumes they may try to "remove" T_2's adaptation (e.g., delete its advertisements). We do, however, assume that a trusted end-user media player; e.g., it uses attestation to a trusted platform or a tamper-resistance mechanism (with the usual caveat that such measures can often be circumvented by highly determined adversaries). If the media player detects usage rule violations it takes the appropriate action; e.g., prohibits the client from downloading necessary media files. To realize secure adaptive content delivery under these assumptions, we need a signature scheme with the following properties:

1 T_2 can delete or insert elements from/to meta-data subject to the usage rule specified by T_1. Rule violation must be detected by the verifier.

2 T_2 can insert additional elements only at positions specified by T_1. The verifier can detect insertions to an un-designated position.

3 Once T_2 commits to the element it inserts, the element cannot be altered or deleted without detection by verifiers. (As in any signature scheme, what happens after malicious behavior is detected is orthogonal.)

The "commitment" above does not bind T_2 to a particular element; instead it forms a secure placeholder into which content can be dynamically inserted.

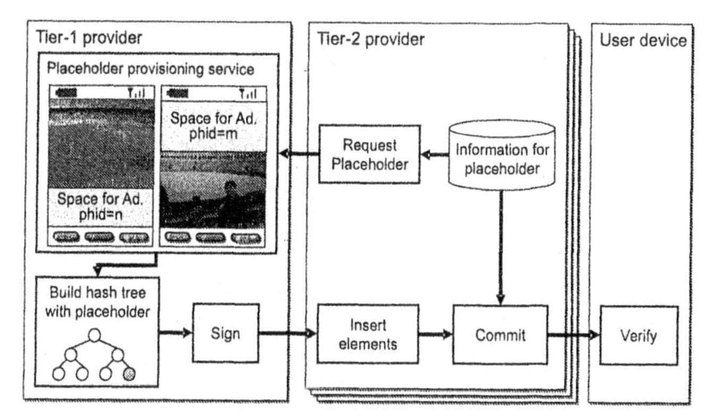

Figure 2. Placeholder request procedure between tier-1 & tier-2 providers; the tier-2 provider sends a request with placeholder information to purchase space.

The next section describes a scheme that achieves these properties. The scheme uses Merkle trees and achieves the first property by binding a hash of the usage rules to the Merkle root prior to signing. The verifier checks both rule compliancy of the modification and signature validation. To realize irreversible inserts, the scheme introduces an extension, called a placeholder, which specifies a position in the meta-data into which a designated entity can insert an additional meta-data element. The placeholder contains information that uniquely identifies the entity who will insert data. After the placeholder is set to the meta-data, T_1 constructs its hash tree and signs the root. Before it signs the meta-data, T_1 must obtain T_2's information for inclusion in the placeholder. This can happen via a directory service or by using a placeholder request procedure between T_1 and T_2. We adopt the second approach, imagining a scenario where T_2 purchases advertisement space by sending a placeholder request message (see Figure 2). Upon receipt of the signed meta-data, T_2 securely inserts an element (e.g., advertisement) to the assigned placeholder.

Although our focus is meta-data adaptation and protection, our system can incorporate the authenticated media-level adaption techniques proposed by Gentry et al. [4] which permit transcoding of the media content itself while preserving end-to-end authenticity.

4. Proposed Signature Scheme

We propose signature schemes that allow one or more T_2s to modify original content by dynamically deleting or inserting elements (subject to T_1's policy), while preserving a receiver's signature verification ability. We first describe Merkle trees and how they permit dynamic deletion. We then introduce placeholders, which allow for dynamic insertion; our main scheme instantiates placeholders using trapdoor hash functions at select Merkle tree leaves. Finally, we discuss two mechanisms that make content insertion irreversible.

Model and Notation. Let $\mathcal{S}$ denote the sender or T_1 who creates and signs the original data and let $\mathcal{R}$ denote the receiver who verifies the signature. The data may pass through a proxy $\mathcal{P}$ such as T_2. Our schemes extend to multiple proxies, but for simplicity, we only consider the case of one $\mathcal{P}$. $\mathcal{P}$ may insert content or remove portions of the data. It further determines what information, if any, $\mathcal{R}$ requires to verify the signature. We implicitly assume $\mathcal{S} \neq \mathcal{P}$, but our schemes work when they are the same. We assume the existence of an open or closed public-key infrastructure where $\mathcal{S}$ has key pair $(\mathsf{Pk}, \mathsf{Sk})$. Here Sk is $\mathcal{S}$'s private key for computing a traditional signature on a message, and Pk is the public verification key. $\mathsf{Sign}(\mathsf{Sk}, M)$ denotes an algorithm that outputs a signature σ on message M under signing key Sk and $\mathsf{Vf}(\mathsf{Pk}, M, \sigma)$ denotes the verification algorithm. $\mathcal{P}$ need not know Pk or Sk. Our schemes may also work with a message authentication code or MAC, in which case both $\mathcal{S}$ and $\mathcal{R}$ share knowledge of a symmetric key (which $\mathcal{P}$ need not know).

Let $\{0,1\}^*$ denote the set of all bit strings. Let M denote the initial content that can be broken up into n blocks which may have different lengths: $M = M_1 M_2 \cdots M_n$, $M_i \in \{0,1\}^*$, $1 \leq i \leq n$. Where convenient, we assume n is a power of 2. In our scheme, the intermediary may choose to either keep or remove an *entire* block, but he cannot perform transformations involving a portion of a block. Let $\mathcal{H}$ denote a *cryptographic hash function* that takes as input a string in $\{0,1\}^*$ and a (fixed and publicly known) v-bit initialization vector (IV), and produces a v-bit output. We assume these cryptographic hash functions are *collision resistant*; i.e., finding two inputs $m_1 \neq m_2$ such that $\mathcal{H}(\mathsf{IV}, m_1) = \mathcal{H}(\mathsf{IV}, m_2)$ is difficult. A practical example of such a cryptographic hash function is SHA-1 [15] which has a 20-byte output and IV.

Merkle Trees, Signing, and Deletion. The Merkle tree associated with M is a balanced binary tree in which each node v is assigned a value $\mathcal{V}(v)$ – we often refer to v and $\mathcal{V}(v)$ interchangeably. There are n leaves, and for each leaf ℓ_i, $\mathcal{V}(\ell_i) = \mathcal{H}(\mathsf{IV}, M_i)$, $1 \leq i \leq n$. For an interior vertex v, $\mathcal{V}(v) = \mathcal{H}(\mathsf{IV}, \mathcal{V}(\mathsf{C}_0(v)) \circ \mathcal{V}(\mathsf{C}_1(v)))$, where $\mathsf{C}_0(v)$ and $\mathsf{C}_1(v)$ are v's left and right children respectively, and $\circ$ denotes concatenation. To sign M, the content creator computes the root value r of the Merkle tree associated with M. The signature is $\sigma = \mathsf{Sign}(\mathsf{Sk}, r)$. Deletion is supported by supplying a modicum of extra verification data so that the verifier can still compute the root of the Merkle tree, as we now describe. First, let M' denote the transformed data after the removal of blocks. The intermediary does the following:

1 Let $S = \{(\ell \mid \ell$ is a leaf of a block to dropped.$\}$
2 If there exist $u, v \in S$ such that u, v are siblings in the tree, then set $S = S - \{u, v\} \cup \{w\}$, where w is the parent of u, v. Repeat this until S has no siblings. Suppose that at the end $S = \{w_i \mid 1 \leq i \leq \rho\}$.
3 Let $\mu_i = \mathcal{V}(w_i)$ for $1 \leq i \leq \rho$. $\mathcal{P}$ transmits M', σ, μ_i, and the tree node position for each w_i, $1 \leq i \leq \rho$.

Verification. $\mathcal{R}$ verifies the signature as follows:

1 For each received message block M_{i_k}, compute $y_k = \mathcal{H}(\mathsf{IV}, M_{i_k})$.

2 Consider the set of all hash values computed in the previous step as well the hash values $\mu_1, \ldots, \mu_\rho$. If any pair correspond to siblings, replace the pair with their hash (which corresponds to their Merkle tree parent). Repeat this step until only one value remains – call it r'.

3 Run $\mathsf{Vf}(\mathsf{Pk}, r', \sigma)$.

We show that $r' = r$, from which it is easy to see why the above algorithm works. If one has all the initial blocks, then the above procedure is the standard algorithm for computing the Merkle tree root. Now, observe that whenever $\mathcal{R}$ receives some hashes $\mu_1, \ldots, \mu_\rho$, these come from $\mathcal{P}$ running the *same algorithm* on the subset of missing frames. Therefore, $\mathcal{P}$ and $\mathcal{R}$ have together run the algorithm on all n blocks which yields the Merkle root value.

Insertion via Placeholders. We propose the CS and HSS schemes for realizing placeholders. The former uses conventional public-key signatures (e.g., RSA) and the latter uses the hash-sign-switch [13] technique. The CS scheme is fairly trivial. $\mathcal{S}$ places $\mathcal{P}$'s public key (or instructions on where to retrieve it) in the placeholder block. $\mathcal{S}$ then creates a Merkle-tree digest and signs as described above. $\mathcal{P}$, in turn, attaches its content and signs it separately. $\mathcal{R}$ checks the validity of both signatures. This approach is less efficient than the HSS scheme which we now proceed to describe.

HSS Scheme. Trapdoor hash functions $H_Y(m, r)$ consist of a public key Y and a trapdoor X; they take two arguments and have following properties:

- If X is unknown, there is no efficient algorithm that finds pairs (m_1, r_1) and (m_2, r_2) such that $H_Y(m_1, r_1) = H_Y(m_2, r_2)$, but $m_1 \neq m_2$, except with negligible probability.
- If X is known, there is an efficient algorithm that given m_1, m_2, r_1 with $m_1 \neq m_2$, finds r_2 such that $H_Y(m_1, r_1) = H_Y(m_2, r_2)$.

One can construct such trapdoor hash functions based on the discrete logarithm assumption (DLA) as follows (see [18] for details). Let p, q be primes such that $q|p-1$, and let g be an element of order q in $\mathbb{Z}_p^*$ – parameters are global. The trapdoor is a value x chosen (randomly) from $\mathbb{Z}_q^*$. The public key is $y = g^x \bmod p$. Now, we define $H_y(m, r) = g^m y^r$, which can be computed by anyone. However, for any given $m_1, m_2, r_1 \in \mathbb{Z}_q$, knowledge of the trapdoor is required to efficiently compute an $r_2 \in \mathbb{Z}$ such that $H_y(m_1, r_1) = H_y(m_2, r_2)$ by setting $r_2 = (m_1 - m_2)x^{-1} + r_1$. To create a placeholder, $\mathcal{P}$ sets up a trapdoor hash function and hashes random values, m', r': $TH = H_Y(m', r')$. It sends TH and Y to $\mathcal{S}$. $\mathcal{S}$ treats the received parameters as a message block, and signs everything using the above hash tree technique. To insert content m, $\mathcal{P}$ uses x to compute r such that $H_Y(m, r) = TH$. These values together with the original signature are sent to $\mathcal{R}$. In turn, $\mathcal{R}$ verifies the original signature using TH as a placeholder, and then determines placeholder validity by checking if $H_Y(m, r) = TH$.

Comparison. HSS is more efficient than CS for $\mathcal{P}$. Assuming the DLA implementation, HSS requires one modular multiplication. CS using 1024-bit RSA keys requires a full-length exponentiation, which involves about 1500 modular multiplications on average. Also, in HSS, $\mathcal{P}$ need not rebuild the hash tree after adding data, but merely attaches the commitment value r to the original signature. $\mathcal{R}$ need only rebuild the hash tree to verify the original signature and hash. In CS, however, $\mathcal{P}$ must re-build the hash tree since malicious entities can replace the added data with any data previously signed by $\mathcal{P}$. $\mathcal{R}$ must rebuild two hash trees from the meta-data with and without the added data. A drawback of the DLA based HSS is that placeholders can only be used once, otherwise x leaks by solving simultaneous equations. A simple modification enables us to use placeholders k times. We generate k public keys $\{y_i = g^{x_i}(\text{mod} p) : 1 \leq i \leq k\}$ and compute hash value $TH = g^{m'} y_1^{r'}(\text{mod} p)$. To use the ith message m_i, $\mathcal{P}$ computes $r_i = (m' + r'x_1 - m_i)x_i^{-1} \bmod q$. $\mathcal{R}$ checks that $g^{m_i} y_i^{r_i} = TH$. The CS placeholder has unlimited reuse.

Preventing Removal. We should also prevent malicious deletion of T_2's inserted content by those who, say, do not want to see advertisements. There are two approaches – each of which is compatible with both HSS and CS. In the first approach, $\mathcal{P}$ signs each of its placeholders regardless of whether it wishes to insert content into the corresponding slot. Then, any placeholder without a corresponding signature constitutes evidence that $\mathcal{P}$'s content was illegitimately deleted. Since only $\mathcal{P}$ can produce signatures corresponding to its own public key (which is embedded in the Merkle tree generated by $\mathcal{S}$), no other parties can remove or modify $\mathcal{P}$'s inserted content without detection.

The second approach, which we have not yet implemented, uses aggregate signatures [19], which is a single signature that convinces any verifier that signer S_i signed message M_i, $1 \leq i \leq n$, for distinct signers and messages. One advantage of aggregate signatures is compactness; ideally, the size of the aggregate signature does not grow at all as n increases. Here, we use a different property of certain aggregate signatures: when two entities (e.g., T_1 and T_2) aggregate their respective signatures, it is impossible for a third party (e.g., a second tier-2 provider or a receiver) to separate or "disaggregate" the signatures. Using this property, T_2 can ensure that its insertion cannot be removed without detection by aggregating its signature on its insertion with T_1's signature on its content. Then, any deletion of T_2's content will be detected by a receiver that attempts to verify the authenticity of T_1's content.

As an example, we consider the BGLS aggregate signature scheme [19], which uses a function $e : \mathbb{G}_1 \times \mathbb{G}_1 \rightarrow \mathbb{G}_2$ called a "pairing", that maps two elements of an elliptic curve group (or abelian varieties group) $\mathbb{G}_1$ to a second group $\mathbb{G}_2$. (See [19] for details.) We assume that all users of the aggregate signature scheme share certain parameters, such as a point P of order q on the elliptic curve, a hash function $H : \{0,1\}^* \rightarrow \mathbb{G}_1$, and a public key s_1P. Similarly, T_2 has key pair (s_2, s_2P). Let M_1 denote T_1's content (including, of course, the placeholder for T_2), and let M_2 denote T_2's content. T_1 computes its signature on M_1 as $s_1P_{M_1}$, where $P_{M_1} = H(s_1P, M_1)$; the tier-2 provider similarly computes its signature on M_2 as $s_2P_{M_2}$, where $P_{M_2} = H(s_2P, M_2)$. The aggregate signature is $S_{agg} = s_1P_{M_1} + s_2P_{M_2}$, and it is verified by confirming that $e(S_{agg}, P) = e(P_{M_1}, s_1P)e(P_{M_2}, s_2P)$. It is impossible (even information theoretically) to recover $s_1P_{M_1}$ or $s_2P_{M_2}$ from S_{agg}.

To prevent the removal of T_2's inserted content, T_1's original signature (i.e., $s_1P_{M_1}$) must be sent to T_2 over a secure channel; otherwise, anyone can replace the aggregate signature with T_1's non-aggregated signature. When combining this scheme with HSS, T_1 generates random values for m' and r', and computes $TH = H_Y(m', r')$ as usual. It then generates and stores the tentative signature s_2P_{TH}, where $P_{TH} = H(s_2P, TH)$. To sign M_2, T_1 transmits the r corresponding to M_2 and aggregates s_2P_{TH} with T_2's signature. If T_2 does not wish to insert content at a placeholder, it need not sign.

Under this approach $\mathcal{P}$'s signature is shorter. The user's verification time is proportional to the number of used placeholders as opposed to the total number allocated. However, verification time may be greater since computing a pairing takes, as a rule-of-thumb, about the same time as five full-length 1024-bit modular exponentiations.

Security Analysis. Our formal security analysis requires three standard assumptions: the scheme used to sign the Merkle root resists existential forgeries under adaptive chosen message attack in the sense of [20]; $\mathcal{H}$ is collision-resistant; and the trapdoor hash function is collision resistant (if the trapdoor is unknown). The last assumption can, in turn, be based on the discrete logarithm assumption. We can theoretically base $\mathcal{H}$ on this assumption as well, though in practice we use SHA-1. The underlying reductions are tight in a concrete security sense. The proof is straightforward and combines techniques from [22] (to address secure removal) and [13] (to address secure insertion).

5. Implementation and Evaluation Results

We built a prototype of our adaptive content delivery system with the proposed signature schemes in Java. We used SMIL [11] for meta-data specifying the composition of media files, and XACML [16] to write usage policies restricting adaptation to the original SMIL file. We adopted XML digital signatures as a basis of our signature scheme for meta-data, and implemented an extension to support Merkle hash trees with placeholders.

Signatures. Figure 3 shows a (simplified) example SMIL document before and after signing. The document includes a placeholder for video with an identifier (`phid`) of 1. The Signature element is written in XML-DSIG with two extensions: a new hash algorithm identifier, `HashTreeConstruction` (for the Merkle tree) and a new element, `TrapdoorHashMethod` (for trapdoor hash function parameters). The policy element specifies allow/deny rules of add and delete operations for each element under the SMIL element. The add operation rule specifies the placeholder identifier and attributes with which the inserted data must comply. The Policy element is bound with the SMIL elements by including its hash value in the Signature element. T_2 sends a SOAP placeholder request message containing the identifer and parameters associated with the placeholder. T_1 copies the parameters from the message to the `PublicValue` element and the `TrapdoorHashValue` before calculating the signature.

```
<?xml version="1.0"?>
<smil>
  <head/>
  <body>
    <seq>
      <par>
        <video src="rtsp://tyer-1/video1.rm"/>
        <video src="rtsp://tyer-1/music1.rm"/>
      </par>
      <par>
        <video phid="1"/>
      </par>
    </seq>
  </body>
</smil>
```

(a) Before signed

```
<?xml version="1.0"?>
<DocumentRoot>
  <Policy/>
  <smil/>
  <Signature>
    <SignedInfo>
      <CanonicalizationMethod/>
      <SignatureMethod/>
      <Reference URI=/DocumentRoot/Policy />
      <Reference URI=/DocumentRoot/smil/head />
      <Reference URI=/DocumentRoot/smil/body>
        <DigestMethod Algorithm="HashTreeConstruction"/>
        <DigestValue> root_node_of_hash_tree </DigestValue>
      </Reference>
      <TrapdoorHashMethod Algorithm="Discrete Log" phid="1">
        <PublicValue> public_values_of_trapdoor_hash </PublicValue>
        <TrapdoorHashValue> trapdoor_hash_value
                  </TrapdoorHashValue>
      </TrapdoorHashMethod>
    </SignedInfo>
    <SignatureValue> Signature </SignatureValue>
  </Signature>
</DocumentRoot>
```

(b) After signed (***Bold: extended part***)

```
<smil>
  <head/>
  <body> <seq>
    <par>
      <video src="rtsp://tyer-1/video1.rm"/>
      <video adaptation="delete"/>
    </par>
    <par> <video phid="1" src="rtsp://tyer-2/xxx.rm" adaptation="add"/>
    </par>
  </seq> </body>
</smil>
```

(c) After transformed

```
<Signature>
  <SignedInfo>
    <CanonicalizationMethod/>
    <SignatureMethod/>
    <Reference URI=/DocumentRoot/Policy />
    <Reference URI=/DocumentRoot/smil/head />
    <Reference URI=/DocumentRoot/smil/body />
    <TrapdoorHashMethod Algorithm=
                     "Discrete Log" phid="1"/>
  </SignedInfo>
  <SignatureValue/>
  <AdditiveSignature phid="1">
    <CommitmentValue>
      Commitment_Value_of_TrapdoorHash
    </CommitmentValue>
  </AdditiveSignature>
</Signature>
```

(d) After commitment

Figure 3. SMIL documents (a) before, (b) after signing, (c) after transformation, and (d) after committment.

Adaptation. T_2 modifies the signed SMIL document subject to the Policy element restrictions. The transformed meta-data is checked against the Policy Element restrictions. If the result is "allow", the added element's commitment value is calculated and set to the element `ArgValue` under the element `AdditiveSignature` element. Otherwise, we interrupt the process.

Verification. The user device verification module is implemented as an HTTP proxy which evaluates a signed document and outputs a SMIL document that can be handled by existing SMIL players such as RealOne [6]. There are three steps in the verification process: signature validation, policy compliance check (identical to what is in the adaptation module), and transformation. The signature validation step reconstructs the hash tree from the leaves to the root. If an element contains an adaptation attribute of "add", it fetches the hash value from the corresponding `TrapdoorHashMethod` element with the same `phid`. After hash tree reconstruction, the value in the `SignatureValue` element is validated. Commitment value for the added element is validated separately. The trapdoor hash value is computed using the added data and the commitment value, and compared with the trapdoor hash value in the Signature element. If the signature is valid, the adaptation by T_2 is checked against the restrictions in the Policy element. The policy compliancy check step in the adaptation process is reused here. If the check succeeds, the signed document is transformed to a standard SMIL format by deleting system-specific elements and attributes. If any of the above steps fails, the verification module sends an error message to the SMIL player and terminates.

Performance. Modules in T_2 are implemented on a 3.06 GHz Pentium 4 machines with 1 GB memory running Redhat Linux 2.4.20. The user device modules are implemented on an 866MHz Pentium III machine with 512 MB memory running Windows XP. Our experiments used 1024-bit DSA-SHA1 in XML-DSIG for both the Hash-Sign-Switch (HSS) and Conventional Signature (CS) schemes. For HSS, the trapdoor hash function also uses a 1024-bit modulus. All results are computed by averaging 10 trials.

Figure 4 shows processing delay in msec of each step in T_2 (left) and the user devices (right). In the figure, "XML-DSIG", "XML-DSIG (hash tree)", "One delete", "One add (Conv.)", and "One add (Trapdoor)" mean processing delay to handle a SMIL document with XML-DSIG, XML-DSIG with hash tree extension but without adaptation, one delete operation, one add operation using CS, and one add operation using HSS, respectively. The SMIL document included 5 leaf elements. In T_2, commitment using CS was implemented using the existing XML-DSIG implementation and took about 439msec for one added element. On the other hand, commitment using HSS took only about 23 msec for the same added element. This commitment step includes insertion of the commitment value to the Signature element. The processing delay of adaptation and the policy compliance check took about 11msec and 10msec respectively, rather insignificant compared to commitments implemented using CS. In the user device, signature verification using the existing XML-DSIG

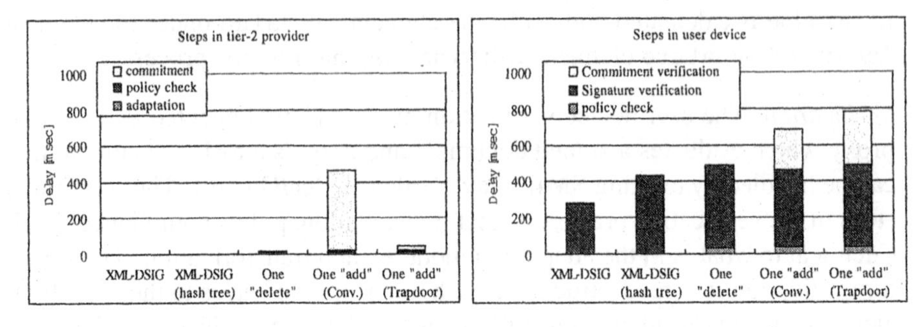

Figure 4. Processing delay in msec of each step in T_2 (left) and the user devices (right).

implementation [9] took 282 msec in our setting. In case of using hash tree construction, the verification delay increased by 52%. The processing delay of the policy check was 38 msec, three times longer than that in T_2 because of lower CPU power. Verification of the commitment using HSS required about 32% more overhead than the commitment using CS.

We see that HSS reduces computational overhead for T_2 to commit to the element added to the original meta-data by 95% (400 msec in our setting). Although this improvement comes at the cost of increased verification overhead on the user device by 32% (70 msec), total end-to-end overhead is reduced by 30% (315 msec). This indicates that the HSS scheme improves scalability and response time of secure adaptive content delivery systems.

6. Conclusions

We presented a protection system for adaptive multimedia content delivery that preserves end-to-end authenticity while allowing content adaptation by intermediaries. We proposed a new multi-hop digital signature scheme, and used it to protect content meta-data and usage rules from illegal modifications. The proposed signature scheme uses Merkle hash trees to allow selective element removal, and achieves secure element insertion by adding a placeholder extension. We also suggested a computationally efficient scheme to instantiate the placeholder based on the hash-sign-switch paradigm using trapdoor hash functions. The proposed scheme can alleviate the trust level from T_1 to tier-2 providers; otherwise T_1 must have complete trust in them not to perform illegal modifications. We envision that this trust alleviation will give flexibility to secure adaptive content delivery services. The evaluation results using our prototype showed that HSS can reduce signature-related overhead in the tier-2 provider (commitment) and end-to-end (signature, commitment, and verification) by 95% and 30% respectively, compared to CS. The proposed signature scheme, thus, contributes to improvement of scalability and response time of adaptive content delivery systems with the content protection scheme.

References

[1] NTT DoCoMo i-mode. `http://www.nttdocomo.com/corebiz/imode`.

[2] M. Etoh and S. Sekiguchi. MPEG-7 enabled digest video streaming over 3G mobile network. *12th International Packet Video Workshop (PV2002)*, Apr '02.

[3] O. Goldreich, S. Goldwasser, and S. Micali. How to Construct Random Functions. *Journal of the ACM*, vol. 33, no. 4, 1986, pp 210-217.

[4] C. Gentry, A. Hevia, R. Jain, T. Kawahara, and Z. Ramzan. End-to-End Security in the Presence of Intelligent Data Adapting Proxies: the Case of Authenticating Transcoded Streaming Media. *To Appear in J. Selected Areas of Communication*, Q1, 2005.

[5] Microsoft Windows Media 9 Series. `http://www.microsoft.com/windows`.

[6] Real Networks. RealOne player. `http://www.realnetworks.com`.

[7] IETF RFC 3238. `http://www.ietf.org/rfc/rfc3238.txt`.

[8] IETF Open Pluggable Edge Services (OPES) Working Group. `http://www.ietf.org/html.charters/opes-charter.html`.

[9] IBM alphaWorks XML Security Suite. `http://www.alphaworks.ibm.com/tech/`.

[10] T. Yuuichi, T. Kaori, O. Takeshi, S. Shinji, and M. Hideo. ASIA: Information Sharing System with Derived Content Restriction Management. *IEICE Transactions on Communications (Japanese Edition)*, vol. 428, pp 1463–1475, Aug '03.

[11] W3C Recommendation. Synchronized Multimedia Integration Language (SMIL 2.0). `http://www.w3.org/TR/smil20`. Aug '01.

[12] R. Johnson, D. Molnar, D. Song, and D. Wagner. Homomorphic signature schemes. *CT-RSA, Lecture Notes in Computer Science*, vol. 2271, pp 244-262, 2002.

[13] A. Shamir and Y. Tauman. Improved Online/Offline Signature Schemes. *Proc. of Crypto 2001*, pp 355-367.

[14] W3C Recommendation. XML-Signature Syntax and Processing. `http://www.w3.org/TR/xmldsig-core`. Feb '02.

[15] National Institute of Standards and Technology, U.S. Department of Commerce. Secure Hash Standard. *Federal Information Processing Standards Publication 180-1*, Apr. 1995.

[16] OASIS Committee. eXtensible Access Control Markup Language v1.0. `http://www.oasis-open.org`. Feb '03.

[17] R. Merkle. Protocols for Public Key Cryptosystems. *Proc. of the IEEE Symposium on Security and Privacy*, pp 122-134, 1980.

[18] H. Krawczyk and T. Rabin. Chameleon Hashing and Signature. *Proc. of NDSS '2000*.

[19] D. Boneh, C. Gentry, B. Lynn, and H. Shacham. Aggregate and verifiably encrypted signatures from bilinear maps. *Proc. of Eurocrypt '03*. LNCS 2656, pp. 416-432.

[20] S. Goldwasser, S. Micali, and R. L. Rivest. A Digital Signature Scheme Secure Against Adaptive Chosen-Message Attacks. *SIAM Journal on Computing*. 17(2), pp281-308, 1988.

[21] OMA. DRM2.0 Enabler Release. `http://www.openmobilealliance.org`. Feb '04.

[22] R. Steinfeld, L. Bull and Y. Zheng. Content Extraction Signatures. *Proc. of ICISC 2001*. LNCS, vol.2288, pp.285-304.

[23] W3C Recommendation. SOAP v1.2. `http://www.w3.org/TR/SOAP`. June '03.

[24] W3C Recommendation. XSL Transformations v1.0. `http://www.w3.org/TR/xslt`. Nov '99.

USING SAML TO LINK THE GLOBUS TOOLKIT TO THE PERMIS AUTHORISATION INFRASTRUCTURE

David Chadwick[1], Sassa Otenko[1], Von Welch[2]
[1]*ISI, University of Salford, Salford, M5 4WT, England.*
[2]*National Center for Supercomputing Applications, University of Illinois, 605 E. Springfield, Champaign, IL 61820, USA*

Abstract: In this article the new trend in authorisation decision making will be described, using the Security Assertions Mark up Language (SAML). We then present an overview of the Globus Toolkit (GT), used in Grid computing environments, and highlight its authorisation requirements. We then introduce the PERMIS authorisation infrastructure and describe how it has been adapted to support SAML so that it can be deployed to make authorisation decisions for GTversion 3.3.

Key words: SAML, Grid Computing, Authorisation, X.509 attribute certificates, RBAC, policy decision making, PDP, PEP.

1. INTRODUCTION

The Security Assertions Markup Language (SAML) [1] has been designed by the Organization for the Advancement of Structured Information Standards (OASIS) to provide a universal mechanism for conveying security-related information between the various parts of an access control system. It is an XML-based language for encoding security request and response messages between the initiator of an access request, the authentication service, the authoriser (termed an attribute authority) and the access control decision function (ADF). Some of these parts of an access control system may be grouped together, in which case they will not need to send SAML messages between themselves, and may use some sort of API to convey the necessary information between each other.

The Globus Toolkit (GT) is an implementation of Grid software, which has a number of tools that make development and deployment of Grid Services easier [2]. One of the key features of this toolkit is secure communications. However, Globus Toolkit has limited authorisation capabilities based on simple access control lists. To improve its authorization capabilities a SAML authorisation callout has been added. The important consequence of this is that it will be possible to deploy an authorisation service that the GT will contact to make authorisation decisions about what methods can be executed by a given client. One such authorisation service is PERMIS [3]. Whilst the original PERMIS Java API was intended for local calls only, and didn't have any network interface, a PERMIS Authorisation Service has been developed to provide authorisation decisions for the Globus Toolkit through the SAML callout.

2. OVERVIEW OF EXISTING TECHNOLOGY

2.1 SAML

SAML is a language for expressing security-related information. It defines message formats in XML for Queries and Responses. It also defines a request-response protocol in SOAP over Http for carrying the SAML messages. SAML Queries are sent to a decision-making service whilst Responses, in the form of SAML Assertions, are returned. These assertions can then be coupled with a further Query and sent to other decision making services to aid them in their own decisions. In the SAML model there are three decision-making services: the Authentication decision-making service, the Attribute decision-making service and the Authorisation decision-making service (see Figure 1). Each decision-making service uses its associated policy and the user's credentials to evaluate the Query. After the SAML Query has been evaluated, a SAML Response is generated and this may be forwarded to another decision-making service, until it finally reaches the Policy Enforcement Point (PEP) of the application, which will determine the ultimate fate of the user's application request. The PEP is equivalent to the Access control Enforcement Function (AEF) in ISO 10181-3 Authorisation Framework [4].

SAML does not mandate any exact sequence of message flows for access control decision making. However, a typical flow might be as follows. A user's access request is presented to a PEP/AEF, and comprises the user's name, the user's credentials, the target to be accessed and the requested mode of access. The PEP could then sequentially present portions of this request to the three decision-making services. Firstly the user's name and credentials are presented to the Authentication Authority, which confirms the identity of the user. Next the authenticated name of the user (or the authentication assertion returned by the Authentication Authority) is presented to the Attribute Authority, which confirms the assignment of certain attributes to the user. Finally the attribute assertions, the name of the target and the requested mode of access are presented to the PDP, which makes an access control decision. The PEP then acts on this decision and either forwards the user's request to the target (if the PDP granted the request) or returns an error message to the user (if the PDP denied the request).

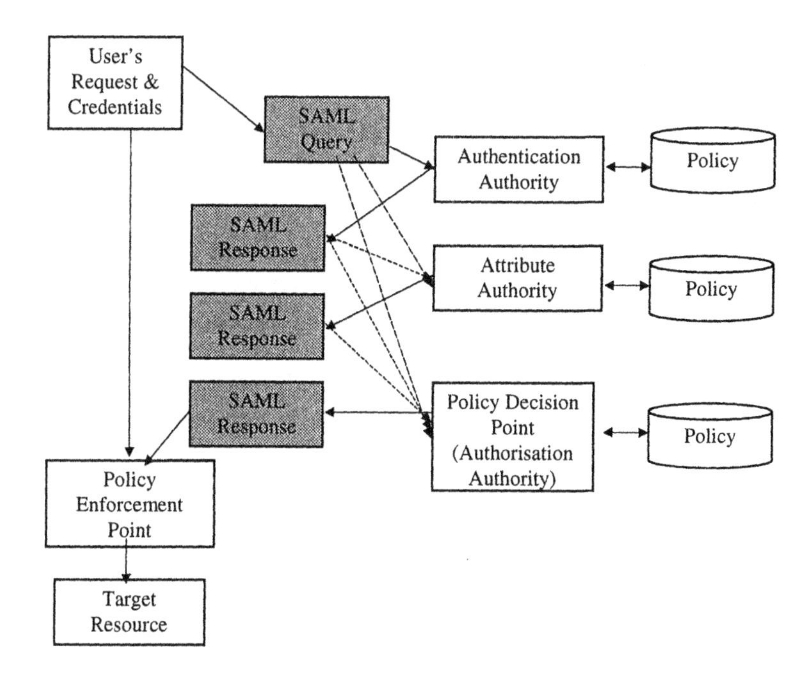

Figure 1. SAML

The SAML messages can be digitally signed, which makes them tamperproof, i.e. the messages can be sent as plaintext across untrusted networks. Alternatively, the SAML protocol messages could be sent as SOAP over Http over SSL, which can also protect them from eavesdropping.

Until quite recently most uses of SAML were limited to authentication and attribute usage e.g. as in Shibboleth [5]. Authorisation decisions were usually made locally either based on the user's identity (in Access Control Lists) or on the attributes/roles of the user (in simple scripts).

As virtual communities and Grid computing started to develop, identity-based systems for authorization became increasingly difficult to manage due to the distributed nature of the user communities. To accommodate these communities, new authorisation systems were required that would make the decisions based on the attributes of the initiator rather than their identity. Another prerequisite for SAML authorisation messaging was that there should be a centralised decision-making point for a number of remote services, governed by the same policy. Thus Community Authorisation Server (CAS) [6], Akenti [7], PERMIS and others started to appear.

2.2 The Globus toolkit

The Globus Toolkit (GT) is a set of tools for building Grids that includes tools for resource discovery, job submission and data movement. Version 3 of the Globus Toolkit (GT3), includes support for Grid Services based on the Open Grid Service Infrastructure (OGSI) standard, which defines extensions to Web Services for lifetime management and stateful instances (among other things outside the scope of this paper). GT3 provides a Grid Service Container to host Grid Services instances, which provides services such as message marshalling/de-marshalling, authentication and authorization.

A virtual organization (VO) is a collection of users and resources, distributed across a number of geographic and administrative domains, which share common policies for access control. Initially access control was solved in GT through the use of simple access control lists called grid-map files, which performed mapping of access rights based on the user's identity. Such simplistic policies were robust, but failed to scale as the VOs grew in size and spanned larger numbers of institutions. To provide more flexible authorisation solutions, it was decided to provide a SAML authorisation callout in GT3 to allow the use of advanced authorization services. The effect of this is that the Grid Service Container would be able to contact the centralised Policy Decision Point to make access control decisions for invocations of services it hosts. In this design the PDP becomes yet another Grid Service, which provides authorization decisions through a standard message format i.e. SAML.

Now it is possible to create a CAS, Akenti, or PERMIS port that would make access control decisions for Grid Services, based on queries and decisions in the form of SAML Queries and Responses which are enforced by the Grid Service Container. A detailed description of the operation scenario is given later, with the example related to PERMIS.

2.3 PERMIS

PERMIS is a policy based authorisation infrastructure, in which a user is granted rights to access a resource based on the authorisation policy for the resource, and the set of attributes (or roles) that the user possesses. A user's attributes are stored in digitally signed X.509 attribute certificates [10], and are allocated by the authorities in charge of the various attributes. Thus a "doctor" role attribute could be allocated by the General Medical Council, whilst a "project manager" role attribute could be allocated by the head of a department. A "date of birth" attribute could be allocated by a national registrar. These attribute certificates are then stored in various LDAP directories.

PERMIS was designed with a Java API between the PDP and PEP providing the access control decisions. Given the name of the user, it retrieves the user's attributes/roles and makes decisions based on them. The authorisation policy, written in XML, expresses which users can be assigned what attributes/roles by whom, and what privileges are bound to each of the attributes/roles. The XML policy is then inserted in an X.509 attribute certificate, signed by the manager who wrote it, and stored in an entry in an LDAP server.

When an application starts up, its PEP/AEF passes to the PERMIS ADF/PDP the name of the manager, the location of the LDAP directory, and the unique number of the policy to be used (each policy is assigned a globally unique number – actually an object identifier [12] – so that a manager can create different policies to be used in different contexts). The PERMIS ADF retrieves the policy X.509 AC from the LDAP directory, checks the signature and policy number, and if both are correct, uses this policy for its decision making.

3. THE IMPLEMENTATION

3.1 Extensions to SAML

A standard SAML Response contains a complete list of all the allowed actions which were contained in the SAML Query. While this is useful in cases where the response is passed to a third party, in the case where the query was generated by the consumer of the response it can introduce unnecessary overhead. In these cases the consumer of the response must parse the entire list of actions, when it may only be interested in a "yes" or "no" answer regarding the entire list as a whole.

For the sake of performance, new SAML Requests and Responses have been proposed – they are shorter and more concise versions of the standard SAML Authorization Decision Request and Authorization Decision Statement (passed inside a SAML Query and SAML Response respectively).

These new messages allow the query to request, and the decision to contain, a simple yes/no response to all the actions contained in the query. This allows the authorization service to easily encode, and the Grid Service Container to easy parse, the response. The specification of these new SAML messages has been written by the Global Grid Forum's (GGF) Open Grid Service Architecture Authorisation working group (OGSA-AuthZ) [9].

3.2 Extensions to PERMIS

As the demand for an authorisation service appeared in the Globus Toolkit, the PERMIS researchers closely collaborated with the GT team to provide practical input into the design of the SAML messages to be used in GT3. In parallel a standalone PERMIS ADF was developed. Whilst the original PERMIS RBAC ADF had to be contacted via its Java API, the standalone ADF has a networking interface, through which it can receive SAML Queries and send back SAML Responses. In addition to this, the PERMIS ADF can pose as a Grid Service, so it can be used as a centralised PDP of a Grid application. It can also easily be embedded as a Service Authorisation – i.e. a PERMIS Authorisation "Callout" can replace the GT3 standard SAML Authorization Callout, and make local decisions for local Grid Services.

The original PERMIS architecture supported only LDAP Distinguished Names as Target identifiers. This allowed PERMIS to group targets into domains for easier expression of the policy. It was noticed during the early development stages of PERMIS that in fact people use various kinds of naming conventions for identifying targets, e.g. IP addresses, DNS names, URIs etc., so the design of the PERMIS API incorporated Principals, as an abstraction for such identifiers. However, the original PERMIS pilot sites did not have any specific requirements about which type of naming to use, and so for consistency purposes target naming was chosen to be the same as subject naming. Since subjects were named using X.500/LDAP distinguished names, then so too were targets.

When porting the code to work with the Globus Toolkit, it became necessary to allow other kinds of naming conventions to be used for targets, specifically because in Globus the intended targets are Grid Services, and they already have non-LDAP identifiers in the form of Grid Service Handles (GSHs), encoded in the form of a URI. URIs are hierarchical names like LDAP DNs, and this helps to group targets into domains (although of course in any particular Grid application the relevant targets at different sites may have totally unrelated URIs). URIs do not provide any further refinements for targets, unlike LDAP, which provides Object Classes to help to further distinguish between the different kinds of target e.g. printers or cpu clusters.

This is one example of identifying targets by their attributes as well as or instead of their names.

Besides changing the ADF interface to support URI target names, the PERMIS policy syntax also had to be extended to support URIs as Target Identifiers[1]. This allows the manager to specify target names as URIs.

The PERMIS ADF assumes the subjects are authenticated, but it can recognise unauthenticated subjects, and now it will return public access rights to such subject names, i.e. it will grant access to the targets that do not require any roles to perform certain actions.

The Java code for constructing subject and target domains is the same, so in principle subjects could also be identified by their URIs. This would allow, for example, particular Grid Services (which are the targets for normal Grid users) to act as subjects and to make requests to other services protected by the PERMIS infrastructure. For example, a Grid service could make a request to an attribute repository protected by the PERMIS ADF, and PERMIS could decide if the particular Grid Service is allowed to retrieve certain user Attribute Certificates (specified as targets), thus enforcing a user's Privacy Policy.

The question of how to locate the credentials of a subject identified by a URL in a repository that uses LDAP naming can in fact be solved in at least two ways. The first and easiest way is to use URLs that conform to RFC 2255 [11]. This specifies how LDAP URLs can be used to retrieve information from LDAP repositories. An alternative way is to embed the URL as the latter part of the LDAP Distinguished Name and to configure the LDAP repository with the prefix DN.

For file-based repositories, e.g. Web-servers or file-servers, it is possible to construct filenames out of the subject's identifier, e.g. an MD5 hash of the normalised subject identifier (either the LDAP DN or URL) can be used to locate the files containing the necessary credentials[2].

The extended SAML Requests designed by the OGSA-Authz group and specified in [9] may contain Attribute Reference elements. In essence these are repository URLs from where the subject's attributes should be retrieved by the Authorisation Service. This is a "semi-push" or "controlled pull" model, i.e. the subject doesn't have to push all the credentials to the Authorisation Service as SAML evidence, or rely on the Authorisation Service to pull whichever attributes it wants from where, but instead can provide a reference to the repositories that contain them. The Authorisation Service will then pull the attributes from this referenced repository. Note that

[1] In fact, any URI can be used, but a specific URI handler must be registered with the PERMIS RBAC at initialisation time.

[2] For example, this is the way some Public Key Certificates are located on some web-servers.

where the attributes are stored as digitally signed X.509 ACs, they are tamperproof and so it is still possible to use such references for making secure decisions. To cater for this extension to SAML, a new parameter to the PERMIS getCreds method has been introduced. It provides the PERMIS Authorisation Service with a list of repositories to contact to get the subject's credentials.

To configure the PERMIS Authorisation Service at initialisation time, it is necessary to specify the URL of the LDAP repository where the policy is located, the Distinguished Name of the manager issuing the policy, and the Object Identifier of the actual policy to be used. These parameters are specified in the GT3 Service Container deployment descriptor. Unfortunately, there is currently no way to make the deployment descriptor tamperproof. Therefore to ensure that the Grid service is always correctly configured, it is recommended that a human security officer should always be present at the service start-up time, to check that the configuration parameters that the service uses are the expected ones.

3.3 Operation Scenario

There are two modes of interaction between GT3 and PERMIS Authorisation. One mode is remote, the other mode is local. In remote mode a PERMIS Authorisation Service is set up to serve a number of Grid Service Containers. In local mode of operation each Grid Service Container has its own PERMIS Authorisation set up as an Authorisation Handler. In local mode there are no SAML messages, and authorisation is done via the PERMIS API, so only a comparison of this mode to the remote mode of operation is given in section 4. The remote mode of operation is described below.

When a subject makes a request of a Grid Service, the subject is typically authenticated by the Grid Service Container using SSL and the user's X.509 certificate (see [8] for details). The subject may also invoke operations anonymously, in which case a special identifier (*) is used to indicate an anonymous user. The service container generates a SAML Authorisation Request, which includes an identifier of the subject, an identifier of the service (its Grid Service Handle, a URI), and the name of the operation being invoked. This information is enveloped in a message containing a timestamp and signature along with other information to protect the message from tampering and prevent replay attacks. This message is sent to the trusted Authorisation Service as defined in the service's configuration, e.g. a PERMIS Authorisation Service.

The Authorization Service parses the request, uses the policy to make an authorisation decision about the request, and returns a response containing the decision (again enveloped in a message which includes a signature and replay protection). Only an affirmative decision will cause the service container to allow for the action requested by the user to be executed.

4. DISCUSSION

The implementation described above should help to provide Role-Based Access Controls in Virtual Organisations built on Grids. Each of the resource providers will write a PERMIS policy for resource usage, and authorise collaborative institutions to issue roles to their members. The collaborative institutions will issue role assignment X.509 Attribute Certificates to their members, and based on these and the policy, the PERMIS ADF will make the authorisation decisions.

The implementation is now complete and pilot testing is due to take place during the next 5 months, so that actual results should be present in time for the CMS2004 conference.

It is still questionable how efficient it is to have such an authorisation service called via SAML/SOAP/Http rather than to have a PDP/ADF called locally via a programmable API. The gain that can be achieved using the centralised PDP is that in single sign-on distributed systems such as the Grid, the authorisation tokens (attribute certificates) of the user would have to be retrieved only once, rather than at each resource of the distributed system. In most cases this might give a doubtful gain in performance because SAML messages still have to be generated for each request.

A centralised PDP should make policy management easier – security managers do not have to change the policy at each PDP. However, the PERMIS infrastructure has already addressed this problem by storing its policy as a digitally signed AC in a central LDAP repository, from where all the distributed systems can retrieve the same policy.

A centralised PDP can provide more user privacy. For example, it is easier to conceal the user's identity in a single trusted PDP (and use a pseudonym throughout the rest of the system), rather than spread this knowledge across PDPs at each resource site.

A centralised PDP makes implementation of the Principle of Separation of Duties much easier to enforce – it is easier to track what roles a user has assumed in the past, so his further requests do not clash (e.g. the Payment Requestor cannot be a Payment Guarantee for the same order, and an Accountant cannot be an Auditor for the same transaction). This is much more difficult to enforce with multiple distributed PDPs.

Having said all this, it should be noted that most authorisation decision systems today are local, i.e. no centralised decision-making is done. Decentralising the decision-making process has its benefits, which are usually connected with the speed of decision making, and the up-to-date reflection of the system's state in the PDP (as contextual parameters).

The Grid environment encourages institutions to collaborate with each other. The links between these institutions may be established in a fairly spontaneous way, and these institutions may already have their own Privilege Management Infrastructures in place. This means that the participating institutions may have already assigned roles to their members. It is important in this case that the collaborating institutions are able to recognise each other's role assignments and optimally to be able to compare the roles issued by the different participating institutions. Currently the PERMIS policy has to be configured with all the different roles, and permissions assigned to each. In the future we expect to be able to express role mappings, and one of our ongoing projects aims to facilitate dynamic cross-institutional virtual organisations using existing PMIs.

5. REFERENCES

[1] OASIS. "Assertions and Protocol for the OASIS Security Assertion Markup Language (SAML)". 19 April 2002. See http://www.oasis-open.org/committees/security/

[2] Globus toolkit, http://www.globus.org/toolkit

[3] D.W.Chadwick, A. Otenko, E.Ball. "Implementing Role Based Access Controls Using X.509 Attribute Certificates", IEEE Internet Computing, March-April 2003, pp. 62-69.

[4] ITU-T Rec X.812 (1995) | ISO/IEC 10181-3:1996 "Security Frameworks for open systems: Access control framework"

[5] Shibboleth Project, available at http://shibboleth.internet2.edu/

[6] L. Pearlman, V. Welch, I. Foster, C. Kesselman, S. Tuecke. "A Community Authorization Service for Group Collaboration". Proceedings of the IEEE 3rd International Workshop on Policies for Distributed Systems and Networks, 2002.

[7] Johnston, W., Mudumbai, S., Thompson, M. "Authorization and Attribute Certificates for Widely Distributed Access Control," IEEE 7th Int Workshops on Enabling Technologies: Infrastructure for Collaborative Enterprises (WET ICE), Stanford, CA. June, 1998. Page(s): 340 -345 (see also http://www-itg.lbl.gov/security/Akenti/)

[8] Von Welch, Frank Siebenlist, Ian Foster, John Bresnahan, Karl Czajkowski, Jarek Gawor, Carl Kesselman, Sam Meder, Laura Pearlman, and Steven Tuecke. Security for grid services. In *Twelfth International Symposium on High Performance Distributed Computing (HPDC-12)*. IEEE Computer Society Press, 2003.

[9] Von Welch, Frank Siebenlist, David Chadwick, Sam Meder, Laura Pearlman. "Use of SAML for OGSA Authorization", Jan 2004, Available from https://forge.gridforum.org/projects/ogsa-authz

[10] ISO 9594-8/ITU-T Rec. X.509 (2001) The Directory: Public-key and attribute certificate frameworks

[11] T. Howes, M. Smith. "The LDAP URL Format", RFC 2255, Dec 1997
[12] ITU-T Recommendation X.680 (1997) | ISO/IEC 8824-1:1998, Information Technology - Abstract Syntax Notation One (ASN.1): Specification of Basic Notation

SECURE ROLE BASED MESSAGING

David Chadwick[1], Graeme Lunt[2] and Gansen Zhao[1]
[1]*ISSRC, ISI, University of Salford, Salford, M5 4WT, UK;*
[2]*Nexor Limited, Bell House, Nottingham Science & Technology Park, University Boulevard, Nottingham, NG7 2RL, UK*

Abstract This paper describes a secure role based messaging system design based on the use of X.509 Attribute Certificates for holding user roles. Access to the messages is authorised by the PERMIS Privilege Management Infrastructure, a policy driven role based access control (RBAC) infrastructure, which allows the assignment of roles to be distributed between trusted issuing authorities, and allows a change of access control policy at runtime. Messages can be sent by roles and users, and can be sent to roles and users. Messages are secure in their exchange between senders and recipients. Details of the security and messaging design are presented.

Keywords: X.509, Attribute Certificates, Role based Messaging, PERMIS, PMI

1. Introduction

Messaging systems like email systems are widely used to enable communication between people. In the setting of organizations, a message is sent to a person with the assumption that the receiver is the person who is responsible for dealing with the message's contents. To some degree, it requires that senders know about the identities of people corresponding to specific duties and issues, and that they can always get up-to-date information on the relationships between issues, duties and the people who are responsible for them.

From a business's point of view, the destination of these messages is organisational roles instead of the physical occupants of roles. A role is an abstract model in an organization, which specifies a set of duties and tasks and can be associated with a set of people in the organization. People are related to the duties and tasks by being assigned as an occupant of the corresponding role. Role assignment is dynamic, and should be instantaneous, especially when a role is being removed from a currently role occupant.

Security is required when the information being carried by a message is important and/or confidential. Message security means various things including: confidential messages can be accessed only by authorised entities, including roles and users; message contents have integrity and are protected from being modified during the course of their transportation; recipients cannot falsely deny having received messages that have been delivered; and the identity of message senders can be verified at any time after the messages have been sent.

Most existing messaging systems provide only person to person messaging and lack the ability to send messages to and from dynamically changing role occupants.

The purpose of the current research at Salford is to design, build and test a secure role based messaging system that can provide for the secure exchange of messages between organisational roles. This paper describes such a design based on the use of: X.509 attribute certificates [9] for holding user roles, PERMIS [1], a role based access control (RBAC) [4, 5] infrastructure, and user and role public/private key pairs. Access to both user mailboxes and role mailboxes is authorised by the PERMIS Privilege Management Infrastructure (PMI), an XML policy driven RBAC infrastructure, which allows the assignment of roles to be distributed between trusted issuing authorities. The design is achieved in a way that has the least impact on existing systems and standards.

The rest of this paper is structured as follows. We present the system requirements for secure role based messaging systems and the current challenges in Section 2, and propose a system design for secure role based messaging systems in Section 3. The details of secure messaging are elaborated in Section 4. We conclude with a review of the related work in Section 5 and conclusions of the system design in Section 6.

2. Requirements and Challenges

This section presents the system requirements and challenges for secure role based messaging systems.

2.1 System Requirements

A secure role based messaging system should have all the following properties:

- Privacy and confidentiality. Messages are delivered in an encrypted manner, and are accessed by only authenticated users and roles through authorised operations.

- Integrity and authenticity. Senders can sign messages, which enable recipients to verify the sender identity. Messages will not be modified during the course of their delivery.

- Time sensitivity. Role occupants are able to access the role mailbox only during the time that they officially hold the role

- Accountability. It should be possible to determine who acted in any specific role at any particular time.
- Scalability. The system should support multiple role occupants both concurrently and consecutively e.g. any current role occupant should be able to access and respond to any of the messages in the in-tray, and read all the responses sent by all the other role occupants in the out-tray.
- Manageability. Managers should be able to dynamically allocate and remove roles from people and they should then immediately be able to access role mailboxes (or not) without having to reconfigure the system
- Distributed management of roles. Different managers in different organisational units should be able to allocate and remove roles from people under their control.
- Policy based access control. Authorisation can be represented by policies, which can be set or modified to specify who is trusted to allocate which roles to which users, and which access rights are given to which roles.
- User friendliness. User friendliness is required for both use and management. It should be simple for users to access messages whilst acting in the capacity of a role. In the case that users hold a number of roles, it should also be simple to select which role users wish to exercise at any particular time. It must also be easy for managers to allocate and remove roles, and for the security officer to set the policy controlling access to the role based messaging system.

2.2 Challenges in Secure Role Based Messaging

There is significant interest in role based messaging. Such a system presents a number of challenges, especially when encryption and digital signing are involved, since keys need to be assigned to a role, even though the role could be occupied by zero, one or several real people at any given time.

Within a large and structured organisation, people often want to send a message to a given role within that organisation, rather than to a specific individual. Unfortunately most email systems are person to person and do not inherently support roles. The gap between existing messaging systems and applications is exaggerated in large organisations, which have complex organization structures and people continually adopt different roles during their professional life.

Two of the current ways of supporting role based messaging are using dedicated role mailboxes and using distribution lists. When using dedicated role mailboxes, role occupants share a role mailbox by sharing the role password or role private key to access the role mailbox. Sharing passwords brings a risk of password disclosure, and the risk will increase when the number of role occupants increases or the change of role occupants becomes frequent. Furthermore, it is difficult to stop someone from accessing a role mailbox after the role has been removed from him or her without changing the role password. Sharing role private keys is a better option if the keys are held in hardware tokens. The tokens can then be physically removed from the role occupant when the role is removed. But if the role private key is held in an encrypted file it is little better than sharing a role password, since the file can be copied at will.

When distribution lists are used, messages sent to a role are copied to each role occupant. One of the drawbacks of this mode is that it does not cater for the temporal nature of role occupancy without significant management overhead. Removed role occupants will continue to have access to the messages that were delivered to the role prior to their removal, while new added role occupants will not be able to access those messages that were delivered to the role before their role assignment was made.

The issue is further complicated when secure messaging is required. Messages sent by a role need to be signed by a role, whilst encrypted messages received by a role need to be read by all role occupants. Role occupants could be given copies of the role private key(s), but the management overhead of these keys, both by the individual and by the administrator would be prohibitive.

Enhancing the distribution list expansion method to re-encrypt the message for each individual role occupant does not allow new role occupants to access the messages that have already been delivered, nor does it cater for role occupants whose role assignments are revoked after messages have been sent but not read and acted upon.

3. System Design

The work reported in this paper is an attempt to develop a framework for secure role based messaging, which is flexible enough to cater for different security and messaging requirements whilst having the least impact on existing systems and standards.

3.1 System Architecture

Figure 1 shows an architecture design for a secure role based messaging system. The main components of the architecture are the Message User Agent (MUA), the Message Transfer Agent (MTA), the Internet Mail Access Protocol 4 Server (IMAP4 server), and the Role Gatekeeper. The MUA is a component that provides users with facilities for sending and receiving messages. It mediates the communication between users and other components, and the communication between roles and other components. The MTA component is responsible for transporting messages. It receives messages from MUAs or remote MTAs, and delivers messages to a remote MTA or stores them locally according to the destination of the messages. The IMAP4 server provides an interface to access electronic messages that are stored in the system. Users and roles use MUAs to retrieve messages from the IMAP4 server. Messages are transmitted between MUAs and MTAs over the SMTP protocol [10], and are transmitted between MUAs and IMAP4 servers over the IMAP [2] protocol.

The Role Gatekeeper intercepts messages between the MUA and the MTA server, and communications between the MUA and IMAP4 server. The communications between the Role Gatekeeper and the other components are secure by means of authentication and encryption of messages or links. The Role Gatekeeper is responsible for all security operations regarding roles.

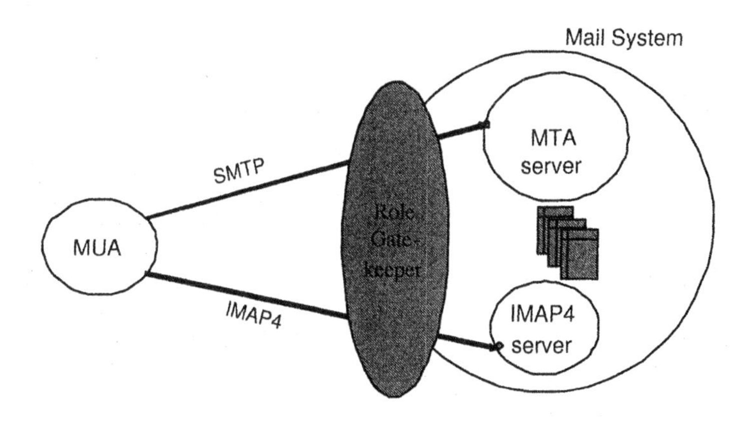

Figure 1. The Secure Role based Messaging System Architecture

3.2 The Role Gatekeeper

Details of the Role Gatekeeper design are shown in Figure 2. The Key components in the Role Gatekeeper include the authentication service component, the encryption and decryption service component, and the PERMIS authorisation service component. The authentication service component verifies the identities of message senders, and the identities of users and roles who are requesting to perform actions within the messaging system.

The encryption and decryption service component signs (and encrypts) role messages if necessary when they are being sent, and decrypts encrypted role messages when they are being retrieved. The encryption and decryption service component has access to the role private keys, so it can sign role messages on behalf of a role by using the role's private key. The encryption and decryption service component eliminates the requirement of role occupants to hold role private keys for signing and decrypting role messages.

The PERMIS authorisation service component authorises all security sensitive operations within the system, ensuring that only permitted operations on messages are conducted in regard to the identity of users and roles. The PERMIS access control decision function (ADF) can reason and decide whether an operation of a user or a role is permitted or not, in regard to a specific resource, which are mailboxes in the case of this work. PERMIS also supports the distributed management of roles.

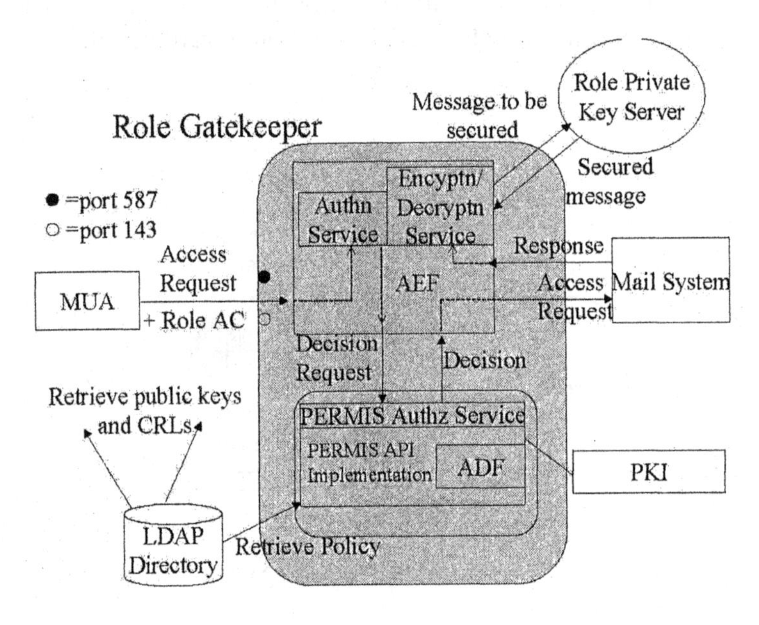

Figure 2. Role Gatekeeper

3.3 Private Keys and Pubic Keys

The proposed design assumes that each role and user is allocated his or her own public/private key pair(s). One key pair is used for digitally signing messages, named signature keys, the other for encrypting/decrypting messages, named encryption keys. The user private keys are held in a smart card, encrypted file or similar that is only accessible to them, while the role private keys are held in a role private key server. Users can access their own private keys, but role occupants have no access to the role private keys. The Role Gatekeeper will access the role private keys on behalf of role occupants when it is necessary to use the role private keys to sign or to decrypt messages. Both the public keys of users and roles are held as X.509 public key certificates [9] in an LDAP directory [18].

3.4 Attribute Certificates

An Attribute Certificate (AC) is a data structure which contains a set of attributes for an entity, and it is required to be signed by an attribute authority (AA), which is an authority trusted by the system or the user [16]. A Role Assignment Attribute Certificate (RAC) specifies a user's assignment of a role. Role occupancy is conferred upon a user by being in possession of an X.509 RAC. Given a RAC and a trusted root AA, called the Source of Authority (SOA) in X.509, it can be verified whether the RAC is issued by a trusted AA or not, and it can also be determined whether a user is assigned to a role. A Role Specification Attribute Certificate [9] or Policy Attribute Certificate (PAC) [16] specifies the authorised operations of a role on a specific resource. In PERMIS, for efficiency reasons, all the PACs are collected together into one PERMIS authorisation Policy Attribute Certificate. A user acting in a trusted role will be authorised to perform a specific operation on a specific resource if the PERMIS policy specifies that the role is allowed to perform the operation on the resource.

4. Secure Messaging

The system framework described in Section 3 works by authenticating users and their roles and authorising their operations, i.e. sending, delivering and accessing messages.

4.1 Authentication and Authorisation

The authentication service component within the Role Gatekeeper is responsible for authenticating both the identity of a user and the identity of a role. Users hold their private keys by themselves, and make them available for the MUA. The MUA can then use the private keys to achieve authentication with the Role Gatekeeper. One of the possible ways is that the Role Gatekeeper requires the MUA to sign a specific message, and verifies the signature on the message. The general submission mechanism is specified in [7].

Role occupants do not have access to role private keys, thus they have no way to prove their role identity by directly using role private keys. In the proposed design, a user gains its authentication as a role occupant by getting its own authentication and then proving its assignment of a role through a valid X.509 RAC. In this way, when a user wants to login in as a role, he/she will first login into the system as a user as above, and then present a RAC to the system, which specifies that the user has been assigned to the role.

The PERMIS component of the Role Gatekeeper authorises operations of both users and roles. RACs and the PERMIS PAC are the most important security tokens for the PERMIS authorisation service component to authorise a user's and role occupant's operations. The authorisation requires a user or role occupant to present one or more RACs, which can show that they are allowed to perform the specific operations. Given the identity, the requested operation and the related RACs, the PERMIS Access Control Decision Function (ADF) can reason and decide whether the request of performing the operation is allowed or not, in regard to the target mailbox.

PERMIS can operate in either push or pull mode. In push mode, the user pushes their RACs to the Role Gatekeeper to present to PERMIS. In pull mode, the PERMIS component fetches the user's RACs from one or more configured LDAP directories.

The way the system works can best be described by considering in detail each of the following three scenarios:

- a user sends a secured message to a role
- a role sends a secured message to a user
- a role sends a secured message to a role

4.2 User to Role

A user (MUA in the figures) wishes to send a secured message (digitally signed and/or encrypted) to a role. In normal email systems, when encrypting a message, the user would first obtain the encryption public key of the role/recipient from the LDAP directory and also obtain the latest revocation information for the role/recipient certificate (e.g. Certificate Revocation List(CRL) from the LDAP directory or OCSP [14] response from OSCP responder) to ensure that the certificate has not been revoked. The user would then digitally sign and/or encrypt the message, and send it to the SMTP server. The order of signing and encrypting would typically be determined by the MUA software, unless it was configurable by the user. ESS triple wrapping [17, 8] states the order should be Sign/Encrypt/Sign. A signature over the clear content, as opposed to encrypted content, has much more value.

In our design, because users do not have access to role private keys, the order of securing messages is important. Digital signing must come first. Signing followed by encrypting allows the Role Gatekeeper to subsequently decrypt and then re-encrypt the message to role keys without invalidating the signature of the sender; otherwise the signature will be invalidated when the message is decrypted. Thus the actual order of events is as follows.

The user creates a message to a role recipient and selects the sign and/or recipient role encrypt features. If sign was selected the MUA signs the message using the user's private signing key. The message is then transferred to the message submission port (587) on the Role Gatekeeper along with the optional recipient role encryption flag. The Role Gatekeeper, upon seeing the recipient role encryption flag, encrypts the message to the recipient role, using the role's public key obtained from the LDAP directory. (Revocation checking is also always carried out, but we will take this as a given and not mention it again). The S/MIME double wrapped message [6, 17, 8] (signed by user, encrypted to role) is then submitted to the SMTP server by the Role Gatekeeper.

We note that the encryption could have been done at the MUA as the recipient role's public key is in the directory and the originating role private key is not used in the encryption process. However, to maintain consistency with the other scenarios, we propose to always perform recipient role encryption in the Role Gatekeeper.

We further note that the link between the MUA and Role Gatekeeper may be encrypted or not to preserve message confidentiality. The security of this link is independent of the encryption of the message to the recipient role. If the link is encrypted this will have been negotiated at session establishment, using for example an SSL/TLS link.

The SMTP system distributes the mail until it eventually ends up in the role mailbox of an IMAP4 server. The secured message sits in the role mailbox of the IMAP4 server until a current role occupant logs in. A role occupant (user) authenticates to port 143 of the Role Gatekeeper and uses SASL [13] to identify themselves. The user then requests to access a particular mailbox using standard IMAP commands. The Role Gatekeeper determines if the user has access to the requested mailbox by determining if the user has an appropriate X.509 RAC. If no RAC is presented, the user's request is passed straight through to the mail server and he/she is only granted access to the default mailbox of their own username (INBOX in IMAP4). Such exchanges are no longer considered by this paper

If a RAC is presented, PERMIS authorises the operations according to the RAC and the related PERMIS policy. If PERMIS grants access, the Role Gatekeeper will log into the role mailbox on behalf of the user, using the role mailbox password that it holds. (Note that users do not know the passwords to the role mailboxes). When the user sends request messages to access the folders within the mailbox e.g. via the IMAP SELECT command, then the embedded folders and mail headers are returned to be displayed on the user's terminal. When the user wishes to fetch the contents of an encrypted message (e.g. via the IMAP FETCH command), then the Role Gatekeeper extracts the encrypted key information, sends it to the key server, and then attaches the response to the message before returning it to the user.

The encrypted key information $E\{Km\}_{Pkr}$ contains the symmetric key used to encrypt the message, Km, encrypted with the public key of the recipient role, Pkr. The key server, which has the private keys of all the roles, is able to decrypt the encrypted key information using the role private key of the role encryption key pair, Prr. It then re-encrypts the symmetric key, Km, using the user's public encryption key, Pku, which it can obtain from the LDAP directory. Note that we are currently working on the design of a policy controlled email system, which will allow some role occupants not to have access to some policy labelled messages, but description of this feature is out of the scope of this paper.

When the role occupant receives the encrypted message, (s)he is able to decrypt the message using their own private decryption key, and then validate the signature of the sender.

4.3 Role to User

A user logs into the IMAP4 server as before, by sending their RAC to the Role Gatekeeper. The Role Gatekeeper checks the validity of the RAC and if OK, allows the role occupant (the user) to download the contents of the role mailbox. The role occupant may now either reply to a message in the inbox, or create a new message to someone, acting in their official role. Once the message has been created, the role occupant selects the sign, role sign and/or encrypt functions, and if sign is selected, the MUA digitally signs the message using the role occupant's own personal private key of the signature key pair. This functionality provides a complete audit trail of which role occupant actually acted in the role at the time the message was signed. The MUA sends the message to the SMTP server via the Role Gatekeeper along with indicators specifying whether the message requires role signature and/or encryption. If this is a new connection between the MUA and the SMTP server (actually to port 587 on the Role Gatekeeper), then the user's RAC is transferred during the connection establishment phase. The Role Gatekeeper validates the RAC of the role occupant (once per session) and if the message is flagged to be role signed, it is sent to the key server for digital signing using the private key of the role signature key pair. If the message is also flagged to be encrypted, then it is encrypted to the recipient's public encryption key by the Role Gatekeeper. Finally it is submitted to the SMTP server. The resulting message may be S/MIME tripled wrapped (signed by sender, signed by role, encrypted to recipient).

When the user downloads the message from the IMAP4 server (in this case the Role Gatekeeper does not interfere with the message exchanges) the user is able to decrypt the message using the private key of their encryption key pair, then validate the signatures of the sender. (We assume here that the MUA is capable of downloading certificates and CRLs from an appropriately configured LDAP directory, and is capable of deciphering doubly signed messages).

In an alternative design that we are also building, the user includes his RAC in the message before signing the message. This binds the user to the role they are signing on behalf of. The advantage of this design is that the message is only doubly wrapped as a maximum (signed by sender and encrypted to recipient) instead of triply wrapped. Further, message encryption can be done by the MUA which relieves the burden on the Role Gatekeeper. The disadvantage is that the message is not actually signed by the sending role, and the recipient has to view the attached RAC to see that it was sent by a role.

4.4 Role to Role

This scenario is obviously a combination of the previous two scenarios. A role occupant logs into the IMAP4 server via the Role Gatekeeper, by passing a RAC at authentication time. If the role is valid, the Role Gatekeeper allows the role occupant to download the contents of the role mailbox. Any encrypted messages are passed by the Role Gatekeeper to the key server so that the symmetric encryption key can be encrypted to the public key of the role occupant's encryption key pair. The role occupant is thus able to read all messages that were encrypted to the public key of the role encryption key pair.

Any messages that the role occupant submits to the SMTP server via the Role Gatekeeper are firstly passed to the key server for digitally signing by the private key of the role signature key pair, and then they are encrypted to the public key of the recipient role's encryption key pair, resulting in an S/MIME triply wrapped message (or alternatively the sender includes his RAC in the message, signs the message and then encrypts it for the recipient role).

5. Related Work

Mont et al [12] describe a role based secure messaging service used in a health care setting. The service employs Identifier Based Encryption to protect messages. Senders decide the permitted role(s) who can view the message, and the messages will be encrypted with a string describing the permitted role(s). A recipient has to be authenticated as a member of at least one of the selected roles by the trust authority before getting a decryption key for the message. This work requires all users to be assigned a role before they can interact with the system, which is not practical to some degree.

Microsoft [11] released Microsoft Windows Server 2003 with a Rights Management System (RMS) that enables enterprises to add security information to files produced using Microsoft Office 2003 applications. The added security allows an author to limit the circulation and operations of a document. A header containing the security control policy is added to the file. The system also provides facilities for administrators to generate templates to define access control policies. One of the drawbacks is that RMS is provided without a mechanism to specify access control policies for groups and roles. Some may argue that Microsoft Active Directory can be integrated with the system and provide mechanism for controlling group permissions. For users external to the enterprise, Microsoft mandates the use of the Passport authentication service, which is a service provided by Microsoft, to allow these users to produce licenses for their files. However, it is not yet clear how the interface between external users and the enterprise is managed and there is no provision for binding users to roles.

MailRecall^{TM} is produced by Authentica [3]. It provides plug-ins for several popular email clients with the ability of keeping e-mail's privacy and protecting emails from unauthorised users, even after delivery. MailRecall^{TM} uses content security policies to determine the expiration of messages and authorize operations on emails. These policies can be configured individually by users or centrally, in accordance with corporate policy. When a message is sent outside the organisation the external recipient can be automatically registered and a browser plug-in is downloaded when the message is opened. The plug-in allows the recipient to view the protected message. Furthermore the web viewer can be configured to prompt the recipient to install the email client plug-in. Although MailRecall^{TM} provides several security control features, it fails to provide facilities to define a security policy at the group level or from a role's perspective.

The Omniva Policy Manager package [15] offers functions that are similar to MailRecall^{TM} , and it is available as a plug-in for Microsoft Outlook. It does provide a means of applying policies to groups of users, using existing directories and external recipients can read, but not directly respond to messages, using a web browser. However, no provision is made for addressing mail to role mailboxes.

6. Conclusions

This work presents a design for a secure role based messaging system, which is based on X.509 role assignment attribute certificates and the PERMIS policy driven role based authorization system. The proposed design has been developed with the effort of making the least number of modifications to the existing Email systems and protocol standards. The assumption is that such a design will facilitate its deployment within enterprises.

We have two variations on the design for sending digitally signed role based messages. We are currently building both systems and will report on the implementation, performance and usability in due course.

Acknowledgments

The authors would like to thank Nexor Ltd who is sponsoring this research.

References

[1] D. Chadwick, A. Otenko, and E. Ball. Role-based access control with X.509 attribute certificates. *IEEE Internet Computing*, pages 62–69, March-April 2003.

[2] M. Crispin. RFC 3501: Internet Message Access Protocol - Version 4rev1. Request For Comment, Network Working Group, March 2003.

[3] Victor DeMarines. MailRecall: Secure E-mail for the Enterprise, May 2004. Authentica, Inc.

[4] David Ferraiolo and Richard Kuhn. Role-based Access Control. In *Proceedings of 15th National Computer Security Conference*, 1992.

[5] David F. Ferraiolo, Ravi Sandhu, Serban Gavrila, D. Richard Kuhn, and Ramaswamy Chandramouli. Proposed NIST Standard for Role-based Access Control. *ACM Transactions on Information and System Security*, 4(3):224–274, 2001.

[6] N. Freed and N. Borenstein. RFC 2045 - Multipurpose Internet Mail Extensions (MIME) Part One: Format of Internet Message Bodies. Request For Comment, Network Working Group, November 1996.

[7] R. Gellens and J. Klensin. RFC 2476 - Message Submission. Request For Comment, Network Working Group, December 1998.

[8] P. Hoffman. RFC 2634: Enhanced Security Services for S/MIME. Request For Comment, Network Working Group, June 1999.

[9] ITU-T. Recommendation X.509, ISO/IEC 9594-8. Information Technology – Open Systems Interconnection – The Directory: Public-key and Attribute Certificate Frameworks, 4th ed., 2000. ITU.

[10] J. Klensin. RFC 2821 - Simple Mail Transfer Protocol. Request For Comment, Network Working Group, April 2001.

[11] Microsoft Corporation. Technical Overview of Windows Rights Management Services for Windows Server 2003, November 2003. Microsoft Corporation.

[12] M.C. Mont, P. Bramhall, and K. Harrison. A Flexible Role-based Secure Messaging Service: Exploiting IBE Technology for Privacy in Health Care. In *Proceeding of the 14th International Workshop on Database and Expert System Applications*. IEEE, 2003.

[13] J. Myers. RFC 2222: Simple Authentication and Security Layer (SASL). Request For Comment, Network Working Group, October 1997.

[14] M. Myers, R. Ankney, A. Malpani, S. Galperin, and C. Adams. RFC 2560 - X.509 Internet Public Key Infrastructure: Online Certificate Status Protocol - OCSP. Request For Comment, Network Working Group, June 1999.

[15] Omniva Policy Systems. Omniva Policy Manager Technical White Paper, January 2004. Omniva Policy Systems.

[16] Rolf Oppliger, Günther Pernul, and Christine Strauss. Using attribute certificates to implement role-based authorization and access controls. In S. Teufel K. Bauknecht, editor, *Sicherheit in Informationssystemen (SIS 2000)*, pages 169–184, Zurich, 2000.

[17] B. Ramsdell. RFC 2633: S/MIME Version 3 Message Specification. Request For Comment, Network Working Group, June 1999.

[18] M. Wahl. RFC 2251 - Lightweight Directory Access Protocol (v3). Request For Comment, Network Working Group, December 1997.

FIVE NON-TECHNICAL PILLARS OF NETWORK INFORMATION SECURITY MANAGEMENT

Elmarie Kritzinger[1] and Prof S.H. von Solms[2]
[1]*School of Computing, University of South Africa, SA.*
[2]*Department of Computer Science, Rand Afrikaans University, SA.*

Abstract: Securing information is vital for the survival of many organizations. Therefore, information must be proactively secured against harmful attacks. This securing of information becomes more complex when such information is transmitted over networks. This paper identifies five non-technical pillars (essentials) for network security management. For each pillar a number of specific actions are specified, resulting in a check list for a high level evaluation of the security status of these 5 pillars in a networked environment.

Key words: Information security; network security; non-technical aspects; information security management.

1. INTRODUCTION

In an increasingly competitive world, the company with the best information on which to base management decisions is the most likely to win and prosper [4]. Organizations must understand that information is a very valuable resource and must be protected and managed accordingly. Security must be considered as an integral part of whole IT governance environment, and must be dealt with in a proactive manner in order to be effective.

This means that information security is fundamental to the survival of any organization which uses electronic information resources. Information security is a discipline which can be divided into technical and non-technical aspects. This division is also reflected in the following definition of Information Security Governance [17]:

'Information Security Governance consists of the leadership, organizational structures, policies, procedures, compliance enforcement mechanisms and technologies needed to ensure that the confidentiality, integrity and availability of the organization's electronic information assets are maintained at all times.'

Aspects like the leadership, organizational structures, policies, procedures and some of the compliance enforcement mechanisms can be seen as the non-technical aspects, while the specific technologies (firewalls, encryption, access control lists etc) can be seen as the technical aspects. The authors do agree that some of these aspects overlap, and therefore fall into the grey area of being technical as well as non-technical. Nevertheless, the major aspects can be categorized as technical or non-technical.

Real Information Security Governance therefore consists of ensuring that both these technical as well as the non-technical aspects are implemented and coordinated in a holistic way. Figure 1 below indicates where Information Security Governance fits into the wider Corporate Governance structure.

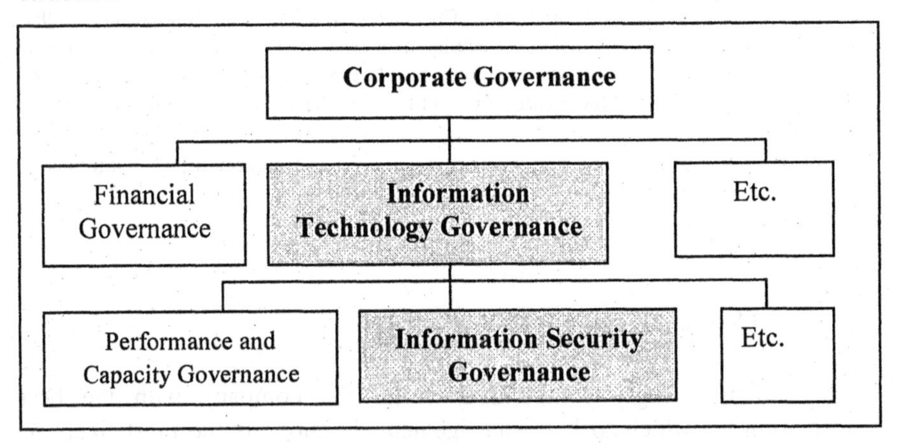

Figure 1. Corporate Governance Structure

Over the last 10 to 15 years, Information Technology in general has evolved from a centralized environment to a more decentralized environment, in which all types of networks (LANs, WANs, and Internet) are used daily to connect systems, work stations etc. to each other.

Managing the security of these networks, i.e. ensuring that the existence and use of all types of networks, do not impact on the confidentiality, integrity and availability of the organization's electronic assets, has become a pivotal part of more general information security governance. The more recent security worries around wireless networks, emphasize the crucial importance of such network security management. Figure 2 below indicates where network security management fits into the Information Security Governance structure.

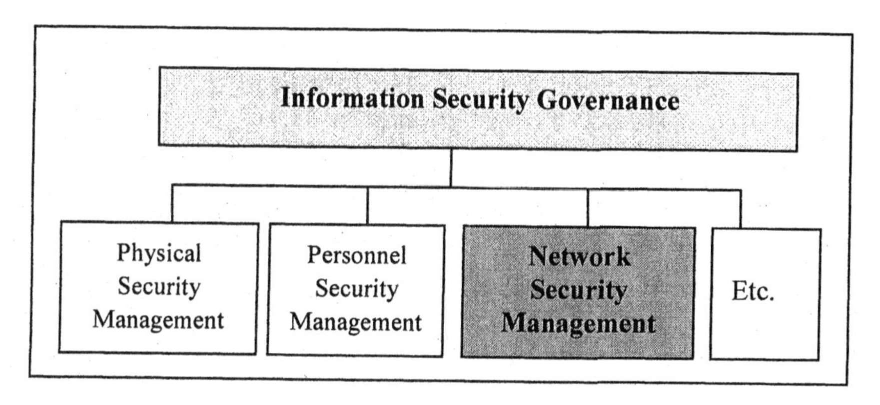

Figure 2. Network Security Management within the Information Security Governance structure

Because of the pivotal role of network security management, this paper zooms into this specific part of Information Security Governance, and defines 5 pillars (essentials) which must be in place to ensure proper network security management. These 5 pillars have to do with the more non-technical aspects of network security management, in line with the division made for Information Security Governance above.

Understanding the importance of these 5 pillars are vital to network security, as too often companies approach network security from a purely technical viewpoint, and do not realize that if the non-technical aspects (pillars) are not in place, huge risks will still exist as far as the use of their networks are concerned. Identifying and highlighting the importance of these 5 pillars are not necessarily a novel idea, as they are discussed and mentioned in most internationally accepted best practices for information and network security management. However, the purpose is to again stress their importance, and to provide a simple way for a network security manager to do a fast high level evaluation to determine the presence and level of implementation of these 5 pillars.

We start off by introducing and discussing each of these 5 (non-technical) pillars, and finish with a checklist that a network security manager can use to see whether the relevant 5 (non-technical) pillars are in place.

2. NETWORK SECURITY MANAGEMENT PILLARS

The five main pillars (building blocks) that the authors claim to be essential for network security management can be defined as:

- Having Top Management's commitment and buy-in for network security
- Having a proper Network Security Policy
- Having a proper Organizational structure for network security
- Having a proper User awareness program for network security
- Having a proper Compliance monitoring system for network security

Combined these five pillars will have a significant positive effect on implementing and maintaining a good network security management program.

Each of these five pillars will now be discussed briefly.

2.1 Having Top Management's commitment and buy-in for network security

In the last decade, boards of directors have experienced many new challenges and demands (such as rapid developments in technology and market conditions) [6]. The document referred to, goes on to state that information possessed by an organization is among its most valuable assets and is critical to its success. The board of directors, which is ultimately accountable for the organization's success, is therefore responsible for the protection of its information. The protection of this information can only be achieved through effective management and corporate governance.

According to Nicholas Durlacher [10], senior executives do not have to take responsibility for all the actions of their employees. However, organizations have the right to require senior executives to justify their conduct and competence formally in the event of any serious management failure that threatens the future of the firm. It is clear that senior managers in many large organizations are now expressing a much greater interest in Information Security than their counterparts of five to ten years ago.

Another author who has addressed the importance of senior management is Lewis [11]. Lewis states that the business should take responsibility for Information Security and appoint an officer whose key responsibility is the integrity of the organization's information. Given that the directors of the company are ultimately liable for business continuity, it is clear that the responsibility for Information Security cannot be removed from the boardroom.

This clearly shows that it is vital to involve top management in all Information Security management procedures and decisions within the organization. The reason being, that they are ultimately responsible for the security of all information in the organization. Because of the increased risks in using networks, Top Management must specifically be aware of the increased risk exposure of the company by using such networks, based on the underlying risks of the Internet, remote dial-ins, wireless networks etc. Without such commitment and buy-in, proper corporate governance will be affected.

2.2 Having a proper Network Security Policy

A Corporate Information security policy may be defined as "compiled documentation of computer security decisions"[15]. These security decisions can be made with regard to hardware, software, networks and information. Such a Corporate Information Security policy must be a maximum of 2 to 3 pages, very generic, and non-technical, and must be signed by the most senior official in the company.

Because of the pivotal role of networks in most companies, and the increased risks arising from implementing and using such networks, a separate Network Security Policy, flowing from the Corporate Information Security policy, must exist. Such a policy must explain the reason why the company uses networks, the risks involved in using these networks, and the responsibilities of employees in limiting these risks whenever using such networks.

This can be a single policy document, but because of the growing importance and risks related to network usage, trying to cover all aspects related to network security in one document, results in a document which is too big and unwieldy. Increasingly companies are creating a set of policies related to network security, including:

- An Internet Usage Security Policy
- An Email Usage Security Policy
- An Encryption Policy
- A Wireless Network Security Policy
- A Malicious Software Security Policy
- Etc.

Such a Network Security Policy, or rather set of Network Security Policies, highlights the importance of security when using networks and makes it easier to enforce proper network security management.

2.3 Organization

According to the International Guidelines for Managing Risk of Information and Communications Statement #1 [8], one of the six major activities involved in Information Security is Roles and Responsibilities. This includes ensuring that individual roles, responsibilities and authority are clearly communicated and understood by all [7]. Therefore, all security responsibilities, roles and ownership must be defined and assigned to all the users in the organization who work with any information resource.

Again, because of the increased use of networks, a clear organizational structure, with a supporting set of roles and responsibilities must exist for network usage in all its forms. This structure must clearly indicate which organizational positions in the company can use which network services, for example, remote login from wired and wireless networks, home access, dial-in modems etc., and what their roles and responsibilities are.

2.4 Awareness

Information Security awareness is a widely publicized and talked-about issue in the business environment. The reason for this is that Information Security awareness is mainly a human-related issue. It is important to realize that "human issues" are the main cause of security breaches [11]. The most effective way to reduce Information Security risks in an organization is to make employees more Information Security aware. This awareness also means that employees must take responsibility for their own actions in the workplace.

Implementing an effective Information Security awareness programme helps all employees understand why they need to take Information Security seriously, what they will gain from its implementation and how it will assist them in completing their assigned tasks. An effective Information Security awareness programme could be the most cost-effective initiative a company can take to protect its critical information assets [16]. This protection can only be provided if there are effective programmes in place to make certain that employees are aware of their responsibilities.

It is the organization's responsibility to make employees aware of Information Security policies and issues in the organization. Without knowing the necessary security controls (and how to use them), users cannot be truly accountable for their actions [15]. Organizations that have implemented strong protection mechanisms and have educated their staff are in the best position to protect their information from unauthorized disclosure or modification.

According to the CCTA [2], the Information Security procedures must be integrated into normal everyday routine, and staff should come to recognize security as an enabler rather than a barrier. The NIST handbook [15] also stresses this "every day routine" by stating that Information Security is an ongoing process. This process of making employees Information Security aware must continue after a candidate has been hired, which includes keeping employees up to date with their IS duties and responsibilities.

Any general Information Security awareness program must, of course, include all aspects related to network usage security, which must not be hidden amongst a lot of other security issues. Again, because of the importance of networks, many companies are realizing that a network security awareness program, separate from the general Information Security awareness program, has significant value. This is enforce by Lewis [14] that states if one can make employees aware of the threats to the network and let them feel part of the network security team they may feel more inclined to help out and point out potential problems before they get out of hand. Greater success is achieved in this way, because employees are specifically exposed to the security risks related to the use of networks, and can therefore evaluate network security as an aspect in its own right.

2.5 Compliance Monitor (CM)

Compliance monitoring (measuring) is about finding out if procedures and processes that should be implemented in an organization are working as they should, and are being complied with. The objects that are monitored can differ from organization to organization; and include products, systems, processes, security program effectiveness and personal competence [9].

Network security in itself can be compromised if there are no mechanisms in place, apart from some annual audits, to ensure that it is enforced and complied with on a continuous basis. GMITS [5] states that Information Security compliance checking (which includes network security) has to occur on an annual basis. A setback with annual audits is that Information Security problems are only identified annually and the organization is open to security attacks daily. In today's business environment, organizations cannot afford to find out, 6 to 12 months later, that an employee has resigned from the organization but still has access to some of the servers. These problems can be avoided by continuously monitoring the network security in the organization.

A comprehensive compliance monitoring environment, to ensure compliance to the policies and procedures mentioned in 2.2 above, is therefore essential. Although many of these compliance measuring and monitoring mechanisms will be technical, the results must be used to check compliance to policies, and to update aspects like the awareness programs. Therefore this pillar is handled as one of the non-technical pillars, as discussed in section 1.

The compliance measuring and monitoring must not only produce technical low level results for operational purposes, but must also be able to produce high level reports which can be used to inform top management, in an easily understandable way, about the risks related to the use of networks in the company.

Such compliance monitoring is essential, because 'you can only manage something if you can measure it'. This specifically holds true for computer networks.

3. THE '5 PILLARED' APPROACH

3.1 Network security management Processes

In the first part of this paper the 5 pillars for network security management were briefly introduced. Each of these pillars can be summarized into a few high level actions that will enforce the role of that pillar.

This section will use an incremental approach to illustrate how these actions can be used to implement (or evaluate the presence of) these pillars in a network security management environment.

Each of these pillars contains one ore more actions that is vital to that pillar. If there is compliance with an action one can move on to the next action. If compliance with one action within a pillar is not complied with, a counter action must be taken (indicated as a "No" in Figure 3). After a counter action is completed, the process starts again at the first action in the specified pillar (or block). If all the actions are complied with within the pillar, one can progress to the next pillar (block).

The order in which the pillars will be addressed is the same order as introduced in section 2. The order of the pillars is very important to follow, for example one cannot monitor a policy or procedures if such a policy or procedure does not exist in the first place. Therefore, the pillars must be kept in the correct order. The action and counter actions for each pillar can be depicted in Figure 3.

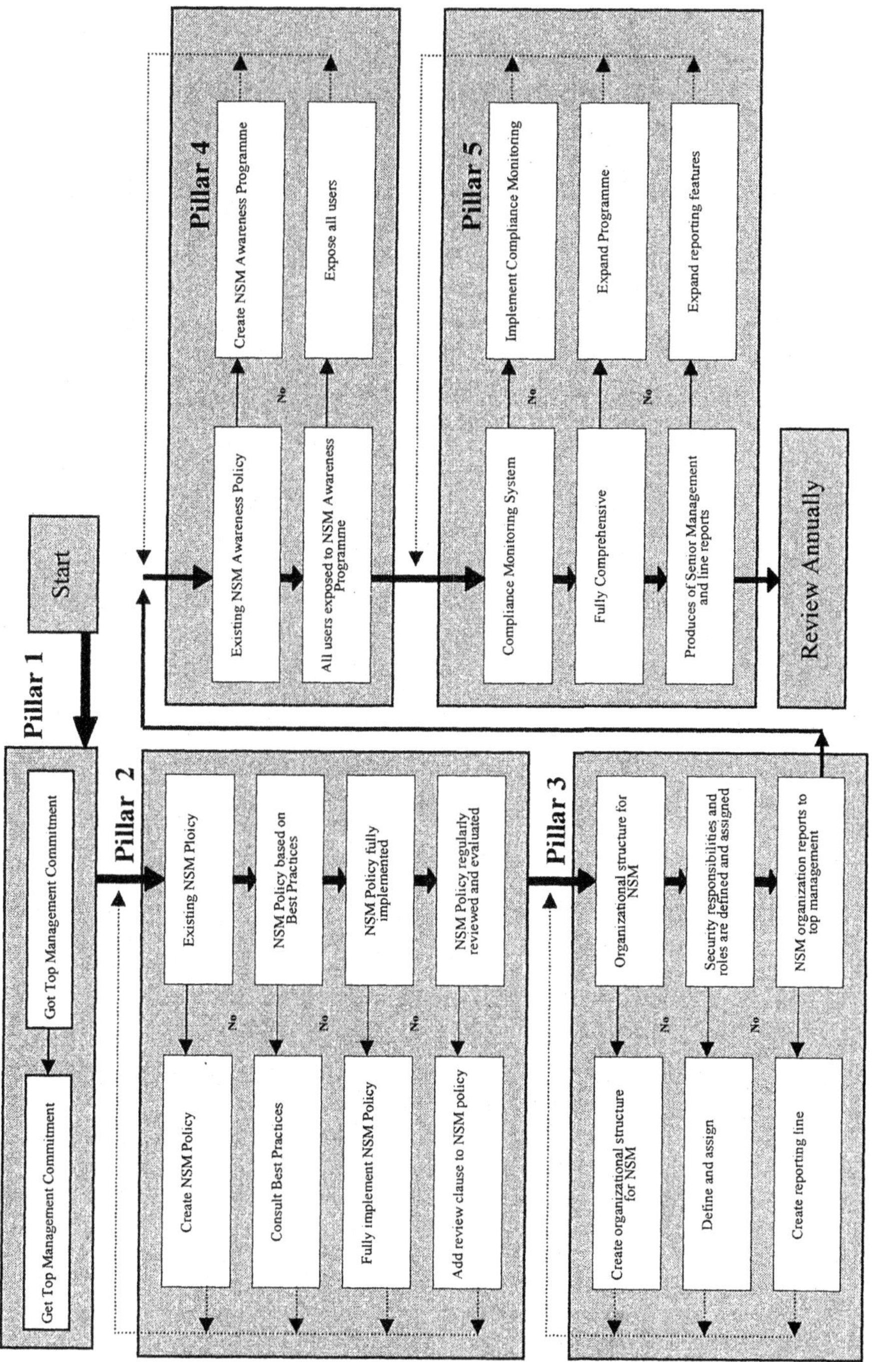

Figure 3. Network security Management (NSM) processes

3.2 Checklist

This section uses the actions and pillars depicted in Figure 3 to create a checklist for network security management. This checklist comprises each of the 13 decision questions from figure 3, and indicates the network security management approach for non-technical network aspects. Before starting to work through the checklist it is important to know that technical aspects such as firewalls protect an organization for outside attacks but leave the organization open to attacks from inside the organization. Insider threats are most often incidental in nature due to the fact that many employees do not know that they are compromising the confidentially, integrity or availability of information. With this check list in place an organization can try to minimize the "incidental" threats by employees.

4. CONCLUSION

This paper introduced the importance of the non-technical aspects of network security management. Five vital pillars were identified and briefly described. Different actions for each of these pillars were also identified. These five pillars, together with the individual actions can be depicted in a checklist with a preset order that must be followed. The importance of this checklist is to ensure that organizations are aware of the different non-technical aspects related to network security management and how to implement and monitor these in an organization.

5. REFERENCES

[1] CCH Enterprises Solutions 2000: *"Security is a management issue, not a technology issue."* Online: www.cch.za/es/news/articles/news59

[2] CCTA - Championing Electronic Government, 1999: Online: http://www.ccta.gov.uk/index.htm

[3] Department of trade and industry, 2000: *"Information Security Management Policy."* Online: http://www.dti.gov.uk

[4] Finne T., 2000: *"Information systems risk Management: Key concepts and business processes."* Computer & Security, 19 (3) 2000.

[5] Guidelines for Management of IT Security – GMITS, 2000 Online: http://www.cancert.ca/Pages/ISStandards.htm

[6] IIA, AICPA 2000: *"A call to action for corporate governance."* Online: http://www.nitc.state.ne.us/tp/workgroups/security.htm

[7] "Information Security Governance: Guide for Boards of Directors and Executive Management." IT Governance Institute

[8] International Federation of Accountants, 1998: *"Managing Security of Information."*

[9] Katzke S., 2001 : *"Security Metrics."*

Online: http://www.acsac.org/measurement/position-papers
[10]Kwok L. & Longley D., 1999: *"Information Security Management and Modeling."* Information Management & Computer Security. Vol 7, 1999.
[11]Lewis A., 2002: "Time to elevate IT security to the boardroom" E-Secure, Volume 1, Issue 1.
[14]Lewis R. 2003: *"The need for Establishing a Security Awareness Training Program."* As part of GIAC practial respository. SANS Institute
[15]National Institute of Standards and Technology 2000: *"An Introduction to Computer Security."* Online available: www.nist.gov
[16]Netigy 2001: *"Information security awareness program."* Online: http://www.netigy.com/solutions/security/sec_foundation/infosec_aware.htm Author unknown.
[17]Von Solms S.H., 2000: *"Information Security - The third wave?"* Computer and Security, Volume 19, Issue 7.

Author Index